Desktop Video Studio

RANDOM HOUSE
ELECTRONIC PUBLISHING

NEW MEDIA

Desktop Video Studio

Andrew Soderberg

Tom Hudson

Sponsored by Apple Computer, Inc.
Multimedia Business Development Group, New Media Division
for the Apple Multimedia Program

RANDOM HOUSE
ELECTRONIC PUBLISHING

NEW MEDIA

Desktop Video Studio
Sponsored by Apple Computer, Inc.
Multimedia Business Development Group, New Media Division
for the Apple Multimedia Program

Produced by G & H SOHO, Inc.

Published in the United States by Random House, Inc., New York, and simultaneously in Canada by Random House of Canada, Limited.

Manufactured in the United States of America.

First Edition

0 9 8 7 6 5 4 3 2 1

ISBN 0-679-75784-8

New York   Toronto   London   Sydney   Auckland

Book Overview

Contents

Foreword

Access, Talent, Imagination, and Change— The Digital Revolution in Video Tools

by Nick DeMartino
—*American Film Institute*

Let's settle one thing right off . . . the digital revolution is not some distant technological prognostication. It is real, it is happening, it is *now*. To the nimble, creative, and skilled go the spoils in a race to create new ways of entertaining, educating, communicating. The victor could as easily be you as those guys whose names grace the pages of the *New York Times, Daily Variety,* or *MacWeek.*[1]

This revolution in moving-image production began in earnest with the public announcement of Apple Computer's QuickTime, the first popularly available, low-cost multimedia architecture for desktop computing. For the first time, a low-cost computer could create synchronized video, sound, text, and graphics. Once brought into the digital domain, all those elements were treated by the computer as a new type of document, allowing them to be stored, manipulated, transmitted, and played back.

---

[1]One definitive piece of evidence that desktop video has "arrived" is the fact that five of the twenty-five innovations nominated in 1994 for technical achievement by the Academy of Motion Picture Arts and Sciences (the Oscar™) were Mac-based: Digital Storyboard, Cinemac; Scriptor, Movie Magic Budgeting, Movie Magic Scheduling, Screenplay Systems; Avid Film Composer, Avid Technology; Ultimatte electronic blue screen compositing process, Ultimatte Corp.; and The Lightworks Editor, Lightworks Editing System, Inc.—*Daily Variety,* September 19, 1994.

As with the desktop publishing revolution before it, the digital media revolution would find adherents only when tools emerged that could help people perform tasks better, faster, cheaper, and more creatively. It took photographers, designers, and publishers willing to experiment with products such as Adobe's Postscript and Photoshop, Aldus PageMaker, and, of course, the Mac OS. Apple evangelized the toolmakers, then the artists. Together, they transformed the world of printed words and images in just a few years. Today, publishing *is* desktop publishing.

Any revolution in moving-image tools and artistry would require technologists to inspire artists and craftspersons working in motion pictures, television, advertising, promotion, corporate communications, public relations, music, and allied industries. That would again require great tools, and some specialized knowledge of this community. This was the role played by The American Film Institute in digital video's earliest days.

The American Film Institute was founded in 1967 to preserve the nation's cinema heritage, to train emerging film makers, and to celebrate the art of the moving image. QuickTime was unveiled to the world at AFI's Los Angeles campus just two weeks after the opening of its AFI–Apple Computer Center for Film and Videomakers. AFI joined with Apple and companies working on the Mac platform literally during digital video's birth pangs. To find its way in a strange new world of bits and bytes, AFI would come to rely on the most adventuresome artists and the most responsive toolmakers.

Within a year, AFI's tiny program became *the* place in Hollywood to learn about the explosion in tools that was very quickly engulfing the mainstream media biz. Today, it's called the AFI Advanced Technology Programs. We continue to provide tools training, now using Windows and Silicon Graphics platforms as well as the Macintosh; we convene conferences, symposia, and weekly "computer media salons" where creative visualists and creative technologists share their coolest stuff and plot mischief. We conduct research activities with a special emphasis on digital imaging.[2]

Some interesting lessons emerge from AFI's experience in training and evangelizing nearly 6,000 professionals in the midst of their real-time digital career retooling. This book may be your ticket to a fascinating journey into your own career future. The experience of others on their own quests may be instructive.

Item One: *It's about talent, not technology.* By expanding access to tools, digital technology levels the playing field.

---

[2]To learn more about the AFI Advanced Technology Programs, call for a catalog at 1-800-999-4AFI.

Whenever the established order is upended, there is room for new voices. Digital technology makes it possible for talent to emerge from new sources, without excessive reliance on vestigial credentials. AFI learned this at the world's first QuickTime production workshop held at AFI in October 1991, months before the tools we used were released.

Participants included: a graphics artist/designer working in advertising; a video producer who had done the trailer for the soon-to-be Best Picture, *Silence of the Lambs;* an ophthalmologist and eye surgeon building a new business in medical education; a video producer for the gas company; an MIT Media Lab grad who would go on to a dazzling career in movie special effects; an experimental video artist who produced a lovely piece about Cristo's umbrellas; a fellow desperate to move from corporate communications into video production; a budding movie producer with a masters from USC who was making a living doing animatics for ad agencies; and a guy who spent the whole time digitizing porno footage of himself and his wife.

The last technology that had reshaped the production business on this scale came in the early 70s, with the introduction of small-format video. A new generation of artists and documentarians reinvented the rules because they understood the revolutionary impact of bringing television into the streets. Portable video and low-cost helical scan editing and image-manipulation systems knocked a zero off the entry cost of TV production. With systems costing $50,000 to $100,000, television production became real for thousands who previously never could have entered a studio-based industry requiring millions. The best of those pioneers produced work that has stood the test of time, irrespective of the tools that they used to bring their talents to the attention of the world.

The same will be true with digital technology. Digital video technology nearly knocks another zero off those capital requirements. Paul and Sarah Edwards include video production as one of the top ten income producers for people looking to start "The Best Home Businesses of the Nineties." They estimate an annual income of $35,000 to $150,000 for desktop video producers, for a maximum startup cost of $22,000.[3] A stupid script, bad camerawork, inaudible sound, amateur acting, and clichéd effects are obvious, no matter how easy the tools are that you use to produce such drek. Ergo:

Item Two: *It's about imagination.* Tools become great only when applied in the real world, when people adapt them to their own purposes in ways nobody else can imagine. To wit:

[3] *The Wall Street Journal,* October 14, 1994, p. R4.

- David Nicksay, former president of Morgan Creek Productions, is a guy responsible for some half a billion bucks in movie grosses as executive producer for 14 pictures, including *Robin Hood: Prince of Thieves*. His wife Heather wanted to retool her career in media production and information systems at the AFI after starting a family. They adapted AFI's model for using database, word-processing, CAD, and other off-the-shelf software in motion picture production with an experiment on the feature *Addams Family Values* at the Paramount lot. A Mac network and a special team incorporated into the process such innovations as pre-visualized effects shots, scanned storyboards for navigating sets that weren't yet built, camera angle and shot plotting, color matching for sets built on different sound stages, visual databases with hypertext access—even automated trucking and hauling. Today, the Paramount Production Resource Center is part of the studio's backlot services department, and the Nicksays teach the computer in film production at the AFI.

- Marcia Reed, a top commercial photographer specializing in movie publicity stills for the studios, got bitten by the interactive bug and developed a digital CD product to promote movies that provides the media with stills, text, and movie excerpts—all accessible digitally at a fraction of the cost of traditional methods.

- Harry Marks, as VP of on-air design and promotion for ABC and CBS, and many other movie and TV clients, is responsible for the look of American television. With high-end broadcast tools from suppliers such as Quantel, Abacus, and Grass Valley, he revolutionized interface design for the world's most ubiquitous medium. With a passion for the Mac, he understood that scalable type, digital video effects, and animation functionality could mean fantastic flexibility and control in such tasks as designing flying logos and layered moving-image montages. It would mean farewell to the wall between "off-line" and "on-line" post-production, because he could create a virtually finished product for the client without the cost, inconvenience, and loss of control of traditional methods.

- Alan Lasky parlayed his knowledge of digital technology into new ways to provide "video assist" services to directors—a quick step into the studio art department at Sony Pictures, where he pioneered "pre-visualization" that helped all the members of a movie's creative team share the director's vision. His mastery of the tools means he can now move seamlessly between the movie set, the special effects unit, the movie post-production process, and the videogame design team.

Item Three: *It's about change*—change in what you need to know, change in how jobs are defined, change in who gets to do what.

Creativity in the digital era may originate from: the software engineer with a new video compression algorithm; a multimedia artist with a hot new CD-ROM title and a clever way to get around the medium's limitations; a software developer with an application that brings new functions to the desktop; a phone company executive with a wild vision for the so-called National Information Infrastructure; a motion picture director, advertising creative director, television producer, or visual effects supervisor with a stupefying new use of digital magic; or a college kid with something to say and a hacker's navigational skills on the Internet.

Talent, imagination, skill, and persistence may not be sufficient in an era of rapid technological change. "It's critical to recognize there's no longer any such thing as job security," said Secretary of Labor Robert Reich. "The most one can hope for is employability security, and by that I mean continually upgrading your skills so you're marketable and ready for that next job." By one estimate, individuals in the high-technology field with expertise in the latest technologies can command up to 50 percent more in salary than peers with more dated technology skills, often having their choice of numerous offers.[4]

At its heart, the digital revolution is fueled by great tools and the access made possible by their relatively low cost and ease of use. Once you set your sights on digital video success, however, you'll still need those time-tested ingredients of talent, imagination, adaptability, and savvy.

If you understand how this revolution is being made, and how you can apply those lessons to your own unique vision, you have an exciting future ahead of you. The lessons you can learn in this superb volume will be an excellent start. Mastery of the tools is the first step to participation in an exciting community that can mean new levels of creativity, technical challenge, and, by the way, prosperity.

Nick DeMartino, Director
Advanced Technology Programs
The American Film Institute
February 1995

---

[4]*The Los Angeles Times,* November 7, 1994, p. 2. "Focus on Jobs" supplement.

Acknowledgments

No book gets written by just the author or authors; books are team efforts, and this one is no exception. There are many people we wish to thank for their time, knowledge, assistance, and understanding when we came home late for dinner. Primary among these individuals is our partner and Art Director, Gordon Soderberg. He took some of the weight off our shoulders during the writing of this book and made it possible for us to step away from our daily business to get this thing done. He is also responsible for some of the custom graphics in the book.

Together, we wish to thank:

- In alphabetical order: Lynn Ackler, Jeff Boone, Nick DeMartino, Steve Demirjian, Karen Dillon, Dan DiPaola, Tam Fraser, Bill Fulco, Jim Griffiths, Jerry Huiskens, Joe Klingler, Roberta Margolis, Sheldon Renan, Greg Roach, Marc Wade, and Garry Weil—for their contributions to this book.

- Mike Roney of Random House Electronic Publishing for his editorial work and for calling us in the first place.

- Dana Morgan for having enough faith in our work to suggest our names to Mike Roney, and for her editorial assistance as Apple liaison.

- Eileen LaPorte and Steve Franzesi of the Apple New Media Division, for their support of the project.

- Cascom International, Inc., for allowing us to use some of their Select Effects™ screens to liven up our screen shots.

- The many software and hardware companies that provided their products for the development of this book. They are listed by name and address in the back of the book.

Andy wishes to thank:

- The two gentlemen who introduced me to and taught me all about radio and television. My thanks to St. Clair Adams for introducing me to film and video. My special thanks go to Robert Berkowitz for being my teacher, mentor, and part-time employer. For two years Bob taught me about radio and television production, and set me on the road to my eventual career in multimedia. Because of Bob and St. Clair, I left high school with high goals and opportunities, much more than just a diploma.
- My high-school-age daughter, Quinn Soderberg, for tolerating the fact that we took over our house with this business for its first year, and for her patience during the time it took getting us out and into our own space so that she can now have parties at home. I dedicate my work in this book to her.

Tom wishes to thank:

- My wife, Patty, for her help, humor, and encouragement over the years and during the writing of this book. I also must thank our two lovely "children," Stanley and Rosie. At no time did they stop their unquestioning love, sloppy kisses, and demands that I rub their tummies, no matter how grumpy I might have become. Now if we could just get Stanley to stop drinking out of the toilet and get Rosie to stop scratching herself in the middle of the night . . .
- I also wish to thank my parents, Russ and Polly Hudson, for teaching me how to diagram a sentence by the time I was nine, and how to drive and parallel park a car before I was of legal age.

Preface

If you are standing in a bookstore, looking for a reason to buy this particular package, then you probably want to know why we believe that our view on digital video is one you should follow.

We don't actually believe that. At least, we don't say that everything we do is exactly what you must do. You need to find your own way, your own style. What we offer is a bit of guidance around the potholes of digital video.

Having said that, let us tell you just a bit about ourselves. . . .

Who Are These Guys?

We, Andrew Soderberg and Tom Hudson (Figure P.1), are two of the partners in Toucan Studios. Over the past fifteen-plus years, we have each

**Figure P.1
Your authors,
Andrew Soder-
berg and Tom
Hudson—just so
you will recog-
nize them if you
ever see them
around.**

**Figure P.2
Gordon Soder-
berg, the face
behind the art.**

worked for various companies within the computer industry, specializing in different aspects of what has become known as multimedia.

Andrew's experience has been mostly directed toward the video side, while Tom has been involved in the creation of interactive, multimedia training programs. Together with Gordon Soderberg (Figure P.2), the third Toucan partner and creative director for the company, we represent more than forty years of experience in the broadcast video and computer industries.

That experience has allowed us to be involved in the evolution of what has become digital video. Andrew spent several years as the QuickTime Evangelist for Apple Computer, working to define the standard and to get it into general use. Tom spent more years than he cares to remember as a senior instructional designer at Apple and was responsible for the creation of many of their self-paced, interactive CD-ROM–based training products incorporating video and audio along with text and graphics.

What Is Toucan Studios?

Toucan Studios is a digital video, multimedia studio located in Cupertino, California. Toucan Studios has been in business since 1993, specializing in the creation of high-quality digital video and interactive multimedia products for corporate customers. The majority of our early work involved the creation of products for software companies and hardware companies.

The results of that work have been seen in everything from trade show video presentations, to demonstration diskettes for software companies, to

**Figure P.3
The equipment
rack in Studio
A at Toucan
Studios. This is
a digital frame
grab from our
first promo-
tional demo.**

screen savers sold internationally, to on-stage displays for a major computer introduction, to the in-box CD-ROMs for Power Macintosh computers, to a permanent display at a famous experimental prototype community of tomorrow entertainment park in Florida.

Our corporate client list includes Apple Computer, Inc.; Berkeley Systems; CASCOM International, Inc.; Connectix; Domark Software; Fractal Design Corp.; The 3DO Company; and many others.

We also have a great company logo (Figure P.4). It isn't mandatory to have a company logo, or even to have a great one. It isn't even necessary

**Figure P.4
The Toucan Stu-
dios logo, which
looks *much* bet-
ter in color!**

to do this as a business, but this logo has helped make us and our products visually identifiable. And it makes a nifty business card, too.

Why Listen to Us?

Like many of you out there, we are a small company when viewed in total number of employees. Possibly *unlike* many of you, we are outfitted with most of the newest software and hardware products available, just as if we were a very big company. Some of this is because we have been collecting and using dozens of different products over the past several years. Some of this is due to this book; many companies have graciously provided us with their products so we could research and use as many as possible during the development of this book. We review and discuss many of these products in Chapters 7 and 8.

What have we learned about having all of this stuff? That's easy. Even if you don't own everything on the market, it is possible to produce quality digital video, even of a quality matching or exceeding that of many large video production houses.

Why? Because the chances are that (a) you started or are starting in this business specifically as a digital video producer, rather than having tried to add digital video to an existing film or video business repertoire; (b) you are computer literate and can readily understand the hardware and software functions and procedures necessary to get good results; and (c) you probably either already work for a company that needs to produce digital video or are running a business that will specialize in certain types of projects.

You may be a hobbyist or home producer, interested in taking your own and your friends' or family's videos and editing and processing them. In this case, you probably have a special desire to create something that you can be proud of and that will impress these important people in your life.

Should you specialize right up front, or take on anything you can get? Unless you have the *luxury* of large amounts of time and money, we suggest that you try to specialize as much as possible. This can help you limit the types and amounts of equipment and software that you need.

Is that really important? Yes and no. For the smaller company, or the individual just starting out, we feel that it is important to find a niche. Money is usually tight for a startup, so you can't go out and purchase tens of thousands of dollars' worth of equipment on day one.

And that's okay! Digital video doesn't have to cost an arm and a leg to get started. There are products for almost every pocketbook. Yes, there are usually more capabilities in the more costly products, but there are techniques you can use to get high-quality results out of low-cost or midrange products.

This book breaks out the different levels of cost, capability, and results for many of the tools available to the desktop digital video producer, and we have been aided in its creation by the gracious editorial contributions of many of the top experts in their respective fields. Their insights into digital and traditional video, both as a process and as an industry, have been of immense help to us. Throughout, you will see short articles by these individuals:

- Lynn Ackler, The 3DO Company: *Alpha Channel/Ultimatte Techniques*
- Jeff Boone, Alaska Software: *Digital Audio*
- Nick DeMartino, American Film Institute: *Foreword*
- Steve Demirjian, Avid: *VideoShop Tips & Techniques*
- Karen Dillon, Radius: *Digital Video Capture*
- Dan DiPaola, Fractal Design: *Corporate Development*
- Tam Fraser, TAM Productions: *Shooting for The Edit*
- Bill Fulco, Network 23: *Compression Technology*
- Jim Griffiths, *FWB: SCSI Considerations*
- Jerry Huiskens, Huiskens Video, *Preparing Video for Digitizing*
- Joe Klingler, Radius: *VideoFusion Tips & Techniques*
- Roberta Margolis, Runway Video: *Moving to Digital Editing Systems*
- Sheldon Renan, Runway Video: *History of Digital Video*
- Greg Roach, HyperBole Studios: *Adobe Premiere Tips & Techniques*
- Marc Wade, Paramount: *QuickTime & HyperCard*
- Garry Weil, *Intel: Cross Platform Development Using Indeo Video*

How to Use the Book and CD-ROM

The book is divided into three parts: Tools and Technology, Techniques, and Product Reviews.

We have attempted to make the body of the book applicable to most possible users, choosing not to devote any section to a particular user level. (When you get to Chapters 7 and 8—the product reviews—you will find that each product has been identified by its appropriate target audience and use.) Where you find a section containing information aimed at a different level of user than yourself, we encourage you to skim through that section so you can concentrate on the sections that are most applicable to you. (You can always go back and read the other stuff later, when nobody is looking.)

Throughout the book, we try to help you better understand certain issues and how to address them as they relate to particular needs. We cover traditional video as an introduction to digital video, since most video content will be gathered using analog video equipment. We present and detail the various digital video hardware and software products available across a broad price spectrum (but remain targeted at the desktop user).

Throughout the first 75 percent of the book we have enlisted experts listed in the previous section to provide their personal and professional insight into particular topics, products, and technologies. If you're looking for the inside scoop and nitty gritty detail, be sure to check out their sidebars.

Before diving in, you may want to decide what you expect to get from this book and how you wish to use it. Most of us start at the beginning of a book and read it through to the end. If you are like that, just keep on reading. The book is laid out in a sequence that looks something like this:

**Part One:
Tools and
Technology**

Chapter 1 includes the evolution of digital video, how to understand your needs first in order to get a better result at the end, an overview of the tools and technologies available to you, and hardware considerations.

Chapter 2 discusses the predominant architecture for Macintosh and Windows digital video: QuickTime. It also touches on Microsoft's Video for Windows, as well as other systems issues.

Chapter 3 covers using specific video compressors, the different desktop video editors available today, working with video and audio, and video cards and other "total" solutions.

In addition to the hints and sidebar articles in Chapters 2 and 3, we profile several dozen hardware and software products, many of which are reviewed in detail in Chapters 7 and 8.

Chapter 4 covers video sources for the creation of digital video—both analog and digital.

**Part Two:
Techniques**

Chapter 5 covers various digital video hints and techniques on shooting your own video, capturing and compressing video and audio, software capture products and techniques, and how to best use different compression schemes.

Chapter 6 is devoted to case studies of many of the different uses of digital video by Toucan Studios in a number of categories. Each case study contains a description of the goal of the project, steps and techniques used to accomplish the project, and a description of the final result.

Where possible, photographs, screen shots, and charts have been added to help illustrate projects.

**Part Three:
Product
Reviews**

No book on a specialty area like Desktop Video would be complete without product reviews, so Chapters 7 and 8 cover dozens of software and hardware products that will aid in the operation of your desktop video studio. These products are not rated one over the other; rather, each is discussed in terms of its unique features and what it does best.

References

Finally, we've included a bibliography, a list of other books you may wish to read, and a comprehensive product and manufacturer address list.

For those of you who want to read up on specifics, your best bet is to turn to the table of contents, or possibly the index, and jump directly to the things that most interest you.

No matter how you approach using the book, we believe that you will want to look through all of the hints and tips.

Using the Materials in the Book

You probably have already put the CD-ROM in your drive; we would like to request that you remove it for now. It contains things to use and practice with once you have set up your desktop video studio.

As you go through the book, you will possibly see things that you already know (feel free to skip) and some things that are new to you. We have to start somewhere, so a level of categorization should help you determine where you fit in the digital video studio matrix. This book contains materials aimed at several levels of digital video producers, several ranges of equipment price, and different categories of use for the end product. A cross-matrix chart (Figure P.5) may help you visualize how these three interact.

**Figure P.5
The user/
price/use
matrix.**

User Type	Price	Usage
Pro-sumer	Entry Level	Desktop
Multimedia Professional	Mainstream	CD-ROM
Corporate Developer	High End	Videotape

We try to associate each piece of hardware and software with all of the categories in the chart so that you can make comparisons and cross-references yourself to get the most from this book.

Let's begin by looking at how you may fit into this matrix and how the matrix fits into the three areas profiled: users, equipment price (hardware and software), and usage.

User Profile

This book is written to address three different types of digital video production facilities or individuals:

Pro-sumer: Not to be confused with consumer, this is the individual working on a single system to produce good-quality but lower-volume digital video projects.

Multimedia Professional: This is the user who creates digital video as a full-fledged business. This type of user, whether one individual or several, generally has more than a single computer, possibly works cross-platform, and may also have some ability to shoot the original video used in their digital video productions.

Corporate Department: Whether you out-source or have your own media department, this degree of digital video usage almost always entails a team of computer- and video-literate individuals working on larger, more detailed projects.

The categories in this book are Entry Level, Mainstream, and High End. These categories span two main areas of interest: user knowledge level and cost of equipment. There are, after all, entry-level products that may be of interest to the high-end video professional, and mainstream to high-end products that are applicable to the entry-level person.

Each level of user generally looks at complete systems (hardware and software) at three different price levels. In Chapters 7 and 8, major products are reviewed and rated according to these user profile levels, and are appropriately identified by the use of a unique symbol (Figure P.6).

Figure P.6 User-type symbols: Entry Level, Mainstream, and High End.

**Book-Disc
Interactivity**

The CD-ROM accompanying this book includes demos, "lite" editions, test drives, and purchasable retail versions of numerous desktop video software products (you'll find a complete list on the inside flap of the back cover). These products are noted throughout the book by a CD-ROM icon in the margin wherever they are first mentioned in a chapter or major section. Whenever you see this icon, you'll know that you can immediately review a version of that software.

What's on the CD-ROM?

The CD-ROM that comes in the back of this book has been produced so that a single version works on both Macintosh and Windows PCs.

For Macintosh and PC users, you should have the following minimum system configurations:

- Macintosh with 68030 or greater processor or MPC-capable Windows PC (i386 or greater processor)
- At least 8 megabytes of RAM
- A CD-ROM drive
- At least a 640 × 480 pixel display

For the sample digital video and audio clips included on the CD, we suggest a slightly different minimum system requirement in order to be fully utilized:

- Macintosh with 68040 running at 33 MHz or more
- 8 MB RAM with at least 5 MB free
- 40–50 MB of free hard disk space
- System 7.0.1 or greater (7.1 or 7.5 or greater processor is recommended)
- QuickTime™ 1.6.1 (QuickTime 2.0 is highly recommended, and is included on the disc)
- Double-speed CD-ROM drive
- 16- or 24-bit color-capable monitor and appropriate video RAM support

PC users must have the following minimum configuration:

- MPC Level 1 (MPC Level 2 is suggested for best performance)
- 486/33 or higher

- Local-bus Video
- 300 K double speed CD-ROM drive
- QuickTime for Windows 1.1 (2.0 is suggested and is included on the disc) or Video for Windows 1.1.1
- Sound Blaster sound card (or compatible)

As you probably have already discovered (see above where we already have assumed that you put the CD-ROM in first before reading anything), the CD-ROM is divided into five major sections:

- *Credits:* This includes a video preface and information on the key people involved with this project.
- *Hypertext book excerpts:* Techniques and product reviews from the book—illustrated and searchable.
- *Tutorials:* Guided learning experiences are included to help you practice some of the techniques discussed in the book. You will also find helpful hints with each exercise.
- *Freebies (clip media and utilities):* There are hundreds of megabytes of clip media, demos, and utilities, including Apple's HyperCard, Quick-Time, and QuickTime for Windows, as well as video and audio clips you can use to practice on. Each clip is between ten and thirty seconds in length.
- *Software store:* The disc also includes full-featured test drives for Apple Media Tool, Adobe Premiere, Adobe Photoshop, Macromedia Director, SoundEdit 16, and Sonic Foundry Sound Forge. Each one may be opened a total of three times before they disable. If you like a particular application and wish to purchase it at a discount, you may do so by calling a toll-free telephone number and charging the purchase to a major credit card. Details are on the CD-ROM.

One Final Word . . .

In whatever spare time you have, experiment, experiment, experiment. We don't have all the answers; nobody does! By experimenting—using the techniques found in this and other books at first and then trying new things on your own—you will begin to arrive at a set of procedures that work best for you, utilizing your unique set of hardware, software, and projects.

Introduction

Humans have always been storytellers
— communicators by nature.

In the beginning there were only words, and very few of those made sense. One day someone got the idea to add pictures to help others understand what the big, hairy thing that just ate old Grunt looked like. Soon, anyone with a cave wall and some limestone or blood or other colorful substance could create visual displays, showing everything from "How I bravely killed the ravaging beast that ate Uncle Grunt" to what were probably the first visual databases of how many hairy beasts the cave owner claimed as property.

This picture-story technique was later fine-tuned by the Egyptians, who added pictures of man-sized cats in King Tut headgear, chorus lines of slaves with broken arms, and other such true-to-life elements.

Fast forward to the 1800s . . .

Humankind, becoming more industrialized and civilized, learned that by making people sit very still for long periods of time in front of a wooden box containing a piece of treated metal or glass, images could be captured for posterity. So was born the camera.

Many people wanted to take advantage of this advance in technology but refused to—or simply could not—sit still for the many minutes it took to capture the image.

One bright individual discovered that exploding small amounts of black powder held in a tray above the camera created enough light so that the plate was exposed quickly enough to avoid getting pictures of people with gunpowder burns all over their faces and clothing.

And he was usually right.

Fast forward to the late 1800s . . .

It was only a matter of time before someone else posed the question, "If I can see one picture of myself, why can't I see many pictures of myself taken in sequence and displayed quickly enough to make other people's eyes and brains believe that there is some sort of realistic motion involved?"

Maybe that wasn't the exact question, but the idea took hold and soon the motion picture was born. For years, the specialized equipment necessary to create motion pictures was available only to the very rich, and to the hundreds of "moving picture" studios popping up in such likely places as The Bronx. The equipment needed to view the "flickers" lay in the hands of the theater owners, their audiences held captive for the duration of each exhibit both by the experience of the spectacle and by the desire to see such scandalous pieces as *The First Kiss* and the marvels of traveling to the moon in a giant bullet as envisioned by some French director.

As the years passed, the picture was joined by sound, then color, and then by various theater-based additives such as smell-o-vision, screech-o-rama, vibrate-o-motion, electro-seat, and the likes. All of these added—some less than others—to the experience of the visuals.

Scanning quickly through the next fifty years . . .

The next decades saw a series of adaptations to the basic theme, but the ability to create and show movies still belonged to the few. Certainly, the invention of the hand-held movie camera was a boon to individuals and small companies wishing to create something visual. Refinements continue even to today, with the 16mm camera giving way to the 8mm camera, then the Super 8mm camera, then on to the shoulder-crushing video camera-with-tape-recorder-slung-over-your-other-shoulder, and on through other formats, to today's Hi-8 hand-held minicam marvels.

Each step in the evolution created new opportunities for those wanting to take advantage of the latest video technologies dealing with the creation as well as the display. With each step came cost advantages, improvements in quality, and new formats—everything leading to what has come to be known as the desktop digital video revolution.

As you read this today, the desktop digital video revolution has already happened. It's over! What remains is a real and thriving market, one that is growing much faster than anyone could have predicted—from the architectural groundwork laid by the introduction of QuickTime 1.0 in January 1991, to today where top-rated television shows are edited with desktop digital systems.

As recently as 1993, shows such as "SeaQuest: DSV" and "Babylon 5" would not have been possible—not for technical reasons, but for economic ones. Not only has creating these "effects" shows become affordable, but the quality of such effects has reached and passed the broadcast-quality threshold.

Yes, there *was* digital video before QuickTime and the Macintosh, but there was never a standard or a platform from which the broad base of potential users could take advantage of digital video.

The same type of people who once said color monitors have no business *in* business are the same nay-sayers proclaiming that digital video will never take off; it will never be as "big" as desktop publishing.

We predict that the desktop digital video market will surpass desktop publishing, and that both of these market segments will blur into a single entity during the coming years as businesses realize that they can get their messages to an ever-increasing segment of customers when all the available tools are used.

We are now into the third generation of hardware and software products based on the QuickTime architecture. There is plenty of competition out there with dozens of products at all price points. Today is the time for people, and businesses, to get on board. And that's where this book comes in; it is designed to guide you through the products, the technologies, and the techniques to help you find the solutions that fit your needs.

Digital video is just another step in the history of storytelling. It brings the ability to create and display the pictures and sounds that make up the stories that we want to tell to the common person.

This book is written primarily to help you understand more about the creation of digital video at the desktop level, but it also includes tricks and tips from the files of Toucan Studios to help you get the best results with your digital video projects. We have attempted to make it both informative and fun.

Learn and enjoy!

Andrew Soderberg and Tom Hudson
February 25, 1995

Part One

TOOLS AND TECHNOLOGY

1

A Digital Video Primer

As with any skill or discipline, it is helpful to have an understanding of the background and history of the subject. This sometimes takes the form of a primer (we prefer the pronunciation as if there were two m's: *prim mer*).

This section of the book can be considered the primer for digital video. It contains information and questions you should think about both when creating your own desktop digital studio and when producing digital videos.

Before continuing, we want to present you with our basic philosophy:

Although you can have just the right computer system for what you normally do, you can never have a system that is too powerful for digital video!

We have about a half-dozen corollaries and contradictions to this statement that appear in the book.

Now to the heart of the matter . . . What is digital video?

It is an approximation of analog video (what we see on TV and in theaters, unless you live in England where it is "on the telly" and in the theatre) using a series of 1s and 0s to create a stream of data that equates to individual color pixels that are displayed on a computer monitor in such a manner that we perceive them as whole images or movies. It sounds easy, right?

Wrong. Other than computing the daily growth in the U.S. gross national debt to the seventh decimal place, it is probably one of the most complex and computer-intensive task you will probably ever have your PC perform (note that we said "probably," because who knows: 3D virtual holograms may be next).

Because of the processing power requirements, it has not been economically or technically possible until recently to find a computer for under $1,000 capable of displaying a digital video movie at a reasonable frame rate and usable window size without any extra hardware assist.

Let's look at what got us to today.

MAKING ELECTRONS DANCE:
A Brief History of Digital Video
by Sheldon Renan

Mr. Renan wrote the first history of experimental films, Introduction to the American Underground Film, *in 1967. He founded the Pacific Film Archive at the University of California–Berkeley. He has written interactive and multimedia since 1981, including "The Treasure Disc," "Murder She Wrote Mystery Theater," and the "Luxor Casino Attractions" in Las Vegas. Mr. Renan also writes more conventional entertainment (the movie* Lambada*) and large-scale multimedia "vision events" for corporations such as Xerox and Intel.*

The roots of desktop video and multimedia reach back over fifty years to the pioneering work of independent film and mixed-media artists. The bleeding edge of artistic vision has been important in creating new ways of seeing and working with video. As the Art and Technology movement of the 1960s made clear, the two worlds fed and cross-stimulated each other.

Experiments in computer-driven film making began as early as 1939 (John and James Whitney in Southern California). By the mid-1950s, artists such as Hy Hirsch in San Francisco were manipulating electrons on cathode ray tubes (and filming the results). And Ernie Kovaks was doing the same thing on the NBC television network and broadcasting the results across America. As video technology developed, it was quickly integrated into the work of performance and mixed-media artists, as well as the work of "underground film makers."

In 1965, when I began research for a history of experimental film, I expected to be looking only at film. But I was soon taken to a townhouse in New York where dwelled Nam June Paik and some forty flickering dysfunctional television sets. Paik had written this manifesto: "As collage replaced oil paint, the cathode tube will replace the canvas."

Time quickly proved Paik correct. Sometimes the images were manipulated by artists with magnets. Sometimes they were programmed with computers. Sometimes they were integrated in interesting ways into live performance art. At one point, Paik was even taping tiny Sony televisions over the breasts of Charlotte Moorman, the topless cellist, in her avant-garde concerts.

Off-On, Scott Bartlett's radical journey to the event horizon of 1960s sensibility, was especially influential. This short film totally integrated and wired together video, film, and psychedelic vision (Bartlett had been host and stage manager for Ken Kesey's LSD-driven Trips Festival). *Off-On,* released in 1967, was widely duplicated and widely imitated. *Life* magazine blew up a frame into a full-color two-page spread for its special Picasso issue.

At the same time, the concept of "expanded cinema" was cooking up a bouillabaisse of multimedia and multiple images. Multimedia drew on a tradition that went

(continued)

all the way back to smoke-and-mirror magic theaters, peep shows, and panoramas of nineteenth-century Europe. Multiple images within the frame were more recent—Abel Gance's *Napoleon* (1927) and the multi-screen expo theaters of Charles and Ray Eames introduced in the 1950s.

As Paik had predicted, all this work became subsumed into the video screen, where images could more easily be combined, controlled, and manipulated.

A more purely electronic vision was emerging by the late 1960s. Steve Beck had begun to create what he called "synthetic video" and to do "video weaving" in real time with circuit and (later) chip design. The Vasulkas and others would soon open The Kitchen in New York.

Experimental film makers such as VanDerBeek, Emshwiller, and Belson began to partner with video artists. And by 1970 Brice Howard had founded the Video Workshop at KQED in San Francisco, giving Beck and other artists access to technology. Brice Howard also wrote *Videospace,* a book that began with these words:

> The mass of an electron . . .
> It is a material with which we can make.

It was also at this point that the microprocessor was being invented—starting the march of Moore's Law[1]—the steadily accelerating power of the computer to make electrons dance.

Advanced technology and artistic vision move forward side by side. In retrospect it is no accident that the Cubism of Picasso and Bracque and Einstein's Theory of Relativity emerged within twelve months of one another . . .

. . . or that individual artists will drive multimedia and desktop video to places that hardware companies could never imagine.

---

[1]"Moore's Law" is the observation by Gordon Moore, a founder of Intel, that the number of transistors manufacturers can place on computer chips tends to double every eighteen months. This effectively doubles the computing power available to end users every eighteen months.

Evolution: From Filmstrips to the Digital Desktop

You have probably heard the term *multimedia* before. Most uses of the term today refer to the combination of audio and video with some text, graphics, and other elements to form some sort of presentation. This may not be a *Webster's Dictionary* definition, but it will suffice for now.

What many people may not realize is that we have had multimedia around us for years and years. For starters, think motion pictures. Even the "silent" pictures were multimedia presentations: the picture, the text dialog, and the in-the-ater organ providing music all went together to make a multimedia experience.

**Figure 1.1
Modern multi-
media evolution.**

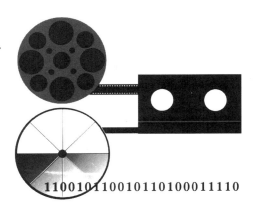

110010110010110100011110

But most of us weren't alive back then. If you are in your middle thirties or greater (not older, *greater*), then you no doubt remember film strips—short, very curled-up pieces of 35mm film with an accompanying record. Visuals, sometimes text, and almost always sound. Multimedia? You bet. PING!

If you've read the Introduction to this book, you already know that humans are storytellers and communicators by nature. We are also users of tools. Along with being one of the things that sets us apart from the beasts, using tools has always been a way for people to get more accomplished within a shorter period of time, and with—hopefully—less effort.

Handwritten correspondence has generally given way to the typed word. The typed word has given way to the word-processed word. And the word-processed word is giving way to the multimedia way of communicating.

Since you already have the basic tool, the computer, why limit yourself to just text? Today's computers are powerful and fast, and most can support the display of video and audio in addition to the text and graphics.

How does the video and most of the audio get into the computer? Via the desktop digital studio. And how does the best digital video and audio get produced? By knowing all the answers before you start.

Understanding Your Final Needs First to Get Proper Final Results

Why do you want to create a digital video?

What are you going to use digital video for?

Who is your audience?

How will you deliver the digital video and how will your audience view it?

In order to determine what is necessary to achieve a desired end result, you should understand your final needs before you begin. By answering these questions before starting, you make it easier to make the decisions about which digital video tools and techniques you should use to produce the results you want. This also can go a long way toward making the final product more effective.

Nobody can expect to be able to answer each of these questions for each project undertaken. But knowing as much before you begin puts you hands and feet above anybody who just dives in and plays it by ear.

Determine the Final Use—From Home to Broadcast

The techniques for producing good digital video of various types are all over the map; finding the right ones for your needs is *job one*. This begins with knowing as much as possible about the final use of the video. For instance, you don't need to use massive amounts of compression if the end result is meant to play directly from a fast hard disk.

You must match the capabilities of the media and the delivery platform to the processes you use. Otherwise, you won't be in business very long.

Just as a quick aside: Expectations can also widely differ from project to project. Clients have hired us for digital video projects requiring full-screen and full-motion display, but the target audience consisted of Macintosh LC computers and single-speed CD-ROM drives. A basically impossible task.

Setting expectations and understanding the limits of the technology is *job two*.

Some things to keep in mind. We expect that you have answered the first question at the top of this section (*Why do you want to create a digital video?*); otherwise, you probably wouldn't be reading this book.

Answering the last question next (*How will you deliver the digital video and how will your audience view it?*) gets you on the right path. What delivery method will be needed for your project? There are several options: videotape, CD-ROM, network, computer-resident. Each format has assumptions and ranges of options. Different types of digital audio and video hardware are needed for the various end results.

Tools and techniques vary depending on whether you create video to be saved back out to videotape, or video to be compressed and delivered digitally—say, on a CD-ROM.

Videotape expects that you will output in full-screen, full-motion video (30 fps). You don't have to, but that's the assumption. This requires the most performance from your system; capturing, editing, and outputting full-screen, full-motion video places you in the mid to high end of the equipment price category. Entry-level digitizing cards, such as Super Mac's Spigot To Tape, can "print to tape," but the quality is generally very low. These cards typically generate a quarter-screen image that is *pixel doubled* to full-screen size. A quick aside: In computers, full-screen generally means 640 ×

480 pixels or 320 × 240 pixels that have been "doubled" to create a full-screen display. As with NTSC television displays, this adheres to a 4:3 ratio.

SUGGESTION: Assuming that you can avoid it, you really don't want to use pixel-doubled video. Unless you have some proprietary technology, the results are usually less than satisfactory.

The CD-ROM has well-defined performance limits, *data rate* (the rate at which data is transferred from the CD-ROM to your computer) being the most important. Although the majority of CD-ROM drives sold today are "double speed" (300 K per second maximum), there are many of the older "single speed" drives (150 K per second or less) in the installed base. In the near future, triple and quad speed (450–600 K per second) CD-ROM drives will become more common.

If CDs are your delivery format, you must assess your viewers' equipment capabilities and set a minimum requirement to view your digital video. Today, 300 K per second is a safe bet for the drive capability, but that translates into different end rate depending on your delivery platform.

Low data rates require that there be some limits placed on the end-result digital video. These limits may be frame rate, frame size, image quality, or a combination of all three. A general rule of thumb is that a 300 K per second CD drive actually can sustain only 240 K per second in a Macintosh system, and 180 K per second in Windows systems. Such data rates can sustain digital video movies at 320 × 240 pixels running at 15 fps using either CinePak or Indeo, two of the most frequently used software formats for *compressing* and *decompressing* the large amounts of data required by digital video..

If you intend to create cross-platform CD-ROMs with digital video content, then you will need to use the lower data rate (Windows is rated at 180 K per second maximum) in order to ensure the best playback results on both systems.

These numbers will get better over time as both QuickTime and Video for Windows and the various CD drivers squeeze out more performance from the CD-ROM drive.

If your digital video production is going to stay on a computer and be played from hard disk, then you have more flexibility than any of the other playback options. You need only be concerned with the target computer's performance level and the hard disk transfer rate (generally fast enough for most applications.)

Another aspect to take into account is the quality of your video source. If you have a poor source, you will get a poor end result. Right now, many of you are sitting there thinking, "But, I generally work with projects where I have no input about the source."

Don't worry. While the perfect world would allow you to always have a say in how the source is created, that isn't a practical expectation. What *is* practical is that you can request the highest possible quality source materials. If that source is a videotape, you can't expect to get a good to high-quality end product from a dub of a dub of a VHS tape. You can get good results from a 3/4 SP or BetaCamSP source.

Yes. We know that that level of equipment is expensive. We don't own a BetaCamSP deck, yet we do a lot of work from BetaCamSP sources. We are blessed to work in an area that has several video rental businesses where we can pick up a deck for the one or two days a month we need it.

You need to know what the final delivery mechanism will be in order to make intelligent choices about how to work with and compress your digital video.

If you remember nothing else from this section, remember this: *No one tool is absolutely perfect for all the different possibilities.*

It is unrealistic to expect that you will run out and purchase half a dozen different software products and several different digital video cards. As you get further into perfecting your handling of digital video, you will find that investing in several titles and possibly more than a single card will give you the variety and range necessary to handle many different types of projects.

Determine Hardware and Software Requirements

There currently are no fewer than three major digital video standards, which you might think of in the same manner as the different tape formats (VHS, Beta, D2, etc.). These include QuickTime (Macintosh and Windows versions) and Video for Windows as well as several proprietary video standards.

Add to this the more than ten major digital compression formats, including JPEG, MPEG, DVI, CinePak, Indeo, Video, Wavelets, DCT, YUV, Raw RGB, etc. (Figure 1.2). If you don't already know about these different for-

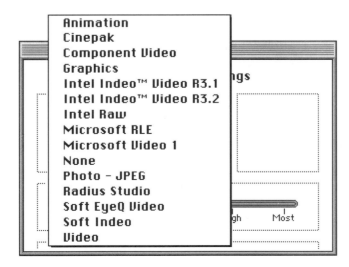

Figure 1.2 Some of the compressors available to you.

mats called *codecs* (short for COMpressor/DECompressor), refer to Chapter 2, "Digital Video Systems," for more detailed information.

There are a lot of possible combinations.

Of course, it is not true that each of the digital video standards supports each of the compression standards. And QuickTime for Windows doesn't allow digital editing work, just playback. (There are exceptions . . . again, see Chapter 2 for more details.)

There are two compressors, Indeo and CinePak, that are available on all three major digital video standards (QuickTime for Macintosh, QuickTime for Windows, and Video for Windows).

Another factor in deciding which tools and techniques to employ is the capability of the display hardware. If your product absolutely must run on an older Macintosh computer, let's say an original Macintosh LC using a single-speed CD-ROM drive, you are going to have to carefully balance the use of tools and techniques to get results that play smoothly while maximizing the playback quality.

And that brings us to . . .

The rubber band analogy of compression. As we have discussed previously, you need to understand the final results in order to select the appropriate tools and techniques for compressing digital video. There are many different possibilities from which to choose, made slightly more difficult by the way in which the various compression schemes work.

Compression is the key factor in the successful processing of digital video for playback on any platform. You must know the capabilities of that platform and compress to meet those needs. Compression is very much like several people pulling a large "rubber band" in different directions. If they

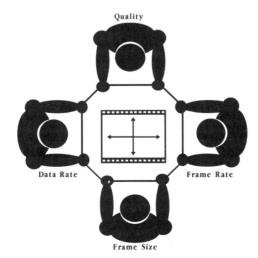

**Figure 1.3
The rubber
band compres-
sion analogy—
pulling evenly.**

**Figure 1.4
When the rub-
ber band is
pulled more in
one direction.**

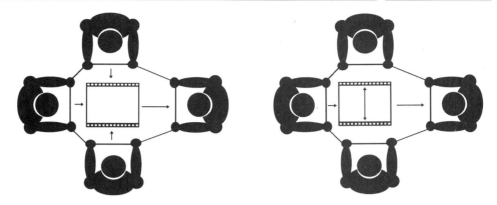

all pull together, the band is evenly stretched (Figure 1.3). They can only stretch the band so far in any single direction before it reaches full tension and pulls some of the other people back toward the center. Sometimes the pull is distributed evenly across the remaining people, and sometimes only one of the remaining people is pulled in, while the others stand their ground (Figure 1.4). The greater the pull by one person, the less the others are able to pull in their own directions.

In digital video, the "people" are actually different factors that act on raw video as it compresses. These factors, or vectors, differ from compressor to compressor; most of the vectors are user-selectable, with some compressors having more vectors to set than others. In some cases, the software being used may preset some of these vectors, whereas another application may require you to set a different set of vectors.

The vectors represented in these figures are not the only ones you need to be aware of when working with digital video. There are others that will be discussed later.

As one of the settings changes, it generally affects the quality of the finished, compressed video. Depending on where each one is set, the others may need to be adjusted to achieve the desired end result.

The most common user-selectable vectors to consider (Figure 1.5) are:

- *Spatial:* the quality of a given image
- *Temporal:* the quality of a sequence of images over time
- *Frame Size:* the X/Y size of the movie (i.e., 320 × 240, 160 × 120)
- *Frame Rate:* the number of frames to be displayed per second
- *Data Rate:* the amount of data to be stored and used per second of video or audio

Let's examine each of these.

Spatial settings are generally rated either as a number between 1 and 100 or as a setting such as Low, Medium, High, Highest. The greater the num-

**Figure 1.5
Various user-
selectable set-
tings.**

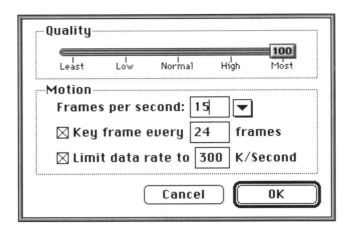

ber or higher the setting, the higher the quality of the end result. Many compressors and applications refer to this as the *Quality* setting. This setting has an effect on the data rate, but its most significant effect is on how good (or bad) the digital video will look when played back.

Temporal settings refer to the group of settings that control the quality of the digital video over time. These include frame rate, key frame rate, and data rate. The key frame/differenced frames ratio has the most control over keeping the compressed image from differing too greatly from the original. If key frames are set too far apart, the compressed video drifts too far from the original. Set them close together, and the resultant data rate distribution causes the Spatial quality to be affected.

Frame Size is one of the largest determinators of how large (in megabytes) your final file is and how it plays (the pixel rate) on the hardware you have. Generally, quarter-screen (320 × 240) and smaller sizes are used for multimedia work.

Frame Rate directly affects the smoothness of your video, but it also affects the size of your finished video file and the amount of data available to provide a good motion picture. Frame rates of under 12 fps create movies that are too "jerky," whereas frame rates that are too high may not allow the movie to play properly on many systems. The sheer amount of data may be too much for the playback platform to handle.

Data Rate is the amount of data per second to which the movie is to be compressed. Low data rates require much more compression and force more source data to be thrown away during compression in order to reach the target data rate (see example, following). Target rates for CD-ROM use range from 90 kps to 260 kps, depending on the platform (Macintosh or Windows) and the CD-ROM drive speed.

Each of these vectors can be set in many steps to vary the effect of that factor on the image being compressed. The trick comes in balancing each of these setting to get the best overall result. We discuss this balancing act in detail in the next chapter.

If we had unlimited space, CPU performance, and data transfer speed (and, of course, budget!), we would not need compressors. We could capture the video and audio at their highest possible quality, size, rate, and so forth, and display them as-is. This would be the digital equivalent of videotape and would be virtually loss-less; what goes in comes out looking exactly the same.

In reality, there are a number of limitations that must be considered when deciding how to set these vectors for the results we want. We must think of when, where, and how the movie will be viewed, stored, and accessed.

For example: Let's say that we want our video to be used with a CD-ROM player on either a Macintosh or PC. The first thing to consider is *data rate;* will this be running on a single-speed, double-speed, or faster CD-ROM drive? Different CD-ROM drives transfer data at rates ranging from 90 K per second to as much as 600 K per second. The most common and readily available drives today can sustain date transfer rates of between 200 and 240 K per second when used on Macintosh computers. Only the very fastest PCs can keep up with this data rate.

This sets limits on how far we are able to "stretch the band" in other areas of compression. A 240 K per second data rate supports a CinePak- or Indeo-based 15 fps 320 × 240 pixel movie with room for 22 KHz 16-bit audio. With these settings (and assuming a high-quality source), the resulting image quality can be very good. If a lower data rate is required—if you must target the video for a single-speed CD-ROM drive—to maintain an equivalent image quality level, one or more of the vectors must be adjusted to a lower setting (such as dropping the audio quality or reducing the frame rate).

Likewise a smaller, 240 × 180 pixel movie at 30 fps with 11 KHz 8-bit audio, set to Highest image quality, will work in the same data rate of 240 K per second.

Although creating a movie with a 240 K per second data rate at 320 × 240 pixels, 30 fps, using 22 KHz 16-bit audio can be done, the rubber band effect snaps the temporal and spatial quality of the movie downwards into the mud! Because the human ear is better able to detect mistakes or errors in audio, in the case of low playback performance QuickTime is designed to gracefully degrade the video frame rate to keep the presentation in sychronization with the audio tracks. Depending on the performance of the playback CPU, you may see frames being dropped in an effort to keep up with the timing. Likewise, audio may be clipped in extreme cases as the slower computer attempts to handle the higher data rate video first.

It isn't (pardon the pun) a pretty picture!

You can't have a CinePak-compressed movie running at moderate data rates with full 30 fps, large screen sizes and high-quality audio unless the source contains almost exclusively solid colors with next to nothing moving in the movie. (But then it wouldn't be a movie, would it?)

Another example: You are preparing a presentation for a client that will ultimately be delivered on videotape. The resulting quality must be high enough for a typical VHS tape player (we're not going on national TV with this one). This basic output "need" is already directing how you will capture and compress your source materials. It says that there is a requirement to use one of the several hardware capture/compression boards available, a hard disk fast enough to sustain a minimum of 2 MB of data transfer per second, and one large enough to hold all the source clips and edited results (probably 1–2 gigabytes).

This setup allows full-screen recording at 30 fps directly to the hard disk. Note that the faster the transfer rate of the hard disk, the higher the quality of the captured video (and the greater the overall storage requirements).

As you increase the quality of the captured video, less compression is applied to the individual frames, and therefore more disk space is required. A single, full-screen frame of uncompressed video requires about 900 K of storage space; a full second of video (30 frames) requires 27 MB of space!

The highest quality JPEG setting (allowing 4:1 compression and discussed in greater detail in Chapter 2) still means that you require 7 MB of storage and playback capability per second of video, much more than most hard drives can handle. Most midrange JPEG cards don't offer the performance to sustain continuous 4:1 compression rates; the requirement for 7 MB per second relates only to high-end JPEG solutions.

Generally, JPEG must be set to a 10:1 compression level to get the data rate down to manageable size. Although this setting causes some degree of degraded image quality on individual frames, the resultant quality when played in real time is still better than most standard VHS VCRs.

Learning how to control the various ways to stretch the rubber band will give you the control you need to create an excellent result for any type of output you want.

Do you always need to know the output needs before you capture and process digital video? Yes, you always must know your output needs before starting!

While this is *always* the hard, fast rule we present you with, remember that we always have exceptions.

Exception Number 1: *There are ALWAYS exceptions to the rules!*

In Part Two, "Techniques," we discuss how you can get around this and other rules. Sometimes successfully, and sometimes less so.

Overview of Tools and Technologies

As with many things in life, the better the source material, the better the results, or as the wise programmer once said, "garbage in—garbage out."

Use the highest-quality source that you can afford. It's as simple as that . . . really!

The basic reason is this: All compression techniques must evaluate the incoming digitized images in order to compress them (several techniques compare sets of many frames before compressing them, whereas others compare contiguous frames). When an incoming video signal contains noticeable noise—drop-outs, color problems, jitter, moiré, color bleed, etc.—these problems become next to impossible to correct once digitized and cause the compressor to not compress the resulting file as small, or as well, as it is capable of.

The results often are unusable.

Keep the source quality as high as your budget allows. Look at everything from the quality of your hardware, cables, etc., on down. Sometimes it is the little things that trip you up. Just because your source comes originally from a 3-chip camera with a BetaCam deck, don't think that you can scrimp on the tape stock. Noise and dropouts—things that are as inevitable as the tides when dealing with low-cost tape—are a big no-no when compressing digital video.

SUGGESTION: Don't recycle your master tapes. Once a tape has been recorded, it is nearly impossible for standard decks to totally erase the old image. Yes, a bulk eraser is better, but the pros don't reuse tapes for production master work, and we follow that lead. The exception is for test purposes or as personal tapes; that's OK, just not for your masters.

If you create digital video for yourself or friends, where you're not making any money and may not need to worry about the highest quality, then a standard VHS or 8mm camcorder is going to be acceptable as the source for movies that will end up processed to smaller than quarter-screen.

When you create movies that are quarter-screen or larger, then an SVHS or Hi-8 source is the absolute minimum. These two source formats give you the signal bandwidth and color stability necessary for capturing good digitized images.

We highly recommend that if you create professional digital video, whether it be for multimedia CD-ROMs or videos for broadcast, you use a TBC (Time Base Corrector). This is used in conjunction with a waveform monitor and vector scope to properly adjust and correct the video signal before it is digitized and compressed (Figure 1.6).

Time base correction is an important step because the quality and stability of a video signal can drift depending on the type and quality of playback deck being used.

**Figure 1.6
Typical Wave-
form and Vector
Scope displays.**

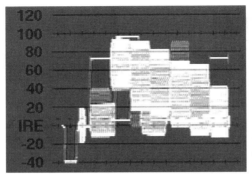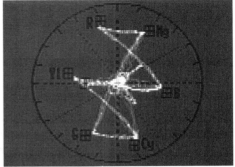

If you produce digital video destined for transfer to videotape that will be duplicated or aired, then we recommend professional SVHS as a minimum tape system, and much better (3/4 SP, BetaCam, Broadcast) if you've got the budget.

The corollary to the "garbage in, garbage out" statement is that "even the best video can come out looking like garbage if some of the processing tools are substandard." Use what is within your economic range, but you can do much to minimize quality loss by carefully watching how everything works together and avoiding the weak links. Some of the small details that can bite you include:

- Cheap tape stock (already discussed)

- Inexpensive, worn, or damaged cables

- Excessively long cables or multiple, interconnected cables

- Dust in your video deck, including dirty heads

- Magnetic interference (unshielded speakers, hardware, and so forth)

We discuss some of the dos and don'ts of selecting your hardware in the section titled "Hardware Considerations."

As important as your selection of hardware are the techniques you employ when using it. Although we cover many tips and techniques later in the book, there are several points that can be made up front.

We have yet to find a good piece of software that doesn't leave plenty of room for user adjustments (see Figure 1.7). These adjustments all affect the quality of the finished product. More detailed information on this subject is to be found by turning back to "The Rubber Band Analogy of Compression" earlier in this chapter.

Regardless of your settings, there are any number of things that can affect how your tools function. For instance, there are several taboos, including:

- Running more than one piece of software at a time (This steals valuable processing time.)

Figure 1.7
Typical adjust-ment settings.

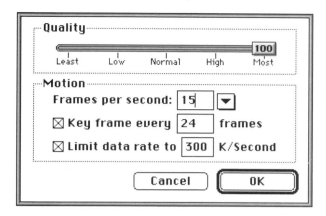

- Running lots of extensions, fonts, and so forth (Shut off anything you don't need.)
- Being connected to, and sharing across, a network
- Having the memory allocations set too low in your applications

We talk about lots of different techniques in this book, but the truth is that you need to experiment to find out what works best for you. Techniques differ depending on such factors as the speed of your computer's processor, the speed and capabilities of your other hardware, your source materials, and the final delivery vehicle.

Use our techniques as a springboard for developing your own. They have been gathered over the past several years, through trial and error, and even through asking others for help.

SUGGESTION: When in doubt, ask others. Nobody has done everything, and everybody has something they can learn from someone else.

We gladly share with others and don't hesitate to call people when we get stimied. So far, we have found very little in the way of professional jealousy in the digital video arena.

Let's all hope it stays that way!

Software Considerations

The software you select for your desktop video studio depends, of course, on the computer platform you plan to use. Regardless of your platform, you must first choose your video *architecture*.

There are several digital video architecture standards in the market—including QuickTime, Video for Windows, and Avid OMF—and several proprietary ones—for example, Newtek Flyerand Matrox.

**Figure 1.8
A QuickTime
playback
window.**

Of these, only one can be said to be a true industry standard. It is in wide use today and supports cross-platform development and playback.

That architecture is QuickTime from Apple Computer, Inc. QuickTime is used on: the Macintosh computer (obviously); on PCs running Windows 3.1 or later, Silicon Graphics systems, and QuickTime's premier compressor, CinePak; and is also used by Next, The 3DO Company, Sega, Atari, Time Warner Interactive, Cirrus Logic, Weitek Comm, Western Digital, and Windows NT systems.

You may already have noticed that this book leans heavily toward QuickTime as our architecture of choice. This is for a number of reasons, among them its cross-platform capabilities. The Chapter 2 sections on QuickTime and QuickTime for Windows contain more complete information on QuickTime as an architecture, and on QuickTime as a development and playback environment on both of these platforms. We have also included QuickTime on the accompanying CD-ROM.

In order to fully utilize QuickTime—or any architecture—you must also use appropriate software and hardware that supports that architecture. Most of us settle on a single hardware setup and vary the software either by project or as new and more feature-rich applications become available. This is the intelligent approach; software changes and is enhanced at a faster rate than hardware.

The remainder of this section discusses the various general categories of software applications used in the production of digital video. This informa-

Figure 1.9 Some current popular digital video applications.

tion, along with the specific software descriptions located in later chapters, will help guide you in selecting the kinds of software tools you need.

Capture Applications

Example: MovieRecorder

A "capture" application is used to record digitized video clips to your hard disk from a digitizer card (see the section "Video-Specific Hardware Considerations," later in the chapter). Most digitizer cards are packaged with a capture application. Sometimes these are simple, no-frills utilities; sometimes they are custom applications designed to take full advantage of the features found only on that card.

One of the things to look for when shopping for a digitizer card, assuming that the basic card features are the same, is the features of its bundled application.

Most of the full-featured editor applications also have capture functionality built into them. The good news is that if the capture card is QuickTime compliant, and the capture application is QuickTime compliant, then they work together even if they are from different companies. (That is the beauty of having a standard like QuickTime.)

In a capture application you set several variables to determine the results you want to get from the video digitizer: window size; frame rate; color depth; audio quality (if any) and sample rate; compression method desired and its intrinsic settings, etc. These settings are discussed in the Techniques section of this book.

A capture application lets you preview the digital video from your video source in a window on your monitor. You cue up the video source and then start recording when you see the section you want.

Some recorder applications (and/or digitizer cards) do not pass video through to the display while they are in the act of recording. This is representative of many less expensive cards. If this is the case for you, we recommend you connect a traditional video monitor to the *preview* (or *second video*) output on your tape source. If you only have one out, some monitors allow video to be "looped" through it to the digitizer. This can degrade the video quality that eventually reaches your card.

The same kind of degradation can result from using a splitter to achieve two video outputs where there is really only one. A good rule to remember is that the fewer components a signal must pass through, and the shorter the route, the better the signal.

All the more reason to have a digitizer solution that allows viewing of the source while recording to disk.

**Players/
Viewers**

Example: MoviePlayer (and several shareware applications)

A player application is designed to view digital video clips from wherever they are stored (hard disk, CD-ROM, etc.). Some players (Apple's MoviePlayer, for example) will allow simple "cuts only" editing using the standard *Cut, Copy,* and *Paste* features of the Macintosh. You can trim video

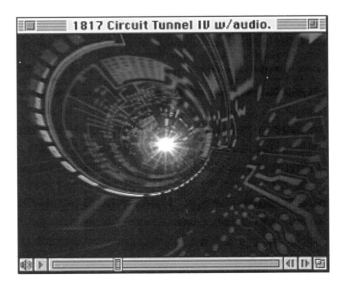

**Figure 1.10
Example of a
player display.**

clips to the desired scenes easily, or make a new movie from several clips by using the *Paste* technique.

A very nice feature of QuickTime is that you can save several different edited versions of your movie clips without modifying the originals *and* without taking up any additional hard disk space. QuickTime allows the player to save a movie alias.

This alias does not contain any movie data, only index pointers to the selected segments in the original movie clips. This allows for endless re-editting before you settle on the results you want.

Editors

Examples: Premiere, VideoShop

Using an editor is where you will spend most of your on-line time. QuickTime editors let you review your raw footage, arrange specific clips in sequence, add backgrounds and special effects, create transitions between scenes, add and mix audio tracks, and save the finished piece in a specific format and frame rate. Unless you have the budget for more than one, you should spend a good amount of time deciding which editor application you will use.

Read reviews, check our comparisons, ask your peers who use these applications. They can be very robust, feature rich, and complex to master. Until the next generation of such software comes along, no one application does everything, nor is everything they do done well.

Evaluate them against *your* requirements.

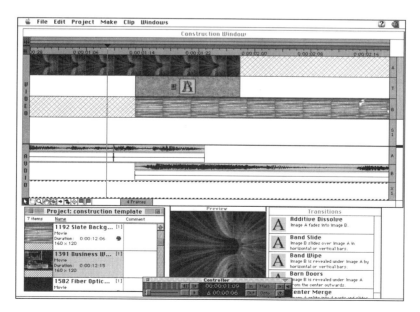

**Figure 1.11
Adobe Premiere:
an example of
an editor.**

**Figure 1.12
VideoFusion: an
example of an
effects program.**

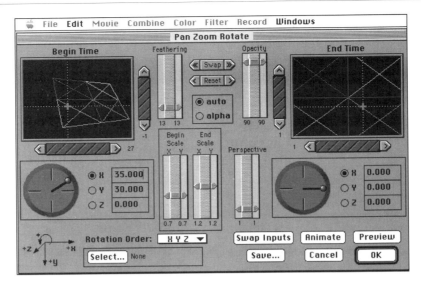

Special Effects

Examples: AfterEffects, AfterImage, VideoFusion, Elastic Reality, Morph

These applications are the desktop equivalent to six-figure digital video editing (DVE) hardware. In fact, they can often do complex effects that cannot be accomplished with the much more expensive equipment. Of course, they can't do them in real time, and that is why the DVE hardware costs so much. But what they may lack in speed (which can be compensated for by using high-performance computers) they more than make up for in flexibility, sheer number of possible effects, and layering capabilities.

Utilities

Examples: MovieShop, MovieAnalyzer, ConvertToMovie

These are the little workhorses of the digital video world. They are often underrated, almost unknown tools that can make all the difference between doing something in just hours versus taking days!

These applications fill a void of features that should exist in more mainstream commercial applications, but don't. Yet. This may be because developers of the mainstream applications are not digital video professionals. They may be great programmers, but they may not have the necessary insight into what working digital video editors really use.

These applications are often unsupported, may have bugs—more often than commercial applications—and generally are targeted at batch-processing tasks. (Batch processing is something the other applications don't get around to until version 4.0.)

**Figure 1.13
MovieAnalyzer:
an example of a
utility.**

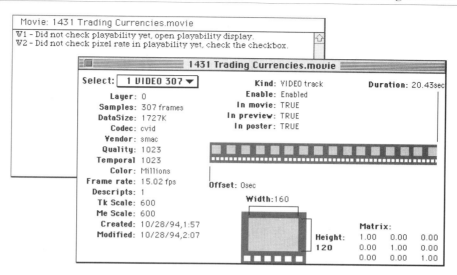

Repetitive processing tasks are the most time-consuming (read: *boring*) things you will do on your projects, yet they are the most common tasks. Since your computer is probably idle from midnight to 8 A.M., that becomes the perfect time to batch process those seventy-two ten-second clips you need to compress for your client, "economically . . . by tomorrow!"

Batch processing is one of those "the more things change the more they remain the same" subjects. When computers (during the era of mainframes) were the domain of big companies, they needed to be designed to be

**Figure 1.14
DeBabelizer:
an example of
a batching
program.**

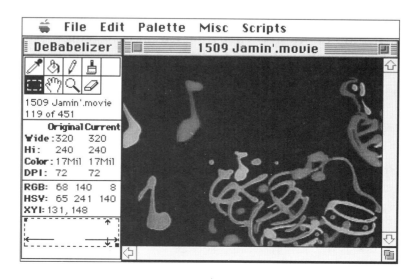

batch processors; access was limited and there were more—repetitive—tasks to be completed than there were terminals from which to process.

The advent of personal computers allows us to do unique tasks to solve individual problems, all in a self-contained desktop box. Now that PCs are more powerful than the first supercomputers—like the Cray—people use them for more process-intensive, time-consuming tasks. That puts us back where we started with the need for batch processing!

Although some developers haven't opened their eyes to this fact yet, batch processing is one of the most important capabilities in which you should invest, especially if your income comes from producing multimedia. We use several good batch-processing utilities including DeBabelizer by Equilibrium, Batch-It! by Gryphon, and PhotoMatic by DayStar.

Apple has been pushing developers to adopt AppleScript, to make their applications compliant. AppleScript lets you create scripts that control an application to do almost any set of repetitive tasks. But who wants to learn a scripting language? (Actually, you may want to look at AppleScript seriously. There are some very strong capabilities in AppleScript that may come in handy. Even if you don't have the time, try to find a local source for this sort of work.)

What developers should be doing—some are, and you should look for this in new applications—is making their applications *recordable*. That is to say, the application "watches" you complete a set of tasks and records them as a script for you. You end up with a new menu item that contains this "batch" of steps that can be applied to an image, movie, document, and so forth, or to a folder full of files!

This is essentially the core of what DeBabelizer and PhotoMatic are all about.

Authoring Tools

Examples: Apple Media Tool, Director, Action!, Producer Pro, HyperCard, SuperCard

Unless you just hand off the movies you make to someone else, you need to think about how to present them. There are many "multimedia" authoring tools available for both Macintosh and PCs. This category is dominated by Macromedia, along with Director, Action, and Authorware. But there is plenty of new competition.

If you haven't already settled on an authoring tool, the issues you should be considering are:

- Do you need cross-platform delivery capabilities?
- Is this for training or presentation?
- Is this a value-added service you provide?
- Does this job need to be done yesterday?

**Figure 1.15
Director 4.0: an
example of an
authoring tool.**

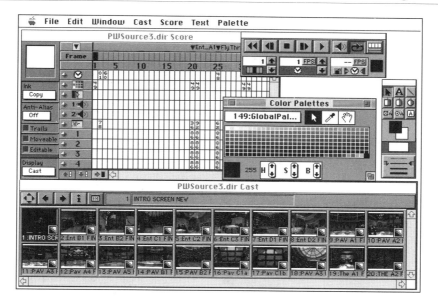

There are two basic types of authoring tool environments—script-based (Hypercard, SuperCard, and others) and media-based (Director, Apple Media Tool, and others). Each has its own pros and cons, and the tools within each category vary widely. If you require a high level of control over your multimedia project interface, you may want to lean toward a script-based tool. If you are a visual type, as most artists and media professionals are, you will want to lean toward the media-based tools.

Apple Media Tool, available for test drive and purchase from the accompanying CD-ROM, is kind of a hybrid, taking advantage of both styles. It is a media-based authoring tool with the ability to be augmented by adding modules created in its custom programming environment. To customize this application does require a "C" language programmer, but it provides the flexibility both kinds of tools offer.

Director, also on the CD-ROM, is the most popular media authoring tool available. It is very powerful, and it is cross-platform. It uses a Cast, Actor, and Stage metaphor, but it has the drawback of a steep learning curve. It offers a great deal of power but can definitely be overkill for most small projects.

Many small businesses are based on offering Director services, so it may be more cost effective to subcontract to a Director expert for a specific project than to start from scratch learning and using Director yourself.

Presentation

Examples: Persuasion, PowerPoint, Harvard Graphics

Adobe Persuasion (that's hard to get used to; as of this writing, Adobe and Aldus have just completed their merger) and Microsoft PowerPoint pretty

**Figure 1.16
Persuasion: an
example of a
presentation
program.**

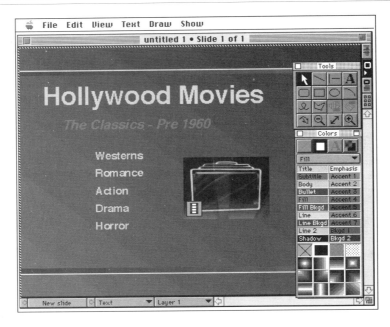

much own the presentation software market on Macintosh. PowerPoint and
Harvard Graphics are among the most popular on the Windows side.
Within their last one or two revisions, these applications have added basic
compatibility for multimedia elements such as sound, animation, movies,
etc. In fact, the most recent versions of Persuasion now offer branching, for
limited interactive capabilities.

For most straightforward (linear) presentations, these applications are all
you probably need. Most offer, and we suggest that you take advantage of,
upgrade programs that bring the latest and greatest to you for a reduced
price. As time passes, we see the presentation and multimedia product markets blurring into one.

These are the basic categories and some examples of types of software we
use in our digital video business. We go into more detail about specific
applications in the following chapters.

A word of caution when dealing with what might be termed "borderline"
digital video software—presentation applications in general being on that
borderline. Be careful about the capabilities a product might advertise in its
list of features. We have noticed that some use the word *multimedia* to
describe their overall functionality. *Multimedia* has become a buzz word
these companies use to sell products. Some of these applications fit into the
multimedia arena, but they may only support a small set of features that

may not meet enough of your requirements to be worth the purchase price. A word of caution: Be sure that a product manufacturer's interpretation of multimedia and what you actually require from a multimedia application are the same.

As with all of your purchases, both software and hardware, look for tools that will meet your needs today and your potential requirements for the future. There are applications out there that may cost a bit more than you planned to spend initially, but their capabilities may be ones that you can foresee growing into.

On the other side of the coin, don't expect the software you buy today to meet all of your needs down the road. You will diversify and take on projects that you may not have dreamed of, yet.

Believe us; we did.

Video-Specific Hardware Considerations

Unless you have an unlimited budget, the hardware you choose today for your desktop digital studio is likely to be with you for some time. Selecting the right hardware products for your current and future needs is very important. Assuming you've done your homework on what you want to do with digital video, you can significantly narrow the range of products you will need to evaluate.

In this section, we break the video-specific hardware products into three categories:

- Entry level (products under $1,000)
- Midrange (products from $2,500 to $6,000)
- High end (products from $10,000 to $40,000)

Entry and midrange products are usually cards that plug into your computer. High-end products are usually full-system solutions. Note that there are many high-end products above $40,000, some ranging into the six figures that, although they technically sit on the "desktop," are not desktop products within the scope of this book. You should also note that there are products we cover in the book that may cost less than $1,000 and are, in fact, very professional and powerful tools.

We have learned an important thing over the past several years: Don't judge a product solely on its price. If a product does a better job, saves time (read: *dollars*), or both, the return on investment (ROI) can make a seemingly costly product relatively inexpensive.

**Figure 1.17
Spigot: an
example of an
entry-level card**

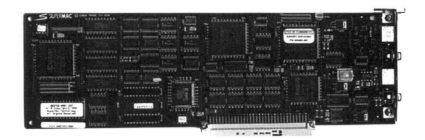

Entry-Level Products

Most entry-level digital video products are digitizer-only cards. By this we mean they capture frames of video, digitize each frame, and then store it to a hard drive. They *do not* compress the digital video; they expect that you will use a software-based compressor built into QuickTime (such as Video, CinePak, etc.).

Some cards can capture only a limited number of frames per second, and/or restrict the size of the window. Don't expect to use one of these products to make the next MTV music video.

Some of the lower-priced cards often do not allow you to digitize audio. In most Macintosh computers, this is not a problem—audio capture capability is built in. But for PCs, you will need a separate audio capture card. (Yes, there are older Macintosh models that do not have audio capability and therefore would also need some form of audio capture card, but they generally are too slow to use for digital video.)

There are many older cards that also offer these features but are no longer on the market (Mass Microsystems, Axion, early RasterOps cards). Generally these entry-level cards are capable of up to 320 × 240 pixel window sizes and speeds of up to 15 fps. Such cards include:

- Radius (SuperMac) Spigot and Spigot to Tape
- Sigma Movie-Movie
- Apple's AV card for the Power Macintosh 6100, 7100, 8100
- The built-in AV capability of Apple's Quadra 660AV, 840AV, and Quadra/Performa 630

Midrange Products

Although we classify these as "midrange" products, they are not midrange quality. They can, in fact, create very high quality output and have been used to create content that has been broadcast on cable and networks.

Midrange products are usually characterized by their single board, "all-in-one-card" nature. They offer digitizing, compression, audio capture, and

Figure 1.18 Radius Studio-Vision card: one of the midrange products.

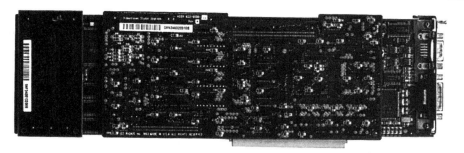

video output in one package. They are based on a widely accepted compression standard called JPEG, but each uses different digitizing techniques—the factor that has the biggest impact on the quality each is capable of producing (all other settings being equal).

Midrange cards include:

- Radius (SuperMac) Digital Film
- Radius StudioVision
- RasterOps MoviePak2
- Truevision TARGA 2000

This level of product is good for everything from multimedia content production to digital editing and mastering of content back to videotape for air.

Some of you might scoff at the idea of using the output from these products for broadcast, but it does happen. Over the past several years we have talked with station engineers who look at the quality of the signal and images that this range of products creates. And the tide has turned from a general opinion of "no way" to being "acceptable for air" as these products have increased in quality.

There are still broadcasters who won't touch these systems—not because of a fear of new technology, but because they just don't make the grade in their book. Strictly speaking, they are right.

What is acceptable, and what is not, is in the eye of the beholder. The JPEG products in this category have gone from producing "less than VHS" quality output of just a year or two ago, to creating a signal and image quality equivalent to that of BetaCam SP.

But here is the disclaimer! *Your actual mileage may vary!* All of the key components of a desktop video studio, including the type of content and source tape format, will have a great impact on the quality of the results you can achieve from products in this price range.

High-End Systems

High-end solutions for the desktop video studio are not the piece-it-together-yourself from every category type we have talked about so far. These are systems that range from $15,000 to $40,000 and more. There typically are two kinds of high-end systems:

- You purchase the system complete from a single provider, where all the necessary components are part of the purchase price. These companies have done all the integration work and come the closest to a plug-and-play desktop video studio you will find.

- You supply a specific model computer, purchase the key components from the "system" supplier (generally a digitizer/compressor card set), and purchase the other components (specifically defined by the system supplier as being compatible) from other sources. Besides creating the digitizing and compression hardware for professional video output, they have done all the hard work of determining the right combination of models and brands of components that will complement their hardware. Every component has been tested to be the optimum choice for the system solution.

The common trait of these two system types is that they are complete, self-contained solutions for producing digital video that, in most cases, is targeted to end up recorded to videotape.

These systems are not well suited for general multimedia work. They may be compatible with QuickTime but often have their own custom software that must be used with their hardware, limiting your choice of software tools. Depending on your needs, that may or may not be a problem.

Figure 1.19 ImMIX Video Cube—a powerful, high-end editing and effects solution.

For our money, if your work is targeted to multimedia projects, then these high-end systems are overkill.

If you produce projects that are destined for cable, broadcast, or high-budget corporate videos, they you should seriously consider investing in a high-end system.

If you are a studio, production company, or corporation with a large media group, then these systems can be cost-savers. Providing desktop production facilities to more people can save big on wasted (read: *expensive*) on-line edit suite time.

General Hardware Considerations

All of the other key hardware components of a desktop video studio can have a significant impact on the quality of the results you can get from a system. Let's look at them in general order of importance.

CPUs

The performance level of a CPU (the processor within the computer) has an impact on the capabilities of the digital video production system you put together. But it may not be as important as you might think. Many of the digitizing cards perform most of their processing right on the card. The CPU in your computer merely becomes a traffic director and file transfer service. If you are going to use a card that falls into this category, maybe what you should be most interested in is not your CPU.

What many people overlook is the basic plumbing of the computer—the performance of the bus (the internal "data highway" and place into which these cards plug). In Macintosh computers, this is known as the NuBus.

**Figure 1.20
The Power Macintosh 8100.**

For example: When the Power Macintosh (Figure 1.20) was first intro-duced, people assumed that everything about these new computers was better, faster, and more robust than the previous generation of computers (the 660AV/840AV). Yes, the CPU runs up to 6x faster (when running appli-cations specifically written for the new RISC processor), but it was slower when running existing applications. In this case, the processor was not the key issue. What was the issue was that the initial performance of the NuBus was only one-quarter that of the previous generation.

Previous Macintosh AV computers had been specifically designed with digital video in mind and therefore had high-performance (up to 20 MB per second) NuBus capabilities. The first Power Macintosh computers were tar-geted for more "mainstream" uses and did not include the same NuBus technology. Don't get us wrong—we like the Power Macs and use them.

The point is that when these machines first came out, they were not capable of handling the high data rates (4 to 7 MB per second) that medium to high-end digitizing cards generate.

This did not go unnoticed or unaddressed. Within several months, Apple and the third-party card manufacturers modified some software drivers to make these cards work in the new Power Macintosh computers.

If there is anything we've learned by watching this transpire, it is that you should always think "holistically" when deciding on the right compo-nents for your system. Look at the whole package from individual hard-ware capabilities to how the software you will use works.

Video Sources

We cannot emphasize this point enough: *Get the highest-quality video equipment your budget will allow.* Even simple things like the quality of the video and audio cables you use have an impact on the quality of your results.

In increasing order of quality, your video sources include:

- Composite video from consumer VHS and Beta equipment is the worst
- S-video (Y/C) from consumer equipment (Hi-8 or SVHS) is better
- S-video (Y/C) from industrial equipment (3/4 SP) is next
- S-video (Y/C) from laserdisc is almost the best
- Component video or Y/C from professional equipment (BetaCam, SP, SVHS) is best

The two most common and optimum solutions for video source material are BetaCam SP and Professional SVHS. Both formats offer the quality, res-olution, and signal strength necessary for high-quality digital video capture. Less common, but equally as good, is Component MII.

We do not cover broadcast equipment in this book, as it is far beyond the book's scope. Assume it safe to say that if you have broadcast video equipment already, well . . . we're very happy for you.

Most tape-based video should be run through a TBC (Time Base Corrector) and adjusted while viewing a waveform/vector scope monitor before going to the digitizer. Improper setup and balance of the video signal can make the output from most professional decks look worse than the cheapest consumer model VHS players.

For entry-level digital video uses, TBCs are not required. We realize that your budget may not support the cost of this type of equipment—typically in the $1,000–$3,000 range—but caution you that your final video quality will not be as good as if you do use one.

We do not cover the use of TBCs, waveform monitors, and vector scopes in this book; there is enough material on them alone for many books. (And they exist already. Look in the "Suggested Reading" appendix for sources on this subject.)

Hard Disk Subsystems

What is a hard disk subsystem? In simple terms, it is part of your computer system you refer to as "the hard drive(s)." Hard disks come in all shapes and sizes (kind of like people), and their capabilities vary based on their intended uses (Figure 1.21).

For our purposes, there are three basic types of hard disk subsystems:

1. *Single drives:* Just your typical hard disk drive. This is a single drive mechanism (regardless of the number of "platters" inside) either

Figure 1.21 Examples of several hard disk subsystems.

installed internally or connected externally to your computer. Also in this category are removable drives. These include high-speed SyQuest and magneto-optical drives, which now offer the significant storage capacity and sustainable data rates sufficient for digital video use. Because of their incremental low cost-per-byte for blank media, they make an excellent archive storage choice.

2. *Mini-arrays:* An array is generally two identical drives, usually in a single box, connected together in such a way that they look like one drive to your computer. The data is "spattered" or split across the two drives in alternating segments.

    (Time for a do-it-yourself analogy to describe how mini-arrays store data: Put your palms together; interweave your fingers (Figure 1.22). Pretend that each finger represents one of ten segments in a simple digital video file. Notice that every other finger is on one hand and the remaining fingers are on the other hand (the different hard disk drives in the array). If you remove one hand, the other hand contains only half of the video file. It can't be used because it represents only every other segment of data.)

    Mini-arrays can give you the benefit of a single, very large, very fast hard disk, at a good cost savings. The drawback is that if one of the drives should fail, all of your data is potentially lost.

    We're not saying arrays are bad—far from it. Mini-arrays are no more susceptible to drive failures than are single drives. The benefits of mini-arrays are that the transfer rate (discussed later in this chapter) effectively doubles by virtue of using both drives in tandem.

    And this is another good time to harp on the fact that, if you consider your data important, you should make sure it is backed up regularly.

3. *RAIDs* (*R*edundant *A*rray of *I*nexpensive *D*isks): These are generally mini-towers containing anywhere from five to ten drive mechanisms.

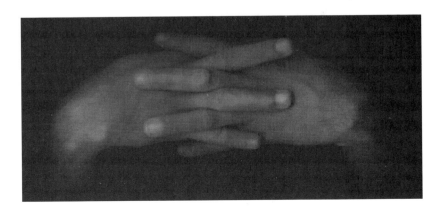

**Figure 1.22
The do-it-
yourself array
analogy.**

They can store between 5 and 20 gigabytes of data. The unique feature of a RAID is its redundancy. If any one drive should fail, the data can be recovered from the other drives. The bad drive is removed, a replacement installed (many RAID drives can very easily be snapped in and out), and the "lost" data is rebuilt from the other drives.

RAIDs are very expensive and are generally used in large networks as part of a server to store data in a near-line capacity.

Single drives are no mystery, and RAIDs are beyond what 99 44/100 percent of us will use, so let's talk just a bit more about mini-arrays. They appear as one of two types: hardware and software. These differ in the following manner:

- *Hardware arrays:* Hardware mini-arrays come in two forms: (1) a single "drive" box that contains two identical drives inside along with an array controller (circuitry) that performs all the work of array management, and (2) a SCSI accelerator card with array capabilities that has two external drives attached to it via SCSI cables.

  These two forms are essentially the same type and are addressed by the computer in the same manner; only the packaging is different. Remember that different brands will have different features and performance characteristics.

- *Software arrays:* Two identical (generally) single drives are connected to your computer in the normal fashion. Software does the job of *formatting* the two drives as an array. The driver software does the job of "spattering" the data between the two drives. This setup can be created fairly simply by the user. Array management software is available at most good software stores.

  The drawback to this method is that software-based arrays are not as fast as hardware-based arrays, since the CPU must find time to perform the array management along with all of its other tasks.

There are many kinds of hard disk subsystems, and their performance characteristics can be all over the map. In 1994, hard disk manufacturers appeared to realize that digital video uses hard disk space the way a person with the flu goes through tissues. We can't seem to get enough storage space; the more we get, the more we seem to need.

This resulted in two things: (1) the cost of hard disk drives has dropped to less than 50 cents per megabyte as of this writing (we expect this trend to continue), and (2) drive manufacturers are building hard drives with specific characteristics suitable for digital video.

All of this benefits you by making your digital video storage devices less expensive. Cost, however, is not the only thing to think about when searching for storage devices. There are many considerations that must be made when purchasing hard disk drives for your desktop video studio. We discuss these in detail in Chapter 3.

To Close This Chapter . . .

We've tried to cover some of the history of digital video and multimedia to give you a background on which to build your future knowledge of digital video. We have touched on types of software and hardware that will be discussed in greater detail later in the book.

As we have stated and restated, it is important to find the right mix of products—both hardware and software—that meet your needs today and that have the capability to meet your needs for one to several years. Any individual piece may be replaced as upgrades or newer and better products become available, but you don't want to be replacing your system every year or six months as inevitable advances in technology arrive. Careful planning about your future needs will help you avoid buyers' remorse as you outfit your digital studio.

Read up on the products; you can usually get free information by writing or calling the vendors—we've included a list of many of the vendors whose products we highlight in the back of the book.

People ask us if they should buy today's model X1, when they just heard that the newer, better, cheaper, faster, whizzier model Z1000 will be coming "soon." The buy-now-or-later question will always be there (the grass is always greener . . .). The only answer we have is that if you don't do *something,* you are going to miss out. It boils down to something called a "lost opportunity cost." That is the price you pay by not having at least some tool with which to perform your work.

SUGGESTION: Before going shopping, make a list of your intended uses for digital video. Have a budget in mind. Don't go shopping when you are hungry (no wait, that's grocery shopping . . .). Ask questions and request demonstrations if you are unsure of a product's advertised versus its actual capabilities.

Whether you go shopping for complete solutions or à la carte, being prepared will make your purchase decisions much easier.

2

Digital Video Systems

Every skilled trade has its own set of systems and tools, and the "skilled trade" of digital video is no different. Systems and tools for the desktop video studio fall into two categories: hardware and software. We've already talked a bit about the considerations to be taken into account when looking for and purchasing these in Chapter 1, "A Digital Video Primer."

Now we'll get into more detail. This chapter contains information about specific digital video systems—hardware and software—along with some hints and tips on how to get better performance from each one. The next chapter addresses specific software and hardware *tools*.

To best understand how digital video systems all work together, we start by talking about the Macintosh and Windows video standard, QuickTime (included on the accompanying CD-ROM).

QuickTime

The QuickTime architecture came from a need to standardize the use of temporal data (dynamic data that is utilized over a specified period of time) on Macintosh computers, allowing applications to work with this dynamic data type in a normal and consistent manner. The aim was to create a standard that could lead the way immediately, and grow as technology advanced.

Before QuickTime, there were several companies that created products for displaying video on a computer screen. Andy was the Director of Marketing at one such company (Aapps Corporation). They created the first digital video TV products for personal computers, called DigiVideo and DigiVideo Color.

The primary problem Aapps faced was in getting all the software companies to adopt *their* application programming interface (API) to take advantage of the capabilities in these products. It soon became apparent that this was an uphill battle. Software and hardware companies zealously guarded their products and technologies; there was very little of the open architecture and compatibility we see today.

Several other hardware companies were also trying to get the attention of the same software developers for their own digital video products. What was needed was an industry-standard API for temporal data. Aapps had been lobbying for nearly a year to have Apple take the torch and create such an API.

Although it may have seemed that they were hitting brick walls at the time, what all such developers learned later was that Apple already had a "skunk works" project team working on the problem. They recognized that nobody was going to come out ahead if there wasn't some way for everybody to work together.

Andy's lobbying efforts on behalf of Aapps led him into the position of Apple's QuickTime hardware evangelist where his first challenge (read: *opportunity*) was to take this new technology and go bang on the doors of all his old competitors to get them to jump onto the QuickTime bandwagon.

As a standard, QuickTime promised that if hardware companies adopted a specific way to interface to the Mac operating system and if the software companies adopted the new standard APIs, then all of these products could magically work together. Users would benefit by gaining access to the world of digital video and audio without the need to understand any more about Macintosh than they already knew, and manufacturers could take advantage of this new world without having to invest in their own development.

As this book can attest, Apple was very successful. At its introduction during the early 1990s during the MacWorld exposition, there were already many dozens of QuickTime products, both new and existing, ready to show. QuickTime was the most successful launch of a new technology Apple ever had. By the end of the first year, over 400 QuickTime-compatible hardware and software products were shipping from hundreds of companies.

Today, QuickTime remains Apple's most successfully adopted technology. In the past two years, Apple opened up the Windows world by creating QuickTime for Windows, a standard that uses virtually the same files as QuickTime for Macintosh allowing easy cross-platform development. Recently, Apple released QuickTime versions 2.0 for both Macintosh and Windows (Apple's seventh revision of the architecture). We discuss much of this "leap of functionality" embodied in version 2.0 later in the chapter.

Although QuickTime's most obvious use is in the display of video and audio, one of the most overlooked things about QuickTime is that it isn't just about "movies." There are many aspects that haven't yet been tapped. QuickTime is actually about temporal data—*any* data that is, or needs to be, dealt with over a definable period of time, in the temporal domain.

What this means in simple terms is that QuickTime movies don't need to contain video or audio tracks.

For example, it is possible to create a movie that only contains a track of AppleScript commands that are designed to be triggered by *time*. As the "movie" plays and each script is reached, it launches and it performs its tasks. The movie doesn't display anything on the screen, but instead has scripts that cause an application to perform some set of functions.

Another less common, but very effective, use is the creation of slideshows featuring JPEG-compressed images that can be called up by frame number or set to run automatically at a specific pace. We have created several product introductions and marketing pieces, designed to be delivered on floppy diskette, using this technique. Along with the slides, we frequently add a narration or music track timed to coordinate with the slideshow.

Applications that have nothing to do with digital video can take advantage of QuickTime's current and future capabilities to offer better functionality to their users.

To better understand QuickTime, let's discuss the basic architecture and some of the special features.

The Technology of QuickTime

Although the typical user only sees the final display of a QuickTime movie, there are four major components in the QuickTime architecture working together in the background—system software, file formats, Apple compressors, and human interface standards.

Although we can't give you a complete white paper on these components here (Apple Multimedia Program members have access to all Apple multimedia white papers), we feel it is important that you get a better understanding of QuickTime in order to help you understand why we suggest some of the techniques and hints in this book.

System software. Three pieces of system software reside at the core of QuickTime. These are Movie Toolbox, Image Compression Manager, and the Component Manager. Unless you are a software developer working on the next great QuickTime application, you do not have to know anything about this core software to take full advantage of QuickTime at the desktop. Just take for granted that QuickTime is there, and that it works.

For the deadly curious, a minimal description of QuickTime's system software components is supplied in the accompanying sidebar.

As with other components of the Macintosh operating system, Quick-

QUICKTIME SYSTEM COMPONENTS

The *Movie Toolbox* is a set of high-level system software services that make it easy for developers to incorporate support for movies into their applications. It includes the routines necessary to create, edit, and play QuickTime movies, and provides the links to automatically interact with the Image Compression Manager.

The *Image Compression Manager* shields applications from the intricacies of compression and decompression through device- and algorithm-independent services. It interacts with the Component Manager to provide this service. It also allows applications to take advantage of the numerous compression schemes that are available now, and to take advantage of future codecs (see Glossary) without having to be modified.

The *Component Manager* allows external resources such as digitizer cards, VCRs, and software extensions to register their capabilities with the system when it is started. Apple has defined classes of components for video digitizer cards, and compression schemes, among many others.

Time works in layers, each layer adding something to the others to provide the overall capabilities of the technology (Figure 2.1). This is especially important when it comes to upgrading QuickTime.

Because of its design, when it comes time to make changes in QuickTime, only the small layers need to be changed rather than the entire architecture. This lets QuickTime address new features such as compressors/decompressors (codecs) without having to make major changes in the code.

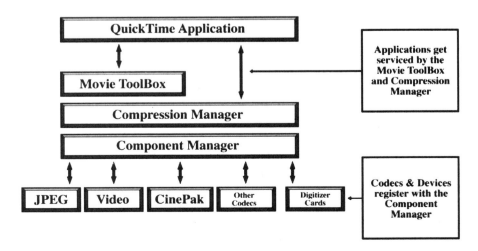

**Figure 2.1
The basic
QuickTime
architecture.**

What this all means is that QuickTime-compatible applications always have access to the best available compression technologies, and that hardware is transparent to the applications. The applications can take advantage of new hardware without modification.

QuickTime is designed to allow your digital video production tools to have a very long lifespan, and your continuing efforts will not be adversely affected by technological progress (read: *outdated by the time you get the product out of the box!*).

File formats. QuickTime supports several file formats, some specific to QuickTime, some in even broader use such as PICT files. Among them are:

- *Movie (MooV).* The Movie file format acts as a container for dynamic data. This is a cross-platform format; a QuickTime Movie file is identical whether found on a Macintosh or a PC. It consists of *tracks*—each track contains a particular data type: video, audio, text, and so forth. Movies can have multiple tracks containing any mix of data and compression types. Or they may have only a single type of data, such as video-only or audio-only.

  In Macintosh, audio track may be added to existing video tracks via normal Copy and Paste techniques. The audio track may be positioned anywhere along the video track and only begins playing when the video track reaches that point. It can't "slip" around—a movie containing a set of video and audio tracks is automatically synchronized when played.

  An index of the data contained in a movie is kept separate, allowing for multiple edits of the original movie without having to copy, move, or delete the actual source data. (If you are familiar with the concept of an alias—especially its "pointing" functions—then you have the basic understanding of how this data file works. The original data stays safe; only a set of pointers describing how to utilize the data is created for each new edit. Once the final edit is chosen, a new self-contained movie may be saved holding a copy of all the edited data.)

  A movie can, in fact, have no data at all, only an index that references some other movie's data. This allows for a movie to contain parts from numerous other movies, or for multiple versions of a movie to exist without duplicating the data, which could otherwise take up large amounts of disk space. A movie can also contain *posters* and *previews* (still frames and short clips that represent a movie when previewing).

  The Movie file format is completely Clipboard- and Scrapbook-compatible; simple cuts-only editing can be accomplished with Apple's MoviePlayer application and the Macintosh computer's standard Cut, Copy, and Paste features.

The QuickTime MooV file format has the ability to handle additional track types such as close captioning, MIDI, and timecode, and is designed to allow other track types to be defined and added to the architecture in the future.

- *PICT Extensions.* Apple has recently expanded the definition and capabilities of its long-standing industry standard graphics file type known as PICT. The extensions now provide the ability to compress and preview PICT files. Because this has been written to conform to industry standards, all current and future applications that recognize and use the PICT file format are automatically compatible with these new PICT extensions. You can view a compressed PICT-image with any unmodified PICT compatible application.

  An image may be saved using your choice of compression, assuming the application has adopted the QuickTime Movie Toolbox APIs. The *preview* feature offers the ability to save a "thumbnail" view along with the actual image. This feature is helpful when browsing for a picture whose name you can't remember, but you will "know it when you see it." Most mainstream graphics applications today offer these basic features.

Apple compressors (Codecs). QuickTime currently offers several compressors to take raw movie data and compress it into files small enough, and at appropriate data rates, for most digital video uses. Compressors are also known as Codecs, short for COmpressor/DECompressor. Some of the better-known compressors are JPEG, CinePak, MPEG, and Animation (Figure 2.2). As discussed in Chapter 1, each compression (and the settings you select for your job) involves trade-offs in frame rule, data rate, file size, and other factors.

**Figure 2.2
Many of the frequently used codecs recognized by Quick-Time.**

Animation
Apple Cinepak
Component Video
Graphics
Intel Raw
Microsoft RLE
Microsoft Video 1
None
Photo – JPEG
Radius Studio
Soft Indeo
Video

The following are descriptions of the different Apple compressors as defined by Apple:

- *Photo Compressor*—The Photo Compressor is Apple's implementation of JPEG (Joint Photographic Experts Group) for high-quality still-image compression. JPEG is designed to compress full-color images and typically gives compression ratios in the range of 4:1 to 10:1 with little or no picture degradation.

  It can compress to 25:1 or higher depending on the image content. Apple's Photo JPEG complies with the ISO (International Standards Organization) baseline standards. It is a *lossy* compression scheme— meaning image data is lost every time the compression is performed.

- *Animation Compressor*—The Animation Compressor is based on RLE (Run Length Encoding) principles to compress computer-generated animation sequences from 1 to 32 bits in depth.

  The algorithm supports both lossy and *lossless* compression. Compression ratios vary greatly based on the content to be compressed. It provides acceptable playback speeds of animation files on lower-performance computers. Using Animation Compression, complex animations can be previewed on a computer without first having to record them to tape frame by frame.

- *Video Compressor*—The Video Compressor (once code-named Road Pizza for the fake squashed rodent on top of the programmer's monitor) is a compression method developed by Apple. This scheme allows digitized video to decompress from CD-ROMs or hard disks in real time, with no additional hardware, on any color-capable Macintosh. Compression ratios range from 5:1 to 25:1. This was Apple's first video-compression algorithm.

NOTE: Apple's Video Compressor is responsible for the coining of the term *Jerkies* given to early QuickTime movies by Todd Rundgren at the first QuickTime Movies awards ceremony. At the time (QuickTime version 1.0), the best digital video you could expect from QuickTime was small (160 × 120) 12 fps movies that tended to drop frames.

As the performance of Macintosh CPUs has increased, the performance of QuickTime has increased through both its revisions and the advent of third-party, full-screen, full-motion compression products.

The "jerky" label has passed into QuickTime lore.

- *Graphics Compressor*—The Graphics Compressor was also developed by Apple. It provides lossless compression of 8-bit (256 colors) images and is ideal for compressing both still images (created by the various paint applications) and 8-bit movies. The Graphics Compressor differs from the Animation Compressor (which can also compress 8-bit data) in that the Graphics Compressor gains compression capability at the expense of decompression speed. A movie compressed with the Graphics Compressor will be about half the size of a movie compressed with the Animation Compressor, but at only about half the playback data rate.

- *Apple CinePak*—The Apple CinePak compressor was a joint development between Apple and a very talented engineer at SuperMac (who went on to found Rocket Science Games). It is based on a combination of a VQ (Vector Quantization) algorithm and Frame Differencing. CinePak significantly increases the image quality, playback rate, frame size, and compression of digitized video when compared to the Apple Video Compressor.

  The CinePak algorithm is highly asymmetric; it takes from three seconds to over a minute to compress each frame of video, depending on the performance of the computer used to compress the movie. The benefit is that it can play back a 15 fps, 320 × 240 (quarter-screen) movie directly from a CD-ROM on an entry-level multimedia-capable computer. Data rates can vary from 100 to 300 kps depending on frame rate, frame size, and the use of key frames.

  On higher-performance computers, CinePak-compressed movies can be played back in quarter-screen size at 30 fps. On Power Macintosh computers, they may be played back as "pixel-doubled" movies at full-screen size.

NOTE: Pixel-doubling refers to the algorithms used to increase display size without requiring additional data. For example, pixel-doubling can take a display of one size, let's say a 320 × 240 movie, and double the screen area covered by that finite amount of data. Each single pixel is now twice as tall and twice as wide as before. The movie covers the entire screen of 640 × 480 pixels, but the file still contains only the 320 × 240 pixel data.

There is a drawback. Because each pixel worth of information now must "cover" this extended area, the picture quality is visually degraded (pixelated) and rarely looks as good as the original. We say *rarely* because solid colors such as white and black can be doubled and still look the same. The real problems come with fine differentiations in flesh tones, shadows, plants, and so forth.

- CinePak has been licensed by SuperMac (Radius) to several other platform vendors (various 3DO game players, Microsoft Video for Windows, Sega, and others) so that content developed on a Macintosh or PC can be ported directly to these other platforms. This provides a very large installed based of units that use CinePak compressed video (read: *potentially lucrative for the desktop digital video studio*).

- *Intel Indeo 3.2*—The Indeo Compressor (aka: DVI) is the latest revision of Intel's video compression algorithm. It, too, is based upon VQ, but it also uses Motion Estimation and RLE algorithms. Using Indeo, digital video can be encoded in real time with hardware assistance to data rates of about 300 kilobytes per second (kps), and can be played back with software only. Off-line, second pass software compression can be performed to get down to 150 kps or less for CD-ROM use. It is about 2x faster to compress (using software) the same digital video source in Indeo than with CinePak. Intel has licensed Indeo for inclusion with QuickTime (Macintosh and Windows versions). Indeo is also available with Microsoft's Video for Windows, and SGI systems.

NOTE: At a given data rate, Indeo is better looking spatially, but at a lesser frame rate than CinePak. Indeo also tends to be better for compressing video with graphics and animation, whereas CinePak tends to be better at compressing "natural" video.

- *YUV Compressor*—The YUV Compressor stores data in the YUV 4:2:2 format. The compression ratio is 2:1. This algorithm is not lossless, but the resulting quality is extremely high. Several Macintosh AV models can digitize directly into this format. It is an excellent intermediate storage format when applying multiple effects or transitions to a digital video sequence.

- *None (raw RGB)*—This "compressor" does not do any compression; it is merely a storage format. The data is stored at 8 bits per pixel for each of red, green, and blue signals. This is also called a "raw" codec. Most video digitizers can capture video in RGB raw format one frame at a time. This is acceptable for capturing still frames. It is also useful as a temporary storage format, as it consumes hard disk space at 1 MB per frame (at 640 × 480 pixels).

In addition to the Apple compressors, there are a few third-party compressors:

- *SuperMac CinePak*—This is the same as Apple's CinePak, except that SuperMac has produced a set of DSP-based accelerator cards to speed up the compression process.

- *Radius JPEG*—The Radius StudioVision card set is based on JPEG, but is used to compress motion video. It is often referred to as "Motion JPEG," but it should not be confused with MPEG (discussed later). Motion JPEG is the application of JPEG to a video sequence. The JPEG compression hardware sees the frames in a full-motion video as a series of stills.

- *RasterOps JPEG*—The RasterOps MoviePak II card set is also based on JPEG to compress motion video.

There are several other products and many types of compression algorithms offering varying degrees of QuickTime compatibility. Someday, there may be a single be-all, end-all of compressors, but we believe that time is a long way off.

Every compressor has its relative strengths and weaknesses. Finding the right one(s) to meet your needs, and the needs of your particular projects, is one of the inexact sciences. Hopefully, some of the information in this book will help you, but a lot of trial and error will go into finding what is right for you.

Audio. QuickTime can support many audio tracks within QuickTime movies, whether they be monaural or stereo sound, or multiple languages. The audio can be of any sample rate, from 5 KHz 8-bit mono voice data to 48 KHz 16-bit stereo DAT music. AIFF (one of several industry standard file formats) audio files can be seamlessly opened as QuickTime audio movies. If the hardware playing the audio does not directly support the sample rate or size, Quick-Time will convert it in real time to the format the hardware requires.

The author of content does not have to worry about the target computer's audio capabilities. Compressed audio is also supported—both Apple Computer's MACE 3:1 and 6:1 compression for 8-bit sound, as well as ADPCM, the IMA (Interactive Multimedia Association) standard. ADPCM provides a 4:1 compression ratio for 16-bit sound.

The user has full control over the volume of the sound being played in a QuickTime movie. The movie controller provides a slider bar for adjusting the volume level.

Using a Macintosh, it is relatively easy to add audio to any QuickTime movie. About the easiest method is to open the video movie in MoviePlayer, then open your audio file (originally saved as either an AIFF file or a QuickTime movie). We'll assume that you want the entire audio file, so simply:

1. Type **Command-A** or choose the Select All feature from the File menu.

2. Type **Command-C** or choose Copy from the Edit menu.

3. Click on the video movie display window to bring it to the foreground.

Figure 2.3
The movie controller slider bar.

Frame Slider

**Figure 2.4
Adding an audio
track to an
existing video
track.**

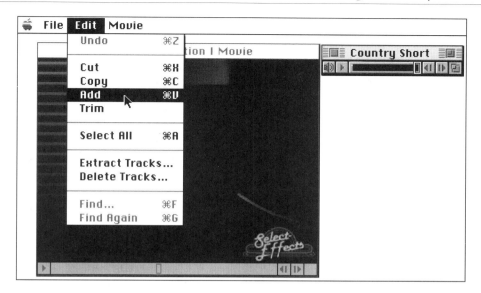

4. Position the movie controller slider bar (Figure 2.3) to the point where you wish to begin the audio insert.

5. While holding down the Option key, pull down the Edit menu (Figure 2.4) and select Add to insert the audio track. (If you do not hold the Option key, this same selection will read Paste and will overwrite the video.)

If your audio track extends beyond the end of your video track, the extra audio will be played with white frames. If you like what you see and hear, save your new movie. If you don't like it, or want to reposition the audio, use the undo (Command-Z) function to remove the audio track before you do anything else.

For cases where you don't want all of an audio track inserted into your video, just use the slider bar on the audio track's display box to locate the desired start point; hold down either Shift key and move the slider bar to the desired end point—you can even let the audio play as you decide where the proper end point is. From that point, follow preceding steps 2–5.

By the way, this same technique works in the reverse direction, adding a video track to existing audio.

**Human
Interface**

Just as Apple refined the Graphical User Interface into the Macintosh OS and set guideline requirements for consistency between applications, they have done the same with QuickTime for dynamic media. They have specified several standard user interface elements to provide users with a consistent way in using QuickTime from application to application.

Figure 2.5
The movie
controller.

- *Movie Controller*—This provides a consistent method for controlling a QuickTime movie. The standard controller (Figure 2.5) lets a user adjust volume, play or stop the movie, and jump or scroll to any frame in the movie.

- *Standard File Dialog with Preview*—This allows an application to provide the user with a preview area for viewing "thumbnails." (See Figure 2.6.) These are movie previews and sounds that can be accessed before loading a particular file.

- *Standard Compression Dialog*—This dialog (Figure 2.7) lets the user change the desired compression method and settings, and allows for previewing the effect of those settings before committing to compressing the file. The small window in the upper-right corner of the box shows the middle section of the video and how the setting will affect it.

   Depending on the type of compression selected, certain other selections may be grayed and unavailable to the user.

   Advanced users may want to try one of the hidden features of the QuickTime interface. When using certain codecs, the Quality setting bar actually adjusts the spatial and the temporal quality at the same time. ("Spatial" refers to individual frame quality and "temporal" refers to the quality of a series of differenced frames over a period of time.)

   This trick only works with those codecs that use differenced frames and offer temporal settings, such as CinePak, Indeo, and Video. Codecs that are frame-specific, like JPEG, do not allow this.

Figure 2.6
The standard
file dialog.

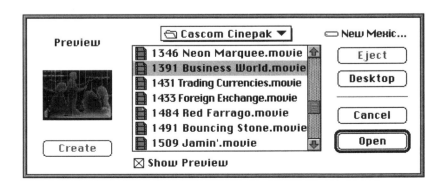

**Figure 2.7
Standard
compression
dialog.**

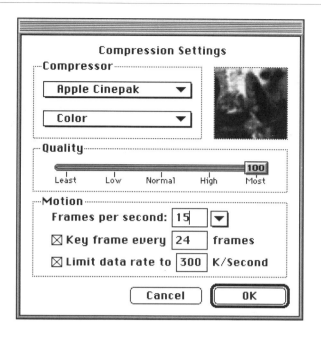

When choosing your compression codec and making the appropriate settings, try holding the Option key as you move the Quality slider bar. This gives you access to both the Quality and Temporal settings and allows you to adjust them separately. Experiment with this. Depending on your actual video, this may allow you to achieve some good results, achieve some not-so-good results, or see no change.

We must emphasize that this is an advanced technique and is not to be done all the time (codecs are generally designed to properly balance the quality and temporal settings). This is also something to which you must dedicate some time if you wish to properly investigate it. You may need to compress and compare the same piece of video using dozens of different setting combinations before you see any *usable* difference.

- *Standard Video Digitizer Dialog*—This dialog panel allows the user to choose the compression method, source, and sample settings for video and sound capture. The capabilities of these settings can be extended by individual hardware and software developers, yet they provide a predictable user interface for setting the capture devices.

Although we show the specific dialog boxes from VideoFusion, there are three different groups of settings that must be individually adjusted to get the optimal results from a video capture. They are Input Source (Figure 2.8), Compression (Figure 2.9), and Image (Figure 2.10).

**Figure 2.8
The Input
Source dialog.**

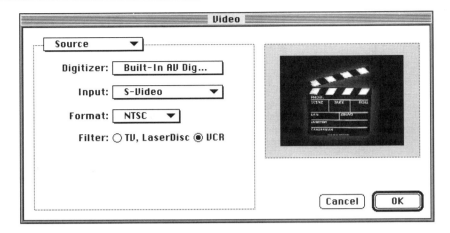

**Figure 2.9
The Compres-
sion dialog.**

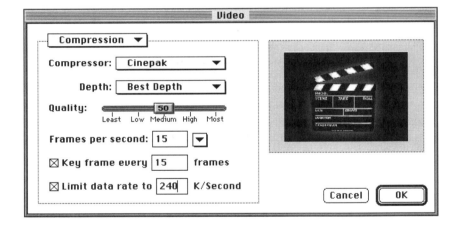

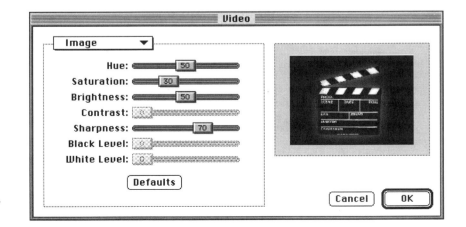

**Figure 2.10
The Image Set-
tings dialog.**

**Figure 2.11
The Audio CD
Import dialog.**

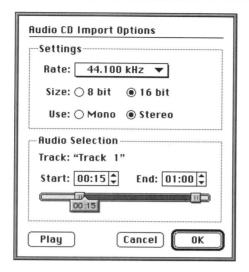

- *Audio CD Import*—This dialog allows a user to import and convert Audio CD tracks directly into QuickTime movies. (See Figure 2.11.) Once in the QuickTime format, these may be edited using standard Macintosh Cut, Copy, and Paste techniques. QuickTime audio tracks may be superimposed and synchronized directly over QuickTime video movies, as discussed in the "Audio" section, preceding.

**QuickTime
2.0 Additional
Features**

Other recent developments in QuickTime have been included in the new fall 1994 release of QuickTime 2.0. Most notably are the support for MIDI, MPEG, and timecode track types. Other features include Burnt text, custom color tables (for 256 color systems), Drag and Drop, native codecs, and many other programmer-oriented features. QuickTime's performance characteristics were also greatly improved in version 2.0.

Using a new capability called the *DataPipe,* QuickTime 2.0 is better able to manage the computer load, allowing better movie playback with better frame rates and larger frame sizes. All the Apple-supplied codecs have been made "native" to take advantage of PowerPC performance benefits (CinePak compression is three to four times faster on a PowerPC-based Macintosh when compared to a 68040-based Macintosh).

Version 2.0 includes MIDI music track support with a sampling of many instruments provided as part of this support. MIDI music files can be imported into QuickTime movies and then easily edited without a user's needing any special knowledge of MIDI.

MPEG data can be contained in QuickTime 2.0 movies. Additional hardware is required to play back MPEG-compressed movies, but as of this writing, such equipment is quite affordable—running as low as a few hundred dollars for a hardware card. MPEG compression can also be achieved with QuickTime on the Macintosh or PC, but it requires extensive time to accomplish and is costly. Real-time hardware compression systems for MPEG are urrently in the $15,000 to $30,000 range.

Timecode can be stored in a QuickTime movie; this track type is a superset of all known timecode formats, meaning that industry-standard SMPTE timecode is now supported. Of great importance, if you edit a movie that also contains a timecode track, QuickTime maintains the correct references.

The Text track capability now supports anti-aliased, pre-rendered text. Such text is also searchable. QuickTime supports the System 7.5 Drag and Drop feature. The movie controller will allow a movie to be dragged onto another movie for editing.

QuickTime 2.0 also provides an environment robust enough for professional video editing, with support for 60 fps video and high data rates (greater than 3 MB per second). This requires the use of QuickTime 2.0 compatible digitizing and compression hardware from third parties.

QuickTime for Windows 2.0

One of the great things about the QuickTime architecture is that it has the identical file structure on each supported platform. QuickTime 2.0 for Windows is no exception and now includes support for Fujitsu's FM-Towns and Apple's Set Top Box in addition to the traditional Macintosh and Windows platforms. QuickTime is a reference standard for multimedia. A single multimedia application can be produced and delivered on both the Mac and the PC. This gives you access to the largest single market of multimedia consumers.

As with the Macintosh version, QuickTime for Windows supports both movies and pictures. We won't repeat all the features for QuickTime for Windows in this space since they are virtually the same as in the Macintosh version. There are a few differences between the versions for the two platforms, however.

Worth pointing out is that because of the nature of the PC/Windows environment (OS developers don't have tight control over the kinds and capabilities of hardware users might have), there are minimum requirements of the various computer subsystems for QuickTime for Windows to perform optimally.

We won't go into these requirements in great detail as the availability, versions, and supported products change too often. We recommend that you review the documentation supplied with QuickTime for Windows which specifically lists, in several addendums, the various video, graphic, and audio card products supported or even accelerated when used with the software.

QuickTime for Windows requires a minimum of any 386SX PC running Windows 3.1 or later. For best display capabilities, we recommend a minimum of a 486*xx* system with Vesa Local Bus video, a dual-speed CD-ROM, and a 16-bit "Sound Blaster" compatible audio card.

If you can afford it, a Pentium-based system is a great way to go. Microsoft and many PC developers have created a pair of "standards" called MPC1 and MPC2 to help simplify your decisions on what is required to make a PC multimedia-capable. Although QuickTime for Windows will work with MPC1-based PCs, we recommend that your PC meet the MPC2 standard for optimal performance results.

NOTE: Be very sure your CD-ROM drive is rated as a "multimedia drive" and adheres to the MPC2 standards; there are some drives in the PC world that claim to be multimedia-capable, but actually are not able to transfer the 300 KB sustained data rates of the MPC2 standard.

QuickTime for Windows does not yet (as of this writing) offer broad support for the full capture, compression, and editing capabilities of Quick-Time for Macintosh. This is not to say that you can't author QuickTime for Windows content on a PC—you can. The available application choice is just considerably narrower.

At this writing, the following products provide capture, editing, animation, and authoring capabilities that are compatible with QuickTime for Windows.

- Intel's SmartCap application can digitize and compress Indeo movies and save them into QuickTime for Windows format.
- Autodesk Animator can be used to create animation.
- Adobe's Premiere 4.0 for Windows (included on the accompanying CD-ROM) can convert the animations and allow you to manipulate and edit your digital video, graphics, and audio into QuickTime movies.
- Macromedia's Director 4.0 for Windows (included on the accompanying CD-ROM) lets you author multimedia applications using QTW content (which can also be used on the Macintosh).
- Microsoft's Visual Basic can be used to author multimedia applications that use QTW content.

There are also several utilities available to convert most PC multimedia file types into QuickTime movies or compressed pictures. There are even utilities to easily convert Microsoft's AVI files into QuickTime movies. These utilities are often shareware and can be found on most commercial on-line services such as Compuserve and America On-Line as well as on the Internet. You'll find a few of these in the Freebies section of the accompanying CD-ROM.

Capabilities for PC developers to make products that create and edit Quick-Time for Windows content are expected in future releases of QuickTime for Windows, thus allowing the wide range of multimedia tools available on the PC to be upgraded to take advantage of QuickTime for Windows.

The important thing to remember is that the resultant content, the movie or picture file, is identical on both platforms. Playback of content—so far, the vast majority of the multimedia-capable PC installed base is used for playback only—is the same across the two platforms.

Whither Thou Go-eth, QuickTime?

From day one, the architecture of QuickTime was not meant to be static. QuickTime has gone through several changes, has been made cross-platform, and continues to embrace new and different codecs. What's new and next on the horizon for QuickTime? Several exciting advances are in the works, and a few are already integrated in retail products and in test markets. These include:

- QuickTime VR
- QuickTime Interactive
- QuickTime Support for Enhanced CD/Interactive Music
- QuickTime Set-top Boxes

Although these products are not yet commercially available, we can tell you a little bit about each of these four new extensions of the QuickTime architecture.

QuickTime VR. QuickTime Virtual Reality is a new software technology from Apple Computer, Inc., which brings VR experiences to ordinary personal computers, requiring no special hardware, software, or accessories. QuickTime VR is a new piece of system software that lets Macintosh and Windows users experience spatial interactions using only their computer, with a mouse or trackball, and a keyboard.

QuickTime VR has two faces: (1) a 360° panoramic movie technology that allows users to explore spaces and (2) an object movie technology that allows users to examine objects close up and interactively.

Viewers can explore virtual spaces and objects as if they were in the actual area. As users change their scenic view—turning left or right and looking up or down, even zooming in or out—the correct perspective is always maintained. Users can also manipulate objects, looking at them from the front, back, top, bottom, or any other angle of interest.

QuickTime VR is not something that anyone can go out and purchase and just plug any QuickTime movie into. QuickTime VR is a technology that Apple is licensing to third-party developers in the form of a runtime engine and a set of authoring tools. This lets content developers, production companies, and software developers create exciting new multimedia products, typically in the form of CD-ROM titles, in a wide range of markets.

The possibilities of QuickTime VR to enhance the user experience make this a very attractive technology for developers to investigate. Its potential uses include retail, interactive multimedia titles, virtual travel, science and medical applications.

QuickTime Interactive. QuickTime 2.0 also creates an infrastructure for development and delivery of interactive television applications through MPEG (Motion Picture Experts Group) support and network enhancements. QuickTime 2.0 supports MPEG compression, widely regarded as the industry-standard method of delivering video into the home for interactive television applications such as video on demand and home shopping.

The MPEG standard, by itself, allows only playback. With QuickTime 2.0, however, users of MPEG-based devices will also be able to edit, search for, and interact with video information.

QuickTime Support for Enhanced CD/Interactive Music. In late 1994, Apple Computer, Inc., announced its plans to support an emerging industry standard that combines audio and computer technology in a single format, and will make it easier for music professionals to use Apple technology to create interactive music products.

One of Apple's own descriptions, which brings all sorts of possibilities to our minds, is: "Imagine playing your favorite audio CD, then watching the artist describe his thoughts behind the music. Or, sitting at your desk, watching the Fourth of July Boston Symphony concert—complete with fireworks exploding across your computer screen." Such popular uses as karaoke may now appear on CDs.

To those of us who invest in laserdiscs that feature extra tracks full of supplemental information such as publicity stills, reprints of the movie's script, and even alternate audio tracks with interviews of the director and stars, this is the boon we have been waiting for in the CD world.

The first thing Apple announced is its support for the emerging standard for enhanced CD; a compact disc can be played not only by a standard audio CD player, but also in a CD-ROM player attached to a computer. Companies in the music and software industries have been working together recently to create a standard for a new generation of such enhanced compact discs, sometimes referred to as "CD Plus."

Using QuickTime, multimedia and music professionals can create material that incorporates video, graphics, animation, and even text with their sound, all on a single multipurpose CD. Because of QuickTime's cross-platform capabilities, they will be able to deliver their content to many different plat-forms—including Macintosh and Windows computers and enhanced CDs.

QuickTime Set-top Boxes. One wave of the future that cable television and telecommunications companies are investigating and testing are set-top boxes capable of receiving highly compressed data, storing it until it is needed, and allowing random access to that data.

What that means is that you could call and order a specific movie to be downloaded to your box—it arrives in just a few minutes—where it remains until you want to watch it. Then, because you have all of the movie in digital form inside the box, you can access any individual frame, anywhere in the movie. You could play the movie from any point or repeat interesting parts—it is even conceivable that you could play the thing backward!

Apple and other companies have been building, testing and even installing such set-top boxes in the United States and overseas since 1993. Certain areas of the east coast of the United States and a group of British Telecom subscribers already use Apple set-top boxes. The architecture these boxes use for decoding and playing the data is a version of QuickTime.

When will these boxes become standard issue to the average television viewer? Some industry pundits believe this will happen by 1997 or 1998. You will see more and more advancements in QuickTime as an architecture as well as new software and hardware developed to take advantage of QuickTime capabilities.

Video for Windows

Another digital video standard has emerged recently from Microsoft. It is called Video for Windows (VfW). VfW differs from QuickTime (both the Macintosh and Windows versions) in that it is not a cross-platform standard, and unlike QuickTime for Macintosh, it uses a single data track rather than a data fork. In this area, it is similar to QuickTime for Windows.

This book is QuickTime-centric, so we will not go into a long explana-tion of Video for Windows. We do, however, cover the steps necessary for converting QuickTime movies to the Video for Windows AVI (Audio Video Interleave) file format and Video for Windows to QuickTime, playable on either the Macintosh or Windows PCs. This information may be found in Chapter 5, in the "Polishing for Best Results" section.

Like QuickTime, Video for Windows should be thought of as the player for the video—in this case, in a Windows environment. Where QuickTime uses the MooV file format, the file format used by VfW is AVI, referring to the fact that audio and video tracks are interleaved into a single data track.

Version One of VfW was released in November 1992. It was designed to display 320 × 240 movies at 15 fps, using one of three compression codecs: CinePak, Indeo, or Microsoft Video 1. Since that time, VfW has been revised to take advantage of new computer and CD-ROM capabilities available to the PC user.

The most recent set of specifications for VfW is the MPC Level 2 spec. Chances are that much of the Windows-based video you create in AVI format will be aimed at this specification. MPC Level 2 requires that you have a system with:

- 486SX CPU running at 25 MHz or greater
- 4 MB of RAM
- 160 MB hard disk drive
- 16-bit sound card
- 640 × 480 × 65,536 VGA capabilities
- A double-speed CD-ROM that is rated as multi-session ready
- SCSI controller (to connect the CD-ROM drive)

To achieve the best results, it is recommended that you have:

- 8 MB of RAM
- Double-speed CD-ROM that features XA audio
- *Accelerated* 640 × 480 × 65,536 VGA capabilities

Most Macintosh users may not see any advantage to having a competing format to QuickTime, but unlike QuickTime, AVI was specifically written to take advantage of the Windows environment. Actually, something we said a few minutes ago is not really absolute. We stated that AVI is not a cross-platform standard. Although it is strictly true, don't go away with the impression that AVI files can't be used on a Macintosh.

Along with the technique of converting AVI files to QuickTime, you may also create QuickTime aliases that point directly to the original AVI file. This has its advantages.

Let's say that you create a set of videos that are meant to go onto an ISO-9660 (Windows) CD-ROM. Your client suddenly decides to make the disc a hybrid HFS (Macintosh)/ISO-9660 disc. Do you have to convert and store out both versions of your video files? No. Simply use a utility to create a set of Macintosh QuickTime aliases. Name them appropriately and place them in a folder. When the user boots the disc in a Windows PC, the directory of the folder that contains the AVI files will be accessed. When a Macintosh user boots the disc, the "Macintosh" folder is opened and the videos are accessed using the aliases.

Playback Platforms

As we covered earlier, creating digital video content needs to be based upon your destination requirements. You make your decisions about what types of codecs to use, what data rate, frame size, and so forth, based upon the target platform. The various output targets have a wide range of capabilities or limitations, or both. If you know how your digital video will be used before you begin, you will save yourself headaches and lost time later on.

You don't want your clients complaining that they could not view your movie properly because they have a lower-performance CPU than you had anticipated. QuickTime has come a very long way in making even the most entry-level computer capable of playing QuickTime movies reasonably, but *only* if the movie has been processed and compressed to the appropriate level for playback on those machines.

Don't get us wrong—you don't have to go out and characterize every different possible computer that your movie might be used on. You *do* need to know something about what the majority of end users will have.

There are two ways to go:

1. If you know the capabilities of all the systems your movies will be used on, you can characterize the lowest-performance computer system to be *target,* and make the movie fit to that low mark. This totally ignores the capabilities of what may constitute the vast majority of your users. The up side is that everyone can view it; the downside is that the quality of the resultant movie may be very low.

   or . . .

2. Characterize a reference system that contains a set of "minimum daily requirements" (or MDRs—see Figure 2.12) for movie playback and publish this information along with the finished content. With this scenario you define the system requirements that are necessary for proper playback. The up side is better performance and higher-quality results because this reference is higher than the lowest common denominator.

   Everyone knows what is required because you have provided that information. The down side potential is that you might set a minimum that is higher than the equipment of many of the targeted users, with the result that if they do not upgrade to the MDR, then the movies will not play back optimally.

**Figure 2.12
Example of
minimum
system require-
ments.**

Feature/Level Requirement	Minimum Value
CPU Processor Level	68040
CPU Speed in MHz	25 MHz
System Software Version	7.5
QuickTime Version	2.0
Monitor Color depth	Thousands
Available Free RAM	5 MB
Available Free Hard Disk Space	<movie size>
CD-ROM Transfer Speed	300 kps

Evaluations and trade-offs are done every day by software and content developers all over the world. If software publishers tried to make their products work perfectly on every machine out there, no matter how old, then everything would still be black and white, running in 64 K of RAM, and would have to fit on a single-sided floppy disk.

Corollary to Our Basic Philosophy Number 1—*You can please most of the people most of the time; the rest need an upgrade.*

The list in Figure 2.12 is by no means exhaustive; these are the most common benchmarks to use. Your list of MDRs may be more or less than this example list. And those of you who are creating digital video for the PC world will want to spec out appropriate requirements including soundboards and other special hardware and software.

Where creating MDRs for various platforms can get really tricky is if you have Macintosh users and PC users that must use the *same* materials. More about this later.

Let's discuss the various targets and what considerations can be made for each.

**Computer-
Based
Playback**

If your digital video is staying on your computer hard disk, or is destined for someone else's hard disk, then you have quite a bit of latitude on how you process and ultimately compress the movies. What we are talking about is hard disk–based digital video. The key issues are CPU performance, compression acceleration (if any), and hard disk drive performance.

There may be no reason to take the extra time to compress to CinePak unless you really want to or if you have a very long video piece that would exceed the drive capacity of your target systems. You may find that using the Video codec lets your video play sufficiently well from the hard drive. Assuming that the target drives and systems meet the MDRs, your video will work just fine. You may also decide to capture the video using an accelerated JPEG card and applying no further compression. (Your target audience will need that same card in their systems, though, for proper playback.)

NOTE: Even if your video will ultimately be played directly from a hard drive, you may want to consider using the CD-ROM as the delivery media. Your target users will need to copy the files to their hard drives, but this is a viable alternative to having to download to dozens, hundreds, or even thousands of individual drives.

If you plan on providing the movies to others for playback from their hard disks, then you basically only need to consider the CPU and hard-disk performance of their computers. Most older hard disk drives (two to five years old) offer in the sub-400 MB capacity range and have data transfer rates of 450–700 kps. Most hard disks that are 500 MB or greater, and most newer drives, have data transfer rates greater than 1 MB per second, about the minimum necessary for basic digital video playback. (See Chapter 3 concerning the difference between data rate and sustained transfer rate.)

If you create a 320 × 240, 15 fps movie using the Video codec, your data rates can range from 300 to 750 kps (based on content). A higher data rate movie may not play properly from a lower performance hard disk because its data transfer rate might be less than the movie requires. The results will be frames of video dropped during playback.

If you have higher-performance digital video needs (full-screen video), then you either need to require the use of high-performance (read: *PowerPC or Pentium-based*) computers, or must require the use and standardization on one of the accelerated JPEG compressor cards. (Be advised that you cannot mix and match the different brands; whatever you use for your compression will be the requirement for the playback.)

It is possible to play back full-screen (640 × 480) digital video on a high-performance computer using software only. The "trick" is to produce the movie at quarter-screen and set the playback size at full-screen. This results in *pixel-doubling* the digital video during playback. One potential drawback is that the resulting movie will look like lower-quality VHS video. At a distance it will look good, but at two to three feet—normal viewing distance at the desktop—you will see the "big" pixels.

Another issue is the use of color palettes and built-in color capability. In the Macintosh world, most newer systems (post–Macintosh IIci) come ready to support thousands or even millions of colors on standard-size monitors (16-bit and 24-bit support). However, in older Macintosh computers, in

Macintosh computers using large-screen monitors, and certainly in the majority of the installed Windows world, the available color support may only be 8 bits (256 colors or grays).

QuickDraw and QuickTime automatically handle creating a 256-color palette on the fly as the movie is being played on a Macintosh, but that may not be the optimum palette for that movie.

QuickDraw dithers the colors pretty heavily. Windows does not have Apple's QuickDraw technology, so the movies are dithered to the standard Windows palette and playback is slower. The end results can look pretty poor—hence, custom 256-color palettes that are attached to movies to improve the image quality of movies being played back on 8-bit systems. For details on making custom color palettes for 8-bit displays, see the section in Chapter 5 on "Polishing for Best Results."

CD-ROM

Defining the settings for CD-ROM playback are fairly straightforward. The limiting factor is the data transfer rate of the target CD-ROM drive. As we pointed out earlier in the book, there are several different drive speeds (150, 300, 450, and 600), measured in their maximum K per second, available on the market. The largest installed base as of this writing is those with a capability of transferring 300 kps—sometimes known as "double-speed" drives. As prices continue to fall, and as technology marches on, the average speed of the installed base will increase.

In 1995, companies such as Apple will begin shipping 4X speed CD-ROM drives. With the projected growth of new CD-ROM drive installations, we anticipate that by the end of 1995 there will be many millions of double-speed and 4X drives in use; single-speed drives will drop to the minority.

The benefits of CD-ROM are the massive amounts of information (640 MB) that can be stored and the very inexpensive cost of producing quantities (less than a dollar each in large volumes). Even CDR (recordable CD-ROMs) media one-off blank discs are less than $15 each. In quantities, these CDR discs will probably hit the $10 range by the end of 1995, and the cost of the equipment needed to "cut" these discs may drop to the range ($1,500 to $2,000 for hobbyist-quality and $2,500 to $4,500 for semi-professional equipment) where most video professionals can afford to own and use a CD one-off machine. Be advised that there are two different "lengths" of CDR discs—the CDR-74 which comfortably holds about 640 MB of data and the CDR-63 which holds about 550 MB. We always use the CDR-74s.

When Video is the source, optimal CD-ROM playback (the best balance of quality and performance) is achieved only when using the CinePak or Indeo codecs. These were designed for use with CD-ROMs and provide data rates in the 100–400 kps range. This can result in quarter-screen, 15 fps movies, with good-quality audio, playing back smoothly from a CD. The choice of CinePak or Indeo is up to you. Our own A-B comparisons show them to be fairly equivalent from a novice user's point of view. We discuss codecs later in the book.

The use of other codecs may or may not be suitable for CD-ROM play-back. The Animation and Graphics compressors can produce data rates within the CD-compatible range, but their rates vary widely based on the source data. They can end up much higher than the average CD data rate. Care and testing should be done with these or other codecs and your own materials to determine their worthiness for CD-ROM use.

Except for still images or movie archiving, JPEG should not be used as a codec for movie playback from CD. Although JPEG can generate data rates low enough for CD-ROMs, JPEG is a slower-than-realtime decompressor. Without hardware assist, or unless the movies are very, very small, JPEG movies won't play back properly from CD-ROM.

Utilities such as MovieAnalyzer—a part of the QuickTime developer kit— evaluate the movies you produce and provide you with the information you need to determine their CD playback-worthiness.

Videotape

Outputting digital video to videotape can free you of some production and compression issues but puts requirements of its own in your decision path. Gaining the necessary signal output to record to tape from your desktop system can be as inexpensive as "free"—several computer models come with AV I/O built in—or can cost many thousands of dollars extra. What will work for you depends solely upon your videotape output quality requirements.

If you need professional to broadcast quality output, then you should be using one of the many high-end system solutions ($12,000–$40,000). If you require industrial to professional quality output, then one of the midrange card set solutions ($2,000–$6,000) can provide the desired results.

But if you are on a budget, and if video equal to the quality of a home VCR is sufficient, then any of the AV computers (offering either composite or S-Video output) will allow you to "Print to Tape" quite sufficiently. Additionally, for non-AV computers, there are inexpensive D-A (Digital-Analog) converters that will create a composite (or S-Video) NTSC (or PAL) signal from your computer's monitor-out port. (Products that fit into this category may be found in Chapter 8 toward the end of this book.)

If you plan to create high-quality, full-screen (640 × 480 or 768 × 524), full motion (30 frames or 60 fields NTSC—25 or 50 for PAL) digital video for output to tape, don't even think about it unless you're using a midrange to high-end solution. This is definitely not entry-level territory. There are a couple good entry-level products (some software, some hardware) that will give you full-screen output, but the output will not be full-resolution or full-motion. Apple's MoviePlayer application will play back full-screen (pixel-doubled from quarter-screen CinePak movies) digital video that can be recorded when used with any of the output options.

In the lower-cost range, Radius offers the Spigot-to-Tape product which features built-in video out capabilities. *(Please see its individual review in Chapter 8 toward the end of this book.)*

Such products offer full-screen (via pixel doubling), 15 fps output. Not to get too judgmental here, but these are only good enough for home movies or the price conscious student director. Don't expect Hollywood to call back after sending a tape from one of these. These are fine products; we just wouldn't recommend your using them for that special corporate board meeting presentation that next year's budget is riding on.

Cross-Platform

When you work within the QuickTime domain, any of the many codecs supplied with QuickTime are completely cross-platform compatible. Most video content is compressed with either CinePak or Indeo, graphics with the Animation or Graphics codecs, and pictures with JPEG. If you need to convert QuickTime digital video for use in the Microsoft Video for Windows environment (AVI file format), then the two codecs of choice are, once again, CinePak and Indeo.

VfW fully supports both CinePak and Indeo. CinePak- or Indeo-based movies can easily be converted between the QuickTime MooV format and Microsoft's AVI format using a simple utility. Using a Microsoft utility, it is possible to transcode a QuickTime movie based on any QuickTime codec to either of Microsoft's own codecs, Video 1 or RLE.

Microsoft's Video 1 codec is roughly equivalent to QuickTime's Video codec. The Microsoft RLE codec is equivalent to the QuickTime Animation codec.

Digital video that is to be used cross-platform generally is also going to be placed on a cross-platform CD, usually in an HFS/ISO 9660 hybrid format. The issue here is that PC-based CD-ROM drives have lower data transfer rates than their Macintosh counterparts. This is more often due to a poorly written software driver for the CD-ROM device than on the actual hardware. On average (as of this writing), double-speed CD drives on PCs can sustain only 180 kps data rates compared to 240 kps averages on the Macintosh. You must consider this when preparing your digital video content for final compression.

Other Platforms

Creating video at the desktop for the typical cross-platform is easy. Creating digital video for other platforms can get a bit tricky; it all depends on what "other" platform you may be targeting for your digital video. QuickTime is available on several platforms beyond Macintosh and PCs. These include the Fujitsu FM-Towns and the Apple Set Top Box used by British Telecom and being tested in the United States.

Additionally, SuperMac (Radius) has licensed CinePak to several other platforms for digital video use. These include 3DO-based units manufactured by several different companies. So when you are planning to create digital video content, be sure to check the requirements of the target platform; but it's a pretty strong bet that QuickTime and CinePak are your likely candidates.

One new product, announced by Apple at the January 1995 Macworld, is the Pippin home entertainment/education unit. According to specs, current HFS CD-ROMs designed for use in a Macintosh computer require only a minimum of adaptive work to be usable in this new machine. One Apple source claimed to be able to rework more than a dozen CD-ROM presentations in a single day.

Hardware Production Systems

This book emphasizes creating digital video on a Macintosh, even if it is to be used on a Windows PC. This is not to say that you can't do it the other way. It's just that we have found that (1) the best and easiest tools are available for the Macintosh, and (2) the most viable platform for the creation of video is a graphics-based platform (also known as the Macintosh).

In this section we cover the various computer systems we feel are good platforms for the various usage types; entry-level, midlevel, and high-end. We actually lump the midrange and high-performance systems together, because the distinction is not in the CPU, but in the subsystem (memory, hard disk, accelerators, and so forth).

Let's start with the computer models.

Computer Models

Entry-Level AV Macintosh Computers

There are two computers that fall into this price-sensitive category. Both offer many of the same features as the higher-performance models, but they generally use lower-speed processors and may offer less RAM and small hard disk drives as their standards. These are:

- Quadra 630AV
- Quadra 660AV

These are two full-featured, digital video-capable computers. Both offer the standard Macintosh AV capabilities of video and audio input, and support most monitors at reasonable bit depths. We have used both and recommend them to others.

High-Performance AV Macintosh Computers

There currently are three main Macintosh computers that fall into this category, each one offering good speed and capabilities. They are:

- Quadra 840AV
- Power Macintosh 8100/80AV
- Power Macintosh 8100/110AV

The processor speeds of these models—particularly the Power Macintosh computers—make these fine, upgradable computers for the mid- to high-level desktop video studio.

In addition to these models, there are other mid- to high-performance Macintosh computers that may be used for digital video. For those without the AV package, you will need to purchase additional boards such as a video/audio capture board. Among these computers are:

- Performa 630AV
- Quadra 700, Quadra 800, Quadra 900, and Quadra 950
- Power Macintosh 6100 and Power Macintosh 7100

Of course, there are other entry-level Macintosh computers that can be used with the same requirements for adding optional cards and capabilities. Although we don't recommend them for the serious desktop video studio, if you already have one and want to create digital video as a hobby, there is no need to run out and buy a whole new system.

- The Performa line
- The older Macintosh II line

One thing we want you to be aware of is that the Performa line of computers tends to utilize microprocessors known as LC processors (68LC030, 68LC040) that do not contain a math coprocessor. Although these LC chips are fine for most home and education uses, you may find some video and audio software that will not run on them.

Windows-Based PCs

We suggest that if you are doing any multimedia development in the Windows environment, you do it with one of the following configurations. Anything with lower CPU performance is probably wasted dollars and time. If you develop video for playback on unknown PC systems, then we suggest that you get an MPC level 1 computer system for testing purposes. It can double as a good office machine for word processing and general use in its off hours. The systems we suggest are:

- 486DX66-based models
- Pentium 60- or 90-based models

As of this writing, Intel is suffering PR nightmares over a math calculation bug that surfaced in the fall of 1994. In fact, IBM announced that they would stop shipping Pentium-based computers until there is a fix. By the time you read this book (spring of 1995 or later), Intel is expected to have new Pentium CPUs available to the computer manufacturers.

Don't discount computers with the Intel Pentium chips. There is a large installed base of units out there with the chips.

Peripherals

CD-ROM Drives

Don't start without one! If you don't have a CD-ROM drive with your computer, you won't be able to see all the great applications and content we have for you on the CD that comes with this book! You paid for it; you ought to take advantage of it.

But seriously, CD-ROM is not the future—it's *today!* Any serious digital video development can't be done without one. This is because many of the applications for digital video production are available only on CD, and your content or multimedia production may most likely end up on a CD. Buy a double-speed (300 kps) or faster drive. It should have 64 K (preferably 256 K) of cache RAM minimum.

For simplicity's sake, and since AV-capable Macintosh computers have the space for it, we suggest getting an internal CD-ROM drive. Even if you don't buy your computer with one already installed, it is generally cheaper to purchase an internal drive than an external drive. (External drives include the case, power supply, and cables that you don't need inside the computer, which ups the cost by as much as $100.) Whether you get the tray type or CD-caddie type of drive is of no consequence. It is only a matter of availability and personal preference.

Hard Disks

Earlier in the book we discussed the various hard disk subsystem types. That discussion was not exhaustive; there are other things you should consider when selecting your hard drive(s): Size, speed, access rate, and other issues surrounding hard disk drives used in digital video are as much as or more important than the size.

There are even, as one of our guest writers covers, some platform considerations you should become familiar with as you outfit your desktop digital studio. This section provides more insight into these other areas.

There are several things to look for when purchasing a hard disk subsystem.

Software. Hard disk formatting and driver software are very important, yet often are not considered as an issue when purchasing a drive. The unfortunate fact is that most drive manufacturers supply some form of formatting and driver utility software that isn't worth the floppy disk it is copied on. It isn't that they are trying to shortchange you; it is generally due to the competitive nature of disk drive sales. Good software costs money, and royalty payments eat into ever-decreasing profit margins.

We strongly recommend that you invest in a high-quality commercial hard disk formatting package. While you're at it, get a good utility and backup package as well. *Hard Disk Toolkit* from FWB, *Norton Utilities* from Semantec, and *Retrospect* from Dantz are excellent choices in the formatter, utility, and backup categories, respectively.

Size. Drive capacity has been growing almost exponentially. At the same time, the overall size of the drive mechanism has been shrinking at a startling rate. What was standard fare just a year ago is a bulky, small-capacity drive by today's comparison. (Warning . . . Here comes our version of the "I walked to school uphill both ways in driving snow, barefoot" story.) When we first used hard disk drives (circa 1974), they could hold 50 MB of data and were the size of commercial washing machines!

Today a "standard" single drive is about the size of a good pulp paperback (not a Danielle Steele novel; they are too thick for this comparison) and can hold up to 2 gigabytes of data (more than 2,000 Danielle Steele novels!) (Figure 2.13).

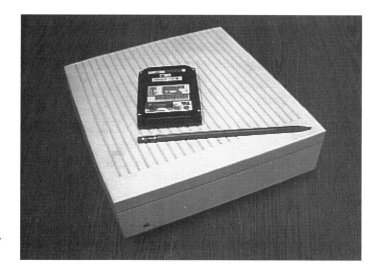

Figure 2.13 Hard-disk shrinkage in just the past few years.

When looking for a drive, ask yourself if the drive is large enough for your needs today and at least a year or two down the road. You can determine this by calculating how much space is needed for the kind of digital video projects you create. Here's how:

1. Decide on the results of your digital video (full-screen, quarter-screen, print to tape, press to CD-ROM, etc.).

2. Decide how many minutes of total video you will usually create (both source and edited results time) on a typical project. You may also want to choose how much data you want to keep "on line" at any given time. To be fair, you could create your project sequentially, breaking it up into smaller portions. If you have only enough space to capture five minutes of video, but your project calls for fifteen minutes, just capture and process it in three or four smaller portions.

3. Decide on the compression format(s) you will be using for your projects.

Once you determine these variables, use the chart in Figure 2.14 to help determine the amount of space you will use for a project.

At the CinePak compression rate of storage space consumption, a CD-ROM (640 MB) will hold forty-five minutes of video; Indeo compression is very similar in file size, and therefore storage requirements, to CinePak at the same settings.

All of these numbers are averages and can be higher or lower based on your content (once again, mileage may vary). And this chart is by no means complete. There are dozens of possible variations. There are also many other compression schemes that we discuss in the QuickTime chapter.

By the way: JPEG-compressed video at a ratio of 10:1 is an excellent source standard for producing digital video that will eventually be compressed using CinePak or Indeo for delivery and playback on CD-ROMs.

The bottom line is this: Almost any project can require up to a gigabyte

Figure 2.14 Compression versus time comparison.

Compression	Size	Frame Rate	MB/ Sec.	MB/ Min.	1 GB Holds . . .
Raw (no compression)	640 × 480	30	27	1600	40 seconds
JPEG @ 4:1	640 × 480	30	4.5	270	4 minutes
JPEG @ 6:1	640 × 480	30	2.7	162	6.5 minutes
JPEG @ 10:1	320 × 240	15	0.85	50	20 minutes
CinePak @ 240 kps	320 × 240	15	0.24	14.4	71 minutes

minimum as you capture your raw video and audio. If you can take on multiple projects, or fit into the midrange to high-end category of user, having just a single 1 gigabyte drive may leave you short. Entry-level users may be able to perform all their work using as little as 500 MB of dedicated disk space.

As of this writing, 1 gigabyte hard drives sell for $450–$650 for basic drives with reasonable levels of performance (speed, access rate, etc.). Hard drives designed for and sold as "digital video ready" draw a premium. The higher-capacity 2-plus gigabyte drives and arrays are more costly today. We suggest that you look at buying at least one 1 gigabyte drive for starters to add to the drive already inside your computer. And think seriously about a second 1 gigabyte drive.

Smart comparison shopping can result in savings of 10 to 20 percent.

Corollary to Our Basic Philosophy Number 2: *Too much hard disk space is never enough.*

Speed. Drive platter rotation speeds generally range from 3600 rpm to 7200 rpm. If you are creating full screen full motion video to tape, make sure the drives you select run at 5400 rpm or better.

If you are not going to be capturing full screen, 30 fps video, then higher rotation speed is not as big an issue for drive selection. In this case, drives in the 3600 rpm to 5400 rpm range should suffice. However, when in doubt, err on the side of higher speed.

Seek time. Seek time is the delay in moving the drive head from data track to data track across the disk. Seek times vary from 6 ms to 15 ms. The faster the seek time (the smaller the number), the better. Many drive makers advertise their average seek time as the amount of delay as the heads move from the inner to outer tracks on a hard disk.

For digital video, you want a drive that offers a seek time that is 10 ms or faster.

Access time. Access time is the period of time required to access any section of the disk drive. This comes into play during both read and write cycles. As with many other hardware considerations, digital video needs drives with fast access rates. Access times on current drives range from 12 ms to 40 ms.

Many companies advertise their "seek time" as their access time, because this generally shows the drive to be faster. Technically they can get away with this, but they shouldn't. The seek time is the most optimal measurement and rarely (if ever) reflects real-world use. Be sure that when you are comparing drive specifications, you are not comparing apples and oranges.

Unless you are constantly vigilant about keeping every bit of data on your drives contiguous (defragmented), your drive will be writing one part of a captured video in one location on the disk and other parts in other locations.

This is bad! It can be avoided, but it often happens when you least expect it.

About the only way around that is having hard drives with the fastest possible access time. This will not alleviate the problem, but it can help.

Data access on hard disk drives is getting faster and faster. Where older drives had access times of 30+ ms (completely unacceptable for digital video but perfectly okay as a file backup source and for other computer uses), access times in newer drives has come down to the range of 10 ms to 20 ms.

For digital video you want a drive with an access time that is under 15 ms.

Transfer rate. This is the amount of data the drive can read from or written to the drive in a specific period of time (usually rated in Kilobytes per second, or Megabytes per second). Many drives actually have different transfer rates for reading and for writing and often are advertised listing only the faster of these two timings. Such ads may also talk about "burst rates" and "sustained rates" of data transfer.

Follow the *sustained rate* as a benchmark. For projects requiring the transfer of large chunks of data per second, such as Print-to-Tape scenarios, you need a drive that can sustain a transfer rate of 2 to 6 MB per second. Only the more expensive single-drive hard disks currently on the market can sustain more than 3.5 MB per second.

To reach the faster required transfer rates for the highest-quality digital video output, you probably need to purchase a hard disk array (discussed earlier in Chapter 1).

Entry-level users and those creating smaller videos using reduced frame rates can operate successfully with drives running at sustained data rates in the 1 to 2 MB per second range.

Quality (the track record). Getting your money's worth in a hard disk, as with all of your digital studio purchases, is very important but should never be a goal at the expense of possible data loss.

Losing a gigabyte of data due to a hard disk crash can really screw up an otherwise good day.

It's not a matter of *if* it COULD happen, but *when* it WILL happen. Believe us, this *will* happen to you at some time in your life! The only protection is to back up your data regularly (and we don't mean weekly). We don't get into archiving in the book other than to suggest it, HIGHLY!

Quality and reliability must be very high on your selection criteria list. Hard disk drives are one of the few moving parts inside your computer; make sure you get warrantees and buy from a dealer or reputable mail-order house that is very service minded.

A dead or "down" hard disk can destroy a project. Ask friends and associates about the track record they have had with hard disks. Stay away from drives that have a bad track record.

Things to look for in a disk drive go beyond speed and quality. Also look for some of the bells and whistles when making a purchase decision. We like to look for what might be called Key Features.

Disk drive key features. There are a number of features we consider "key" when we look for a hard disk drive. Consider these the "bells and whistles" to look for. Among the chief of these are:

- *Disk Cache:* Read and write caches are now common in most disk drives. A cache provides faster throughput of data to and from the computer. Cache sizes typically range from 64 K to 512 K; some drives offer even more cache capacity. A write-thru cache is important for digital video applications. Generally, the larger the cache the better. Of course, drives with larger caches typically cost more.

- *Auto Termination:* SCSI termination can be a topic unto itself. Designed originally to standardize and simplify, it can end up being a nightmare.

  Before telling you why we believe auto-termination is great, here's just a brief course on SCSI. A SCSI chain (a series of SCSI devices, hard disks, scanners, tape drives, etc.) is connected together in series fashion. Each device is connected to the next in a "daisy chain." In any SCSI chain there must be termination (anything from resistor packs installed on a hard disk's controller board, to external terminator blocks) installed at each end of the chain. Most drive manufacturers supply one form or another with each drive. The most common hard disk problems stem from improper SCSI termination.

  So, what is "termination"? Basically, each end of the data path needs to be "terminated" (or blocked) to prevent data signals from being bounced back from the end of the path. If each end is not terminated, it can cause severe data corruption. The drive (or computer) cannot tell which of the signals is the correct one and could mix the bounce-back data with the original.

  Most good drive manufacturers provide detailed documentation, with each drive covering the various setup combinations. We recommend that you follow the setup instructions provided with your hard disk. We also recommend that you consider using drives with the newer "intelligent" termination, as these can greatly reduce the potential for severe migraines!

Generally, the computer's internal hard disk is one end of the chain and can be assumed to be properly terminated. If you add additional internal drives, then you must remove the termination from these drives. (We highly recommend that any work done on the inside of your computer be handled by an authorized service provider.)

When adding external SCSI devices, only the LAST one in the chain is to be terminated. All others in between this last device and the computer must not have termination. Most conscientious drive manufacturers provide detailed documentation with each drive, covering the various setup combinations.

Here is why we believe auto-termination is so great. To solve the termination problem, several manufacturers have developed "intelligent" termination. This auto-termination circuitry senses whether termination is required or not, and at what level. (Some models of Macintosh require double termination, the Mac IIfx being one such computer.) As long as the intelligent drive is at the *end* of the SCSI chain and the other devices are not terminated, then most problems can be eliminated.

- *Thermal Recalibration:* All disk drives do thermal recalibration. This is what keeps the drive's heads in alignment as the drive heats and cools over its usage cycle. This function happens automatically and periodically (every few minutes on average). Thermal recalibration takes time, though, and if you are digitizing some video when the drive decides to do a thermal recalibrate, your drive can begin to drop frames of video during recalibration.

  This is *not* a good thing when you're building your next Emmy nominee.

  The solution is to use drives designed specifically for AV use. They have been redesigned not to perform this function while a large, continuous data transfer is in progress. They wait for a pause in the action to perform recalibration. Many drive makers are now advertising specific models of their drives as "AV" specific, and a modified thermal recalibration is one of several features that make up an AV disk drive.

Corollary to Our Basic Philosophy Number 3: *All other things considered equal, go for the speed.*

As we mentioned earlier, you may want to think about more than just the drive specs. The drive connections are also important, as the following sidebar indicates.

SCSI CONSIDERATIONS

by Jim Griffiths

Mr. Griffiths is employed at FWB, Inc. in the Channel Marketing/Strategic Relations department. Mr. Griffiths is the technical lead for the Sales and Marketing departments due to his extensive experience in technical support and independent consulting. FWB, Inc. is an award-winning maker of high-speed storage solutions for the Macintosh, and soon the Windows platform.

You've bought your computer (we'll assume it's a Macintosh) and digital video card and are thinking about which hard drive to buy. How much storage do you need? How fast should it be? Is it compatible with your computer for achieving the best speed possible?

Since this book contains information to consider when selecting a hard drive for desktop video, I won't go into that. Suffice it to say that digital video work relies on an incredible amount of input/output, and will generate files of tremendous size. Because of this, your *platform* decision must also make your storage needs a fundamental consideration.

If you digitize lower-quality video for multimedia applications, CD-ROM games, or training films, then a high-speed drive system becomes less of a necessity to your work. Fast single-mechanism drives become a more viable alternative since there currently are several on the market that can capture and play back video at speeds up to 4 MB per second. This often is the ideal solution for those users who do not need the fastest solution immediately (or cannot afford it), but who will want the increased performance down the road.

SCSI Performance

(NOTE: The performance numbers discussed in this section refer to raw sustained transfer rates. Please remember to reduce these numbers by 50 percent to provide a proper estimate for QuickTime-based digital video world.)

The same drive should perform identically on all Macintosh models, right? Unfortunately, this is not so. The reason is that your Macintosh model's SCSI chip and its surrounding architecture can vary dramatically from other Macintosh models.

The Macintosh Plus, introduced in 1986, was the first model to include a connection for SCSI hard drives. The maximum transfer rate through its SCSI controller was limited to 1.25 MB per second. Today's Power Macintosh 8100 has a SCSI controller that will allow up to 4.4 MB per second to pass through it. A Quantum hard drive mechanism that can transfer data at 3 MB per second will be able to perform at its full speed on the Power Macintosh, but will be limited to a little over 1 MB per second on a Macintosh Plus.

A Seagate Barracuda drive, which can transfer data at faster than 5 MB per second, will not even reach its full potential on the Power Macintosh because the native

(continued)

SCSI bus is slower than the drive. Since most RAID systems will easily exceed 5 MB per second and can climb as high as 13 MB per second, the native SCSI bus on most Macintosh computers will be too slow to realize the array's full potential.

Because of this, dropping a digital video board and a fast hard drive into a Macintosh IIci (2. 1 MB per second SCSI transfer) will not allow you to achieve the same results as you could on a Power Macintosh. Even adding a CPU accelerator card will not help since this will only speed up the processor, not the SCSI subsystem.

The solution to this problem is a SCSI accelerator card. Available in both NuBus and PDS varieties, these boards provide a separate SCSI bus using a significantly faster controller chip than the Macintosh motherboard. They become ideal solutions for those using older Macintosh models or arrays for high-end desktop video work. With most SCSI accelerator boards, the Mac's motherboard SCSI is recognized by the CPU as being electrically and logically separate from the SCSI accelerator board. This means that you can have up to seven SCSI devices on the native SCSI bus *and* seven more on the SCSI card, for a total of fourteen devices.

One interesting note is Apple's design of a few Macintosh models with two SCSI controllers, the Quadra 900/950 and Power Mac 8100 series of computers. Each bus allows a maximum of 4.4 MB per second, with a theoretical total throughput of nearly 9 MB per second when using a disk array. The array would have each of its two mechanisms connected to a different SCSI bus, preventing data from encountering a bottleneck while trying to get through a single SCSI connection. With real-world sustained transfers of 7 MB per second, this can allow you to achieve digital video performance of nearly 5 MB per second without the cost of a SCSI accelerator card.

NuBus Performance

To go back to our hypothetical Mac IIci with a digital video board and fast hard drive, the supposition is that adding a NuBus-based SCSI accelerator will close the gap with a Power Mac 8100. Although the SCSI accelerator will close the gap with the Power Mac's native SCSI bus, putting the same SCSI accelerator in the Power Mac will again result in a dramatic performance difference between the two machines.

This is because, just like the SCSI issue, NuBus performance will vary widely from Macintosh model to model. Your Macintosh IIci can pass data through its NuBus at up to 4.5 MB per second, but your Power Macintosh, with its highly advanced NuBus design, should be able to pass that same data through at 33 MB per second. Many users may assume that Apple has gradually increased NuBus performance with each successive generation of Macintosh, but this is not true. Prior to the Quadra 840AV, which debuted in mid-1993, NuBus performance peaked with the Quadra 800 at around 6.5 MB per second. The 840AV shattered this limit with an advanced NuBus controller, achieving maximum sustained throughput of 33 MB per second.

(continued)

The result is a Macintosh platform that allows desktop video users to achieve true broadcast-quality captures and playbacks with the use of high-end RAID systems.

Ironically, the Power Macintosh 8100 has the fastest processor of any Macintosh, but not the fastest NuBus. This distinction belongs to the Quadra 840AV. The Power Macintosh and the Quadra 840AV use the same NuBus controller chip; due to design limitations, the current Power Macintosh 8100 falls about 10 to 20 percent short of the Quadra 840AV's NuBus speed. What can be captured to an array on an 840AV at 6.3 MB per second can only be done at 5.7 MB per second on a Power Mac 8100. A debate currently rages between which to choose: the rendering and processing speed of the Power Mac, or the superior I/O performance of the Quadra 840AV.

In either case, a Quadra 840AV or a Power Macintosh 8100 and the proper RAID system will allow you to do full-screen, broadcast-quality work. But if you own or are planning to purchase a different Macintosh, few other models (including the Power Mac 6100 and 7100) will have the I/O capabilities for this quality of work.

Backups

The final consideration for digital storage options is how to store your data for the long term. Since a digital video file can be as large as 400 MB for each minute of footage, backups and archiving can present a major problem. Removable drives such as SyQuests or magneto-opticals currently have a maximum single-file capacity of a little over 600 megabytes. For the multimedia application developer, this might prove adequate. But for the professional film producer, the only viable solution is digital audiotape (DAT) drives.

DAT drives offer the ability to store phenomenal quantities of information at a cost of a few pennies per megabyte. Although a drive that can store as much as 10 GB per tape may cost up to $2,000, the tapes used are available for less than $30 each. No other storage media on the market today can offer this amazing cost-to-capacity ratio.

Conclusion

Most computer users who venture into the desktop video field believe that their only decision lies in which model and whose digital video card to purchase. Usually, their choice of a storage subsystem is dealt with as an afterthought. Unfortunately, this is a serious error if you plan to do anything other than casual desktop video work. Your choice for storage is interwoven not only with your needs, but also with the platform you choose. It must be stressed that you need to consider your decision very carefully before committing to an entire solution. Research your options, talk to vendors and dealers, and most importantly, query other users before making your final decision. This is the best way to get on the road to desktop video with the least heartbreak, toil, and regret.

A small word of caution when purchasing a hard drive. There are two main bus types for hard drives: SCSI and IDE. Most Macintosh computers use SCSI drives, whereas IDE is the standard in the PC world. You *can* get a SCSI bus in a PC and use SCSI devices, however, and Apple recently began mounting IDE drives inside some of its computers while retaining the SCSI port on the rear of the computer.

Do not mistake the standards and do what an acquaintance of ours recently did. Because IDE drives are generally less expensive and he is price-conscious, he purchased a 1 gigabyte IDE drive for his Macintosh. He tore into the box at work, tossed out all of the packaging, and took the drive home. Once he got his Macintosh open, he saw that the cabling was different and called the store. They told him why the drive wouldn't work in his Macintosh, and that he should repackage the drive and bring it back to the store.

Unfortunately, since he no longer had the packaging, they would not take the drive back. Fortunately, a friend of his was in the market for a large-capacity IDE drive and bought it from him.

This could have been bad, but it turned out okay in the end. He took the money and purchased a SCSI drive and everybody was happier. And he was wiser.

Monitors

There are literally dozens of monitor styles, sizes, and brands. Digital video, with its roots in analog video, is linked with NTSC or PAL resolutions. This means that no matter how high a resolution display you have, say 1024 × 768 (and the display hardware to support it; see the next topic), the video resolution will always have a maximum of 640 × 480 pixels. For you broadcast types, only the very high end systems support 768 × 525 digital video. So, getting a 21-inch color monitor will not provide you with video that fills the screen; it will just give you more desktop real estate to work in.

Full-screen video in the digital video sense is 640 × 480. In years past, high-quality displays were set at a fixed resolution. Then, multisync monitors (those that could display different screen resolutions) typically were of inferior quality. Today, all the name-brand monitor vendors offer very high quality multisync displays and traditional fixed-resolution displays. We have used both types and have multiple monitors on several of our systems, providing us with the most flexibility. Being able to display "full-screen" digital video on a 14-inch 640 × 480 display and have the larger monitor for application windows is great.

Multisync monitors are nice to have because they give you the ability to change resolutions without having to buy another monitor. The drawback to them is that the screen DPI (dots per inch) gets much tighter as the resolution increases. In English this means that objects and text get smaller and smaller at each resolution increase, to the point where text can become very difficult to read and you may not get a realistic sense of what a video actually looks like when displayed at "normal" resolution.

SUGGESTION: If you do create digital video on a multisync monitor running at one of the higher resolutions, *always* check your work with the monitor in the 640 × 480 pixel mode before you "ship" it.

Corollary to Our Basic Philosophy Number 4: *Bigger is almost always better, but you have to be realistic.*

Video Display Cards

Not to be confused with the video digitizer card you will need to capture the video, which is discussed in Chapter 3. Video display cards are what drive the signal to your monitor. This category has begun thinning out, with fewer brands and new models appearing every season. The cards that are generally available are classified as accelerated display cards. They can speed up the QuickDraw graphics functions of the Macintosh many hundreds of times.

Although one of these accelerated cards can increase your display capabilities, having a separate display card is not mandatory because modern Macintosh AV-series computers come with built-in video display hardware. Your monitor connects directly to the back of the computer. You will need one, however, if you intend to connect more than one monitor to your system. You may also want to consider a video display card if you want accelerated graphics functionality or if you want 24-bit color capability which your built-in video may not provide.

Be aware that many of the video digitizer cards double as video display cards; they have both capabilities built into the one product.

Windows users almost always have to add a display card to their system because most PC manufacturers do not build this video support capability into their computers. (This lets them advertise a lower cost for the computer while neglecting to mention all of the other things you need to purchase.) There are also accelerated display cards available for PCs. They are rated in WinMarks, which is a measurement of how fast they process and display Windows graphics to the monitor.

There are several buying considerations for display cards. These include:

- Getting 24-bit color support for Macintosh or SVGA support for thousands of colors (or higher) for PCs.

- Does it minimally support the monitor resolution(s) you have?

- Getting QuickDraw graphics acceleration for Macintosh. (This can add $$ to the cost.)

- Getting Windows graphics acceleration for PCs. (This too can add $$ to the cost.)
- Does it have the correct interface for your Macintosh: NuBus, PDS, or PCI?
- Does it have the correct interface for your PC: VESA Local Bus or PCI?

Speakers and Sound Cards

All Macintosh computers have digital audio sound capability built in; most PCs do not have any digital sound capability at all (generally providing only system beeps and simple sounds). No matter their sound capability, most computers (Macintosh and PCs) have small, low-quality built-in speakers. Because of this, many people buy external speakers. When you search for speakers to use with your computer, make sure they are shielded! The magnets in the speakers, if not properly shielded, can wreak havoc with your monitor (causing colors to wash on the screen nearest the speakers) and have even been responsible for erasing data on floppy disks. This has to do with electromagnetism and other mystical things.

If you can place the speakers on a shelf away from the computer and floppies (we recommend at least two feet away), then you probably are okay with most unshielded speaker systems. But, if you are like most of us who place our speakers just on either side of the monitor to get the proper stereo effect when sitting in front of the keyboard, take heed of our warnings.

The packaging for the speakers should indicate that they have been designed and tested (shielded) for use with computers or monitors.

The speakers should be self-amplified (known as "powered speakers") so that you do not need to buy a separate amplifier. They should have a volume control. Having a left–right balance control and a separate audio CD input is nice but not necessary. Apple offers powered speakers designed to complement the styling and capabilities of Macintosh computers.

NOTE: As we cover elsewhere in the book, use amplified, external speakers with the understanding that the quality and volume level you hear are not what users of your projects will hear unless they, too, have amplified speakers. Always check your project's volume settings using the build-in speaker of your computer. We recommend that you use only the built-in speaker when performing audio editing and equalization.

Sound cards are available for Macintosh, but they are not necessarily required. Some Macs have limited audio input characteristics, mono or fixed frequencies or both. If this is the case with your system and you want to digitize audio at higher qualities and in stereo, then consider a sound card. Take heart that many of the video digitizer cards also digitize audio, thus eliminating the need for a specific sound card.

PCs require the addition of a sound card. The Sound Blaster from Creative Labs has set the standard for sound capabilities, and most applications (and many other sound card brands) tout Sound Blaster compatibility. Be sure that the sound card you choose is at least MPC level 1–compliant and preferably adheres to MPC level 2. Many PC sound cards also offer many options, from wave-table audio to MIDI and SCSI interfaces. These features can double or triple the cost of the card, so be sure that the extra features of a card are ones you want and will use.

RAM as a Peripheral

The base level of RAM that ships with most computers today is 4 MB, which is barely enough to boot the computer. 8 MB allows you to use most traditional computer applications. But if you're going to be serious about producing digital video, even if you're going to just play at it, this is not nearly enough. The facts are simple: digital video applications require lots of RAM.

Memory for your system is usually made up of SIMMs (Single In-line Memory Modules). These SIMMs come in several sizes—1, 2, 4, 8, and 16 MB per SIMM—are the affordable ones. Depending on your system, one or more (sometimes up to 16) SIMMs can be added to the computer. Sometimes they must be added in blocks of two or four (of the same size SIMM). You will need to refer to your computer's documentation or the dealership where you purchased the computer to determine the specifics for your system.

Memory can be a major portion of your system cost. Shop around. As the following chart shows, RAM memory can have a wide range. Understand that RAM chips are commodity items and prices can fluctuate weekly.

1 MB SIMM	$30–$45 each
4 MB SIMM	$125–$180 each
8 MB SIMM	$240–$360 each
16 MB SIMM	$600–$800 each

As we say elsewhere in the book, many applications need large amounts of extra RAM. Even though a simple program may say it only "requires 4 MB RAM," you must remember that your system, extensions, fonts, and so forth, all take up some space. Wht is left over may be only enough to open the application and not enough to fully use it.

Corollary to Our Basic Philosophy Number 5: *If it doesn't come with double-digit RAM, make it so!*

There are other types of peripherals that can be added to your system, such as tape backup drives, cartridge and optical disc drives, scanners, and so forth. Since these usually are not directly involved in the desktop video studio, we do not discuss them in this book.

We do suggest that you look into some sort of backup system for your projects. The two main ones we use are CD-ROM one-offs and DAT backup.

In Summary . . .

As you outfit your studio, choose your systems and peripherals carefully. Even though there is a lot of standardization in the industry, there still are some models of some peripherals that are not designed to work with some computers.

We suggest one other thing . . .

If you will have both a Macintosh computer and a PC in your studio (and haven't yet purchased the PC), we suggest that you have the PC outfitted with a SCSI bus, rather than IDE. This will mean that your peripherals will have greater compatibility between the Macintosh and the PC. The only drawback is that most SCSI peripherals cost a bit more than their IDE counterparts.

Oh, well. It's worth the investment.

3

Digital Video Tools

In the previous chapter we discussed the larger system issues of producing digital video and the architectures that make it all possible. We can now turn our attention to the software and hardware *tools* that you will use in your desktop studio.

These tools vary in their use and capabilities, and they can widely differ in their relative effectiveness for any given project. You will need to choose your tools wisely and spend time learning their individual capabilities and eccentricities. Don't go strictly on price when looking for the right tools for your studio. We frequently utilize several low-cost and no-cost utilities to augment the capabilities of some of the high-priced applications we use. In many cases, this is because the utilities do the same job with less fuss and bother; in some cases the utilities do a better job at their one function than an all-in-one application.

In this chapter, we'll first look at desktop video editors and utilities, and then we will delve into some of the many digitizing and compression cards.

For our money, *this* is where all the fun is—editing, adding effects, and using utilities to process your digital video into its final form. This is where you get to use your ingenuity. This is where you can make a big difference. This is the part of the process that turns the raw into the refined.

The vast majority of products for the desktop video studio fall into this category. The lines between product types blur more here than in any other category. Some applications try to be a one-stop shop for all your capturing, editing, special effects, compression, and utility processing needs. And to a certain extent, some of them succeed in doing that. Others have their niche and focus on performing their specialties.

In our business, we find that we use several different applications that fall into this category, switching between them depending on what is best for a given project. Unlike desktop publishing, where it is unlikely that you would use, say, both Adobe PageMaker and QuarkXpress on the same project, we often find that different job and client needs require that we use various "competitive" editors and effects applications on a single project to get the desired end results.

This doesn't mean that any given application is incomplete, or that you have to go out and buy lots of expensive software. It does mean that each digital video editor has its own strengths, and we combine those strengths to save time and money in the long run. To be fair, we *did* have to put in a large amount of time up front to learn all the different products, but it has been time well spent.

The main idea is to find the tool(s) that fit your requirements (no great epiphany here) and to continue searching for the best combinations. You may find, as we have, that one combination works for many projects, although it fails to produce the best results for others. We once found that a combination of products that had not worked well before was exactly what we needed for a new project. The moral is never to discard or discount something that you tried only once.

In the next few pages we outline what each major type of editing tool does, and what to look for in that type of product.

The following pages focus on a couple of important applications that solve specific problems or offer unique solutions. For the purpose of simplification, we break down these software products into three categories:

- Video editors
- Effects tools
- Utilities

We have also reviewed each of the named applications below. *(Please see their individual reviews in Chapter 7 toward the end of this book.)*

Video Editors

Digital video editors do just that: They electronically edit—cut and splice—individual movie components into an end product, or they take long clips and cut them down to just those portions that will be used in the final assembly. The end product may not be complete; it may require further work using an effects tool, but the editor is generally used first.

Features of a Good Editor

There are many things to look for in an editor. It is important that you choose the right one for you, as it is probably the one application type where you will spend most of your time when producing digital video movies. Although there are elements such as ease of use and interface design that are matters of individual preference, we prefer to judge digital video editing applications in these areas:

- Capture—the support available for various digitizer cards
- File format suport—MooV, PICT, AIFF, PICS, and others
- Edit method—the manner in which the editor performs its functions
- Audio—the control and editing of audio tracks
- Preview—viewing what you have edited before committing to a final
- Transitions—the variety of DVE effects
- Compression—proper implementation of QuickTime compression settings
- Options—the added bells and whistles

Capture. QuickTime makes this virtually transparent, but we have found that some of the digitizer cards offer more features to the user during video capture than QuickTime offers as standard. This is a planned-for feature in QuickTime that allows hardware manufacturers to extend a product's capabilities beyond the base QuickTime level. Applications that adhere to Quick-Time properly take advantage of these extensions seamlessly. In future releases of QuickTime, video capture features will most likely be added.

One thing to look for is the ability to capture from within the editor. This is a convenient feature that can help eliminate a step in the process. (Fewer steps can mean a better end result and can take less time.) One other nice feature is batch capture capability. Batch captures are required for *our* needs but may not be necessary for all users.

File format support. The editor should be able to import and export more than just movies. It should be able to handle sound files in various formats (SND, WAV, AIFF), pictures, graphics, and animation in the PICT and PICS formats.

Edit method. There are several different methods of editing digital video clips together, each having its own merits. We do not recommend one over the other; we have found that different folks work differently and one man's ceiling is another man's floor. As long as the clips go together and look like what we planned, we are not picky about how the editor performs the magic behind the scenes.

You will find that the two main types are timeline-based editors and storyboard-based editors. Timeline editors are the more traditional format (derived from film editing techniques) and offer control down to the individual frame. Storyboard editors are generally simpler to use, as they work from the scene or shot level. Some applications offer both methods.

Audio. The ability to perform simple audio edits, fade in, fade out, and import and export separate audio files is a necessity. Most editors can do standard cut and splice audio editing. We haven't seen one so far that is capable of lots of studio-quality audio processing, although some can do simple fades and dissolves between both video and audio.

If your project requires a higher level of audio processing, such as layering multiple tracks, equalization, combining multiple tracks, and other fancy compound editing of audio, these should be performed in an audio editor program such as DigiTrax or Deck II.

Preview. Previewing your transition selections and edit decisions is a must for even the simplest editors. If an editor product forces you to commit to creating the actual edit prior to being able to view it, walk away. The editor need not offer the ability to create a preview in real time, however. Systems that can create real-rime previews fall into the high-level category and start in the mid–five figures. Expect a good preview to take several minutes for a short piece.

We believe that you need preview capability, and the ability to have a preview without altering the original materials (unless you have unlimited hard disk space to keep backups of your originals, and you make sure to clean off all the unused previews so you don't mistakenly use one in your final, and . . . well, you get the point).

Transitions. Except for utility applications such as MoviePlayer, almost all editors offer some set of transitions (Figure 3.1). Many editors offer every kind of transition under the sun, including the kitchen sink. Having all the standards such as fades, dissolves (A-B *and* B-A), and wipes (up, down, left, right) is a must. Having some of the fancier transitions is nice, but don't overlook a particular package because it can't offer you "semi-transparent triangles sparkling in a shimmering lower-left to upper-right pattern over a user-selectable time" effects. Besides, most of those are intrusive and we avoid them like the plague. See the section on "Techniques for Editing" in Chapter 5 for more details.

As time marches on, more and more applications are using what are known as *plug-ins*. These are additional effects that can be added to the basic functionality of a product, usually by simply dragging them into the

Figure 3.1 Some of the transitions offered in Premiere.

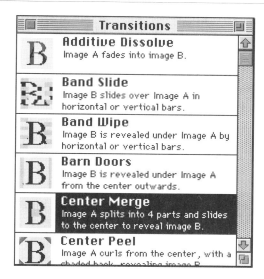

appropriate folder. If you use Photoshop, you should be very aware of plug-ins. Look for editor products that feature this kind of upgradability.

Compression. A proper editor application will provide you with all the options for compressing video when you output, export, or save your movie (Figure 3.2). They may offer the features in a progressive (step-by-

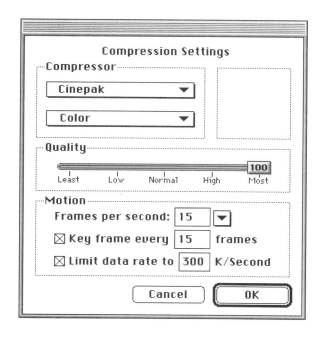

Figure 3.2 The basic setting categories for proper compression

step) manner that gives you control over many of the parameters, the level of control we prefer. You may not want to set *all* the parameters *every* time, but they should be available to you as an option in a dialog box or from the basic menus.

You may find some editor products that let you set your favorite parameters as part of the Preferences settings. You do yourself a big favor by understanding where all the settings are located in your software.

Be sure that the compression schemes used in a particular product are the same ones you use. If a product does only high-quality MPEG compression, but you need JPEG, Indeo, and CinePak, then that product is not for you.

Options. This is where some editor products shine. We use products based on the actual end result required, sometimes favoring a simple "no bells and whistles" application over a more feature-rich one. But there are some of these nonstandard features, or options, that can really make your day. Here are two of our favorites:

- *Output*—Being able to "print to tape" from the editor application is a nice feature. Many higher-end editors are able to take advantage of the video output features of high-end compression cards. Several JPEG cards offer hardware scaling, giving you the ability to output a 320 × 240 movie to tape at full-screen size.

- *Batching*—For us, this is a must-have feature. Almost all of our projects include multiple movie clips. Being able to batch capture, batch process, and batch compress is a major timesaver. Large batch jobs can be left to run overnight, making use of available computer time and speeding up the project completion.

Now that we've talked about some of the generalities, here is an actual product example.

Apple MoviePlayer. This application (yes, it is also an editor) was created to showcase QuickTime and its many features and characteristics. It was also designed so as not to compete with the third-party developers that Apple Computer wants to create great feature-rich QuickTime applications. The end result is a lion in sheep's clothing. Apple's MoviePlayer is a great "cuts-only" QuickTime movie editor. Because of the standard MacOS features of Cut, Copy, and Paste, it is very easy to create finished edited movies using just MoviePlayer.

MoviePlayer supports both audio and video tracks, letting you add, extract, and delete them as you desire. It also features an informative Get Info box (Figure 3.3) that details all of the parameters of each track within the movie.

**Figure 3.3
Two of the
available Info
windows from
MoviePlayer.**

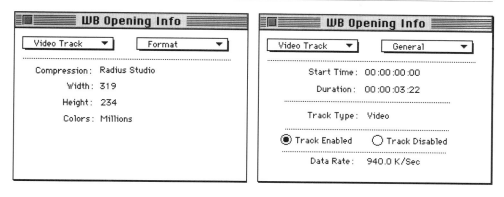

Using the QuickTime feature of saving a Movie alias, it is possible to edit many different versions of a movie, or make many revisions of a movie, without disturbing the original source movie one bit.

MoviePlayer is more powerful than it appears. It has quite a few features that the engineers at Apple added for their own needs that also happen to be useful for the rest of us.

For any developers out there who are familiar with MoviePlayer 1.1, a new 2.0 version is in the works and will offer current as well as some enhanced features.

MoviePlayer is just one of the smaller editor applications available today. There are many other editors on the market, most of which can be termed *mainstream*—meaning those applications available to anyone through retail channels as well as the many catalogs featuring Macintosh and Windows software.

Mainstream QuickTime video editors include the following products, which are reviewed in Chapter 7 of this book:

- Adobe Premiere (available for test drive and purchase in the CD-ROM)
- Avid VideoShop
- VideoFusion QuickFLIX (demo on the CD-ROM)

Effects Tools

There are many different kinds of applications available to add fantastic effects to your digital video movies. These effects include:

- Transitions
- Morphing

- Rotoscoping
- Filters
- 3D rendering
- Keying

And the list goes on and on. Adding effects to your movies is a great way to keep your audience's attention, but they can be a double-edged sword.

When desktop publishing first took off, with a plethora (look it up!) of available fonts, many a newsletter was produced that looked like a ransom note. Using too many or too varied a selection of effects in any digital video can result in something slightly worse than a B grade horror movie from the 1950s.

In fact, it's probably a great idea to create your own bad "video ransom note" with all sorts of effects-combinations in it. This will help get the effects out of your system and will show you what the effects look like and which ones are more appropriate for your needs. So go ahead and experiment! Just don't experiment on your best client's project.

Judicious, appropriate use of effects can make the difference.

One of the "hottest" and most horribly over-used effects today is the motion-image morph. Ever since Michael Jackson did it in a music video, where a dozen people morph into each other as they are singing and dancing, the morph craze has not stopped. When it was discovered that personal computers had the power to quickly and easily re-create these great effects, and at broadcast quality, every ad agency in America had to have their own. The problem is twofold: overexposure, resulting in less impact; and poorly rendered morphs by well-meaning people who just aren't doing it right.

Overexposure means that now there seems to be at least one morph in every television commercial break—everything from men shaving each other's faces to dancing credit cards. You too can join the bandwagon and add morphs to your production. There are several applications available that do very acceptable morphs, but two stand out: Gryphon's Morph and ASDG's Elastic Reality. (This product is so popular that the company renamed itself to Elastic Reality, Inc.) Both of these are on the accompanying CD-ROM.

Morphs aside, several of the mainstream editor applications also have reasonably good effects capabilities. Transition effects are usually included with an editor application.

One application that has taken the opposite approach is VideoFusion, which began life as an excellent effects application that also does a good job as an editor. Its unique storyboard interface design makes it easy to assemble movie clips, add transitions or effects, and output a compressed movie result with little need for video editing knowledge.

Some of our favorite effects packages include the following. (*Please see their individual reviews in Chapter 7 toward the end of this book.*)

Aldus AfterImage
Aldus AfterEffects
Adobe Photoshop (available for test drive and purchase from the CD-ROM)
Radius VideoFusion (demo on the CD-ROM)
Gryphon Morph (demo on the CD-ROM)
ASDG Elastic Reality (demo on the CD-ROM)
Fractal Design Painter (demo on the CD-ROM)
HSC Kai's Power Tools (free samples on the CD-ROM)

Authoring Tools

There are many special authoring tools available for creating anything from slide presentations to multistation kiosks, and from simple icon-based authoring to those full metal jacket, high-level programming languages. Finding the right one for your needs is the subject of separate books published by Random House and others. Let's cover some general guidelines to consider when you're looking for the right authoring tool for your desktop studio.

Question number one should be: Do you *need* to use an authoring tool? Is the end result of your digital video to be a part of some larger multimedia presentation? In many cases your movies *are* the end result. If this is the case, there seems to be little need for an authoring tool. If you are going to output your movies to videotape, a multimedia authoring tool is absolutely unnecessary. In those cases when you do need to put a "wrapper" around your movies, make sure the authoring tool you select fully supports your digital video file format, namely QuickTime.

These authoring tools are what turn your digital video content into a presentable, often interactive, finished product. Check to see that whatever authoring tool you select has been tested with the latest version of QuickTime for your platform. If you need your multimedia piece to be cross-platform, make sure the authoring tool allows you to create two versions—one Macintosh, one Windows—from a single source. You don't want to create it from scratch twice!

Next question: How complex is your multimedia presentation? Is it a "traditional" slide show to which you are adding movies? Do you require interactivity, and at what level? For projects that require basic interactivity within a presentation, products such as Adobe Persuasion or Microsoft PowerPoint may be all that you need; they are already the "standards" in the presentation arena.

Actually, the lines between presentation tools and authoring tools are becoming blurred. In its most recent version, Adobe (Aldus) has added interactive branching features to Persuasion. If you need more complex interactivity, then a more feature-rich authoring tool such as the Apple Media Tool (included on the accompanying CD-ROM) is probably called for.

Several different authoring tool template styles, or creation metaphors, are available. Some are time based; some are object based; some have iconic interfaces; some are scripting based. If you go this route, be aware that products in this category have a wide range of learning curves.

Products such as HyperCard (a demo of which is on the accompanying CD-ROM) and SuperCard, which began their lives as user-friendly database environments, have now become full-fledged multimedia authoring tools. They have become scripting-based authoring tools—full programming environments with high learning curves. They may not have a pretty iconic interface in which to create your shell, but they offer a high level of flexibility in creating custom multimedia productions. Many commercial multimedia software titles have been created using these two tools. Among the best selling CD-ROM titles are Voyager's Expanded Books, develped using Hyper-Card. The two newest versions of SuperCard—2.0 and 3.0—have a very robust set of features and should be investigated.

Choose carefully and know your real needs before deciding between a presentation application and one designed for scripting. You could spend much more time learning and working with the authoring tool than it takes to create your movie content.

Products such as Apple Media Tool, Special Delivery, and MovieWorks all fit into this category. (*Please see their individual reviews in Chapter 7 toward the end of this book.*)

If you are developing for a new or different (non-Macintosh or Windows) platform, even one that uses a recognizable format such as QuickTime, there may be special considerations to take into account. It may be that a particular platform cannot be approached without using an authoring tool. It may also be true that only a limited selection of tools are available for one of these platforms.

If this is the case, you will do yourself a great favor by trying two things: (1) read all of the documentation before you plunge in, and (2) contact the vendors of the platform and of the authoring tool to see if they can refer you to someone in your area.

A final suggestion is that you not try to take on everything by yourself. Learning new environments can be like learning a foreign language. If you live in any sizable area, there probably are people around you who already are experts. We find that it frequently is cheaper in the long run to subcontract out this type of work. It means less money in our pockets, but it provides the client with a high-quality product. And a satisfied client is frequently a return client. Word to the wise!

We have developed a number of projects using authoring tools over the years. Tom was among the first people to use HyperCard to create an interactive training environment while he was a Senior Instructional Designer at Apple. Before there was much brouhaha about multimedia, his product introduction trainings and advanced user techniques CD-ROMs were being used by Apple sales individuals and user groups around the world. (How's that for a little self-promotion?)

Mark Wade, formerly with Apple, has been even more deeply involved in using HyperCard as an authoring environment. He even developed an authoring tool that uses HyperCard as its authoring environment. He began using it before it became a product and continues to use and promote the use of HyperCard in multimedia.

HYPERCARD AND QUICKTIME
by Marc Wade

Marc Wade has been a producer in the Paramount Media Kitchen, developing prototypes and pilots for on-line services, interactive television, and other new media. Prior to that, he spent five years creating innovative business learning applications at Apple Computer, Inc., most recently as the Multimedia Designer for the Worldwide Performance Systems group. Marc has a degree in Computer Science with a special interest in programming languages and authoring tools. After two decades of software design and development using various high-level languages, when faced with a new task, he says that he usually starts out with Hypercard. Marc is co-author of The Multimedia Adventure, *an introductory guide to interactive multimedia development.*

Hypercard changed my life.

When I saw the first public demonstration of Hypercard in 1987, I knew that my dozen years of software development experience had led me to that moment. Hypercard was the perfect tool for creating applications for learning, reference, and entertainment; I wanted to work at Apple and use Hypercard all the time.

My enthusiasm propelled me into a lengthy job search that resulted in a position at Apple as Senior Media Engineer in the Training department. I moved my family to Cupertino, and for five years I created interactive multimedia applications and prototypes used for training Apple's worldwide sales and support staff. Here are some examples of projects my group worked on, including discoveries we made and tips for using Hypercard and QuickTime together effectively.

(continued)

Macintosh Fundamentals

Our first multimedia training applications used Hypercard to control a laserdisc player. *Macintosh Fundamentals* displayed information on the Macintosh screen and showed video clips on a separate TV monitor to emphasize or further illustrate the training material. It was an effective use of multimedia technology, but it required a big hardware investment to deliver the information to the user.

Subsequent applications eliminated the TV screen by requiring an expensive video digitizing card that displayed the video directly on the Macintosh screen.

Call Planning

When QuickTime was announced, we were able to create and deliver multimedia content without extra hardware. We could put video clips (albeit small ones) in a window directly on the Macintosh screen. The first QuickTime-based training project within Apple was *Call Planning,* an example of a bite-sized "learning granule" showing salespeople how to work with customers.

The design was similar to what we had done before with laserdisc. The user was shown a video clip, then presented with a question. Based on the answer to the question, one of three video clips was shown. In several instances we showed a customer making a statement, then offered the user a choice of three different potential responses. The user could view the outcome of each response just by clicking a button.

Since this was developed using a pre-release version of QuickTime, the optimum video window size was a tiny 160 × 120 pixels. To disguise the small size of the video, we shot our video in a "limbo" set—characters and action in the foreground against a solid black background. We placed the QuickTime movie on the screen surrounded by a larger black region. This hid the boundaries of the movie, making the movie appear larger and completely integrated into the card design.

One of the best tricks we found in developing this application was the use of QuickTime movies as a timing device. When a movie is playing, you can send the movie window a frame number, and a message. Once the movie gets to that frame number, it sends the message to your Hypercard stack. We used this to display a text outline of the narrator's script in sync with the audio track. As she hit certain key points, the QuickTime movie told the stack to display the next page of the outline, often by going to the next card in the stack.

We also adapted a trick we'd used with laserdisc programs: putting a clip's name in a hidden field on the card.

Let's say each card in the stack plays one movie. One approach is to create an individual button on each card that contains the name of the movie file to play.

(continued)

Then, if we had to change a movie or shuffle the order the movies played, we'd have to reprogram all the affected buttons. Instead, we created a background field that contained the filename on each card. Then we created a single background button that read that field and played the movie. To make any changes, all we had to do was type the new movie information into the field; no scripting changes were needed.

To facilitate development, we created several "tool" scripts and buttons. Since there were several hidden fields containing important information, one script showed and hid these fields, making them accessible to the developer. One script did an "answer file," retrieving a movie's filename and placing it in the field; another fetched the current frame number from the QuickTime movie, putting it in a field when needed. These tool scripts were kept in a separate stack, called "devTools." When we were doing development, I'd just type "start using stack devTools" in the message window and the tools were available.

LaserWriter Service

For the *LaserWriter Service* course, we created a prototype that allowed the user to practice making a service call to repair a printer. One section allowed the user to choose from a list of questions to ask a customer what was wrong with the printer.

We used QuickTime movies to show the customer's response. Another major section simulated the process of taking the printer apart. We shot more than 100 still frames of a LaserWriter in various stages of being disassembled and from various angles. These video frames were assembled into a QuickTime movie. Each card in the stack represented one stage of the printer repair process: taking the cover off, removing the toner cartridge, disconnecting the power supply, etc. When the user made a selection that removed a part or changed the view, the stack went to the card that corresponded to the new state of the printer.

Each card knew the frame number of the movie that corresponded to the view desired, and simply showed that frame. QuickTime was a good way to manage the picture information, compress it into a small file size, and display the new view very quickly.

Desktop Seminar: QuickTime

We realized that Hypercard and QuickTime gave us a very effective multimedia delivery tool. Our group created the *Desktop Seminar* concept as a way to deliver information to every desktop within Apple using interactive multimedia. The display of text, graphics, and QuickTime movies was synchronized with narration. Our first Seminar described QuickTime itself, demonstrating to our sales and support personnel how it

(continued)

could be used. Refining an earlier concept, we used a QuickTime movie containing just the narrative audio track as the timing mechanism for each topic or chapter.

By providing controls to move forward and backward in this audio track, then tying the display of movies and graphics to the frame number currently being displayed, we gave the user complete control over the pace of the presentation. We chose to open the audio movie as "invisible" and created our own buttons and progress bar. This let the user control the presentation, but allowed us to constrain the user's movement within our own limits—making sure he or she jumped to the beginning of a sentence, for example.

Once we saw how well this concept worked and how well it was received by our audience, we decided to create a set of tools to create more Desktop Seminars.

Desktop Seminar Toolkit

The *Toolkit* is a series of Hypercard stacks that provide a developer with everything needed to create a Desktop Seminar. The final seminar stack is 640 × 480 pixels, requiring a 13-inch monitor and 8-bit color, but the authoring tools can be run on a 512 × 342 monochrome Macintosh. One stack, called the *Guide,* takes the developer through the steps of creating the Seminar: writing the script, connecting media elements, choosing background artwork, and so on. Another stack, the *Shell,* contains all the software necessary for presenting the Seminar, but holds no content. The Guide stack extracts the information from the authoring tools and places it into the empty Shell, creating the final Seminar. All the software necessary to run the Seminar is provided inside the Shell.

Apple shipped the Toolkit with the Hypercard Player application since that is all an author needs: no programming is necessary to create a complete Seminar.

If an author does want to customize a Seminar, the Toolkit provides over 15,000 lines of HyperTalk code that the author is free to adapt or supplement. Some typical customization efforts include adding new functionality, providing connections to other applications for reference materials, and creating new interactive exercises. One key factor in our design was to force all our code to the lowest level possible. That is, all of our handlers are in the script or background level, leaving the card scripts empty for customization.

Tips and Tricks

During the creation of these and other projects, we discovered many little tricks that made the development and maintenance process easier. As mentioned, pushing the handlers down to the lowest level is one trick that can save considerable time and effort. If you create a script to perform a specific function, such as playing a movie, see if you can make it more general.

(continued)

Sometimes a slight change will allow you to reuse a button or script, and that can be a big time saver.

Defining a global variable that keeps track of the name of the currently displayed movie (we called ours *currentMovie*) lets you create general controls that can send messages to the window referenced by that variable. You can create general buttons to rewind, play, pause, and close the current movie just by using this global variable.

If we had a number of cards that each played a different movie in a different place on the screen, we created a button on each card in the desired location. Then the general "open" script showed the movie in the location of that card button. If we needed to move the location of the movie, all that was needed was to move the button—no script changes.

The QuickTime Tools stack that comes with Hypercard is an extremely useful tool for learning how to control movies. At the simplest level, you can use the stack to do all the work for you. The QuickTime Toolkit card lets you define the name of the movie, the style and location of the movie window, and more. A button is created using your specifications, and you can simply paste this button into your stack. Of course, by looking at the button script you can see how it's done and can begin writing your own scripts from the example. The Advanced Options card shows you how to set the movie rate, start and end time, audio level, and other parameters. The QuickTime XCMDs included with this stack give you all the functionality you need to create useful stacks that present QuickTime movies.

Many of the stacks we created present full-color backgrounds and colored animated buttons. We accomplished this through various methods, using different XCMDs and tricks, some of them quite complex. The Color Tools stack (also included with Hypercard) has simplified this process, making color support available within the Hypercard environment.

One trick for creating animated colored buttons is to create a tiny three-frame QuickTime movie in the shape of the button. Let's say you need a 3D colored button that shows and hides a text field on a card. Design an icon for the button (which can be a rectangle of any size), then draw the icon in three states: OFF, ON, and DOWN. In the OFF and ON states the button will appear to be "up"; the ON state should be highlighted somehow, perhaps with a bright color. In the DOWN state the button will appear to be pressed down with no highlight color. Create a QuickTime movie from these three frames, one for each state.

When the card is first shown, hide the text field. Open the movie and place it where you want the button to appear, showing the frame number of the button in its OFF state. Define a global variable for the current state of the button, called "button-State," and set it to OFF. Define the movie so it passes mouse clicks to the card. In the card script, handle the mouse clicks inside the movie window. When the user clicks down in the window, change the frame number of the movie to display the

(continued)

DOWN state. It will appear to the user that a real button has been pressed down. When the mouse is released, check the buttonState global. If it is OFF, then change the frame number of the movie to show the button in its ON state, making it appear that the button has popped back up. Set buttonState to ON, and show the text field. If the global is ON, change the frame number to show the button in its OFF state, set the global to OFF, and hide the text field. This simple technique gives users definite feedback on their actions.

Now, a few comments on delivering a Hypercard/QuickTime application on CD-ROM. Give your movies meaningful names (instead of some complex code names) to make them easier to identify and manage during the development process. Consider grouping your movies into folders and organizing them in some logical manner (by chapter or topic, or some other category).

There are several good sources of information on creating QuickTime movies to be played from CD-ROM, but here's something we learned the hard way. Slower-speed CD-ROM drives will sometimes skip the first bit of audio when a movie starts playing. Leaving a second of "dead air" at the beginning before any sound starts playing will give your audio a cleaner start.

If you are playing movies one after another, here's a performance trick: Open the second movie before closing the first. That way your user doesn't have to stare at a blank screen while waiting for the second movie to appear. When you close the first movie it will be hidden behind the second. It won't make your application run faster, but it will look that way to your user. Just make sure Hypercard has enough memory to have both movies open at once.

When your stack is finished, save it as a stand-alone application. This will run much more efficiently from the CD-ROM than a stack that needs the Hypercard application to run. If there is an order that your movies will play, place them—in that order—on the CD-ROM to reduce seek time and improve performance.

One of the most powerful aspects of Hypercard (and one that I use all the time) is the ability to write scripts that modify objects in the stack. If I have to change the text style of a dozen fields, or move a hundred buttons one pixel to the left, it's no problem: I just create a button to do it. A simple script and one mouse click and the work is done. Under script control you can change the size, shape, location, and style of buttons and fields, cut and paste cards, move graphics, and change the script of any object. This simple capability is the one that keeps Hypercard at the top of my list of favorite tools.

I continue to use Hypercard and QuickTime extensively to create interactive story-boards and prototypes of new multimedia applications. This combination of tools is very useful for everything from quick interactive sketches to proofs of concept to user interface tests to complete commercial applications.

It is our guess that the majority of you, and the majority of your work over the next few years, will be aimed at Macintosh and Windows platforms. This makes things fairly easy. The authoring tools are solid and are being enhanced continuously. All you need to do is master your craft and learn how to make cross-platform files.

Okay, so maybe there is a bit more to it, but these two platforms have about the most complete set of tools and resources around.

When you reach the point where you want to take on other platforms, we suggest that you do so only after researching the available tools. Of course, things will probably change in the next two to three years so that tools will become available that make developing for all platforms as easy as working with QuickTime.

Utilities

A good selection of utilities can make all the difference in the world when it comes to providing your viewers, clients, and yourself with the desired movie results. Content for digital video will come to you in many forms, and likewise your output may need to be produced in more than one format. Digital video utilites are what will rescue you in the end. These include:

- Batch processors
- Image processors
- File format converters
- Movie analysis
- Optimizers
- File editors

The list goes on.

Many of these utilities fall into the category of so-called Shareware applications. These products are called *Shareware* because you can get them free, use them, and share them with your friends and co-workers; if you like them, the author asks that you pay a registration fee. (These fees are usually in the $5–$30 range. Some authors request that you send them a selection of their favorite beverage; these products are known as *beerware*.) Paying the fee and registering yourself as a "legal" user often will provide you with some form of product support and updates (usually electronic) to the latest version of the application (if any).

Shareware applications are generally not sold at retail, but are available for download from many commercial on-line services (for example, America

OnLine, CompuServe, eWorld, the Internet, Genie, Prodigy) as well as via hundreds of public and private bulletin boards. Another great source is via user groups, found in practically every large town and city in the world. Some groups even offer their shareware libraries to members on CD-ROMs.

NOTE: If you don't have an account on one of the several commercial on-line services, get one! It is time for you to get on the Information Highway. Among all the other reasons to have access, here's the one that drives our car: Most developers provide updates to their software products on-line, often for free, and may offer direct links into their technical support organizations. That alone is worth the price of admission.

Shareware utilities spring into being because some enterprising end-user (who also happens to be a programmer) can't find (or won't pay for) an appropriate application that solves a particular set of problems. So they develop their own tools—and *share* them with their friends and complete strangers around the world. Shareware runs the gamut of all computer application uses, but you will find a particularly large selection of shareware programs and utilities for the multimedia arena because it is still fairly new, and mainstream developers have offered only mainstream utilties to date. Many times a shareware application can be as good as or even better than a commercial product equivalent. There have been cases where a shareware application has been good enough, and seen enough general use, to grow up to commercial status.

WARNING: Use shareware with caution. Do not use a particular shareware product on your projects until you first thoroughly test its abilities on test files. Many shareware applications are made available to users long before they are completed. You are the author's product test team, and there may be bugs in shareware application. (Commercial applications are not immune to having bugs either, but are better set up to correct them, or provide your money back.) Check all shareware for viruses! This is not because the author is trying to pass on a virus, but one may have been picked up along the sharing path. Most commercial on-line services that provide access to these products do a virus check before making them available for download, but many public BBSs do not. Be safe, not sorry.

Shareware with a proven track record can be a great asset to you for making movies. Check with your friends or associates for recommendations on good shareware products to use. You can also find comments from other users on the on-line services.

Whether shareware or commercial application, utilities fill a very necessary void in some full-fledged editors. That is no slam on the commercial editor applications or their creators; no product can—or should—do everything. If one did, that application would require 36 MB of RAM, take up 150 MB of hard-disk space, and require a 100 MHz PowerPC chip.

Look for varied software, both full editors and utilities, to make up your software suite. We could try to list hundreds of shareware titles for you here, but the list changes so fast that what we write today may not be around when you read this book. Instead, the following is a list of utilities (some commercial, some not) that offer various sets of capabilities that have been around for a while and appear to be likely to be around for some time to come.

- Movie Recorder—A simple video digitizer application.

- MovieShop—A batch and custom compression utility, excellent for making very good CinePak compressed movies. We have found that it crashes often, but we use it where a single movie at a time needs to be compressed.

- MovieAnalyzer—Determines the performance characteristics of movies. Excellent for determining if movies are CD-ROM compliant. It was designed for single-speed CD drives, so reports are based upon data rates under 150 kps. (See Figure 3.4.)

- Equilibrium DeBabelizer—The Swiss army knife of image-conversion utilities. This application can convert almost any image file format to the format of your choice. It has excellent batch processing features

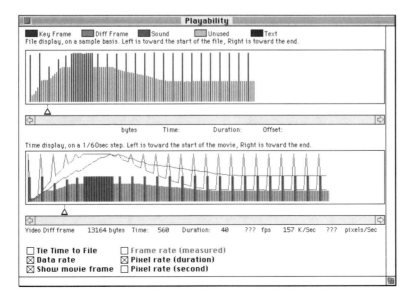

Figure 3.4
One of the data windows from MovieAnalyzer.

but what we feel is a poor user interface. This product was designed by programmers *for* programmers, but we recommend it. The accompanying CD-ROM has both a "lite" version and a full-featured demo of DeBabelizer.

- ConvertToMovie—A simple movie compressor utility. This utility is great for use in transcoding individual movies into other compression formats. It will also convert pictures into movies. It has no batch capability. (See Figure 3.5.)

- ComboWalker—A useful tool for setting various parameters in movies—poster frames, setting file icons, previews, cross-platform, and so forth.

- Copyright/User Data—Allows authors to include detailed copyright information with every track of a movie. It has a cumbersome interface with no batch feature.

- OttoPlayer— Converts a movie into a self-contained, self-playing application. It fades the desktop screen to black before and after the movie, and displays the file name at the beginning of the movie. It is not application-dependent for playback since it creates an actual application shell. This is an excellent utility.

- VideoMonitorPro—A Shareware application for digitzing video.

- MovieInfo—A Shareware application that provides you with a report on all the pertinent information about your movies.

Figure 3.5 Flatten, crop, and resize movies with ConvertTo-Movie.

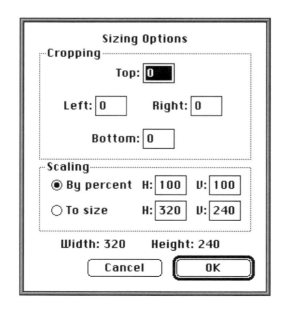

Once you decide on your video editor applications, it becomes a matter of practicing to see what you can do with each one. We have included some techniques in Chapter 5 that you may want to use. Most of them are application-independent.

Although we have spent many years working with desktop digital video, we freely admit that we can't know everything. We are willing to bet that nobody else out there knows everything either. So, we—and we suggest that you, too—frequently ask friends and other professionals for their help and opinions. This is especially useful when you are just beginning to use an application or utility.

We asked an acquaintence at a company that produces digital video editing software to write a few words for us about digital editing. Here is what he has to say:

Y DIGITAL?

by Joseph Klingler

Mr. Klingler was a co-founder of VideoFusion Inc. and a designer/architect/manager of the engineering team that developed VideoFusion and QuickFlix. He also was Director of Engineering at Radius Video Applications Group—formerly VideoFusion Inc. Previously, he algorithmically massaged digital images for medical applications. He has a keen interest in the new aesthetics in imaging and music evolving from the application of digital machines.

Why all of the excitement about digital? Digital anything . . . audio, video, even digital representation of text? Because once a communication medium goes digital, computers can manipulate, structure, modify, transform, transmit, store, retrieve, and yes, even copy it. Unprecedented control.

So how does this level of control relate to video and multimedia movie production? Consider the attributes of a movie that a creator/director might wish to manipulate. There's the order that things happen, the element of *time*. Which shot comes first, which second? This is generally the realm of the editor.

Then there's the visual *look* of the frame itself—the lighting, the color, the texture. Look has long been manipulated by movie makers using optical effects.

Then there's *compositing*—layering one scene over another to convince the viewer that all of the objects were actually in the same place at the same time, essentially creating a virtual set. This also has been done optically for years. But now with

(continued)

digitally synthesized 3D graphics being placed into live video, and the flexible control provided by digital compositing software, the possibilities are expanding rapidly.

Then there's the *spacial* form of the frame. The picture itself can be transformed, stretched, pushed, twirled, distorted like the mirrors in a house of horrors, or mapped onto synthetic 3D objects, video on a sphere, video on a cube, video on a toaster. Or forget distortion—how about just moving the picture in such a way as to simulate the movement of a camera? Zap, instant zoom from still images, motion where there was none, action instead of stills, panoramic moves over large still images creates a camera on wheels. Instantly. Digitally.

So why the excitement about QuickTime? Because it provides a system architecture for the representation of digital movies on the desktop. And digital gives you, the image creator, direct control over these four dimensions of movie creation: time, look, composite, and space.

Add to this the ability to *synthesize* media out of nowhere, the realm of the 3D modeler/animator/rendering software packages, and the ability to *integrate* this synthesized material with recorded footage, and you have an incredible array of tools for creating imagery. Essentially, the computer acts as recording device, palette, image synthesizer, structure manipulator, and image assembler.

So when using digital editor/manipulator/integrator tools like VideoFusion, you can think in terms of these four dimensions of your video. It's not just a series of frames anymore—it's much, much more.

Tools

Look for tools that support each of these dimensions of a movie. And tools that let you efficiently explore and control them to create your finished product.

Look for tools that provide editing capability to help you tell your story. Immediate playback of edits aids your creative flow, and your story emerges from edit after edit. Interactivity is key to keeping the creative workflow going.

Look for tools that can give your pictures the look you want. Also look for filters for color modification, black and white, sepia tone, tints of every imaginable shade, and filters to constrain to NTSC/PAL safe colors if you plan to finish to videotape as your delivery medium. Remember that your computer can display many more colors than a typical tape can record and faithfully reproduce.

Look for tools that allow layers to be created using the magic of alpha channels, which allow you to control frame overlays on a pixel-by-pixel basis.

Look for tools to make your video malleable like clay in the hands of a sculptress. Pixels are square, or at least rectangular, but your images don't have to be.

(continued)

Filmthink

So what do you think of when you think of film? A series of frames playing through a projector at twenty-four frames per second to create the illusion of motion. Yes, this is the final rendering for film, the target distribution media by which the material actually reaches the viewer. Video creates a similar series of frames, but includes a few twists like "fields" and a frame rate of 29.97 for NTSC or 25 fps for PAL. This is the physical rendering of your movie. But beyond the final structure of the result, what is the logical structure that you impose on the movie in order to create it?

Remembering our four dimensions as you construct the images you wish to create in your mind, think about not only a series of frames simulating motion through which you can show action, but also:

1. Transitions, opticals, how you "splice" your clips together—because in digital you can do more than just glue the two pieces of film tail to head and create a splice. Here you're often presented with dozens or even hundreds of predefined transitions. You make choices like the speed of the transition. Too fast and it can be disruptive, too slow and the pacing is off. In *VideoFusion,* you can create custom transitions by creating your own alpha channel movies and using them to achieve the transition. This feature allows you to control precisely how one clip moves into another on a frame-by-frame basis. The 3D with perspective transitions also allow you to add a depth to your movie by bringing new clips in from infinity, or taking them out to a vanishing point.

And you can think about:

2. How to change the look of the picture—convert a recorded video to a watercolor or an acrylic, or a tiled look, or even something simple like black and white, or add film scratches, or tint the entire scene as if it were recorded through color optical filters. Here the ability to access the individual color channels composing an image provides a broad range of control. Experiment with filtering individual channels, such as Slicing only the Brightness channel, and replacing it into the movie.

   Also experiment with combining channels from separate movies to form unusual combinations of colors and motion, or generate new imagery by performing logical operations, such as exclusive-OR (XOR) between independent channels of multiple movies.

   It is possible to simulate many traditional effects using digital techniques—sometimes more inexpensively, sometimes with greater control. But the power of digital is not so much in simulation, useful as that might be, but in the brand

(continued)

new look that digital brings to the table. The look that can only be created with computers and is therefore idiomatic to computers. The look that will ultimately allow filmmakers to create a new digital aesthetic of film.

. . . and remember:

3. Film is solid and stiff, but digital algorithms are a milky soup of semitransparent, rubbery pixels. Thus, an image may be distorted to represent ripples of water or the wave of a flag, or the heat distortion of a jet trail . . . all because algorithms can be used to simply modify the pixels according to the appropriate rules and the viewer associates the effect with what he or she has seen in the real world. (For example, ripples might be water. What else ripples? Certainly not film. At least not prior to digital.)

   Here, time-varying control of parameters is of the utmost importance because you are essentially animating the pixels in your video to make the surface of the video appear to move. So using a warp mesh to mush pixels around on the screen is interesting, but it becomes more interesting if that warp mesh changes from frame to frame, because now the surface of the movie moves and stretches. A warp mesh of this type can be used for simple modifications such as making a portion of the image larger or smaller. And it can be used for interesting animation, such as moving a title through a warp. The title might be standing still and a time-varying warp mesh can be used to distort it one way and then the other to make the letters appear very liquid. Another choice is to use a stationary warp mesh and animate the title so that it moves through the mesh, which will shrink and expand the letters fluidly depending on the shape of the mesh. In this way, you can add new life to titling sequences by breaking the common notion that text is fixed in shape.

. . . and of course:

4. Your film isn't just one piece of film running along by itself; it's really many synchronized pieces running along, layers with individual sizing and transparency control on each layer, and in some cases, like VideoFusion, control of the 3D position of each layer so you can view each from a different perspective and combine them as you like. Audiences are becoming more and more comfortable with rapid action on the screen, from cuts that last only a fraction of a second, to complex semitransparent collages with shadows providing depth cueing.

   Compositing can be considered halfway along the continuum between image processing and synthesis. The final scenes that you create for your films never really existed together in space and time. They existed in different spaces and different times and have been brought together into your final video via the magic of compositing and alpha channels.

(continued)

Project Alpha

This ability to create worlds using compositing is so flexible and so important, let's look at it in more detail. What are alpha channels, and why are they so crucial? Crucial because within them lies the power of compositing multiple layers together with the result that they appear to create a single scene. Note that to be really successful with this kind of compositing, the individual elements must share lighting and camera angle and similar characteristics or the eye-mind combination senses something wrong with the picture and doesn't buy into the belief that all of these things were really happening together at the same time and space coordinates. In other words, *it looks fake.*

So how does alpha achieve compositing? The alpha channel provides the information on how to mix one picture with another, resulting in a blending (or composite) of the two. If the same value is used for all pixels on the screen, then a dissolve results, and no one thinks both scenes happened in one place. However, if only parts of scenes are mixed, say the foreground action with a separate background, then a composite single scene results. This is achieved by providing a third, black-and-white picture called the alpha channel.

Each pixel location of the alpha channel has a value. In an 8-bit alpha these values range from 0 to 255. So at each pixel location the value of the alpha channel tells the software how much of each of the background and foreground picture to mix together to form the output. Imagine an alpha channel that contains a pure white circle. Where the white occurs the foreground picture will be shown, and where the black occurs the background picture will be shown. If the foreground picture is a photograph of the planet earth from space that aligns with the circle, then the picture of the planet will be inserted into the background.

So why *eight* bits? Transparency and edges! If the alpha channel is gray instead of white, then those areas will be a blend of the foreground and background, creating semitransparent foreground objects that allow the background to show through. But what happens at the edges? If we just insert the planet picture, there will be an abrupt transition at the edges, possibly jaggies (those stair steps that occur when trying to cram round images into square pixels), and the final output will have the look of someone cutting a picture out of a magazine and pasting it in. We smooth the alpha channel so the values at the edge aren't 255, but rather gradually fall off from 255 to 0, creating a soft edge blend where the two pictures come together.

We see *both* pictures a little bit, and the hard jagged edge is softened. This yields a more realistic version and a more believable output picture. Creating exactly the right alpha channel has a tremendous effect on the quality and believability of the output.

These channels can be created by hand, a frame at a time, for precise results using a process called *rotoscoping*. Or they can be generated by 3D animation systems at the same time as the 3D objects are created. In addition, 2D picture files can

(continued)

be created with alpha channels using some paint programs. Alpha channels are ubiquitous, and many programs handle them quite nicely. Becoming skilled with the use of alphas will allow you to create interesting, believable, composited scenes in your movies.

In addition, with the channel processing capabilities of VideoFusion, almost any filter can be used to create an image that can then be inserted as an alpha channel. Consider, for example, extracting the brightness channel from a video of clouds and using it to composite one movie over another. A soft, floating, fluid composite of the foreground and background emerges, with the position of the clouds controlling the exact nature of the composite.

Use alpha channels to mix your pictures a pixel at a time using complex alpha channels and make your own magic happen on the screen.

In Summary . . .

In summary, there are several good digital picture-manipulation tools available, including *VideoFusion*. Note that these tools, being all digital, extend well beyond the traditional video notion of "editing." Editing is important, but it is only the beginning of what's possible in the digital domain. Locate these tools, learn them, grow with them as they evolve to provide creative artists with a new digital medium onto which to project their dreams.

For the cost-conscious entry-level individual, you will probably want to find a single, multipurpose video editor and effects application. We suggest that you augment that application with utilities, probably Shareware, to really round out your capabilities. Also, just because you start out with one program, don't let that limit you in the future. Continue to investigate all sorts of applications.

You may find, on one of the electronic services, sample versions of some programs. These generally are disabled in some fashion, such as not allowing you to save your results, only view them; or to be used for only a short period of time—say, thirty days—or a limited number of uses. These sample versions allow you to experiment without committing.

We applaud all of the companies that provide such sample versions of their products. As you must know by now, the CD-ROM that accompanies this book contains a number of demo and "try me before you buy me" applications. Along with these applications, we have included some sample video files (precaptured) for you to experiment with.

Understanding Video Compressors

We cover the use and selection of video compressors in general terms elsewhere in the book. In each of those locations we have attempted to avoid detailed explanations of all the inner workings of the compressors and the deep mumbo-jumbo jargon surrounding each one. As desktop video producers, we find that we have only a cursory need for understanding how these things work, as long as we understand all the issues about using them.

But we recognize that there are some who may really like to know the details.

For those of you who are *not* interested in the nitty-gritty of compression technology, or have an acute aversion to acronyms, you may want to skip over the next sidebar article. (You don't know what you're missing, though.) But, if you are a little adventurous, or want to know why your movies compress the way they do, then you will learn quite a bit from this piece.

This guest author also discusses what goes on behind the scene in broadcast video, something that desktop video producers are likely to become more involved in during the coming years.

VIDEO COMPRESSION ALGORITHMS . . . WHAT DO ALL THOSE ACRONYMS MEAN?
by William J. Fulco

Bill Fulco is CEO and chief scientist of Network XXIII Corporation, a video technology, tools, and titles company specializing in authoring and teleconnected gaming technology for large-budget Hollywood multimedia and videogame projects. Prior to that he was the founder and chief scientist at New Video Corporation. Bill specializes in video compression and processing algorithm design and implementation. He is a contributing editor to Converge, The Multimedia Developer's Resource. *He has been a member of industry standards committees including the IMA Open Architecture committee, the ANSI X3L3/MPEG committee, and the SMPTE N15 committee. Bill is also speaks at many computer-industry trade shows, and is a working costume designer in Hollywood and a stand-up comedian. This sidebar article is based upon an article Bill wrote for "The Digital Video Forum" in* Converge, *in August 1994. (For information on* Converge, *see Appendix A.)*

Listening to the advocates of various video compression algorithms, you might get confused. I'm going to get technical to help you understand details of various compression algorithms on the market today. I hope to impart a *general* understanding

(continued)

of how video compression works and show that it's not a black magic process that only people in white lab coats .with pocket protectors can master.

In the lab, computer scientists can tweek and tune the parameters of compression algorithms to peak performance. In today's QuickTime (Macintosh and Windows) and Video for Windows desktop video world, there are not many ways to control the compression process. As it turns out, the most important parameter is the choice of compression algorithm. On industrial-strength video compression machines that do MPEG or PLV compression, a compression artist has much more latitude to make adjustments to the compression process. This flexibility comes at a price, however. These systems use computer, video, and audio equipment costing millions of dollars.

As desktop video advances, two things will happen. Simpler desktop video compression programs will most likely disappear, their functions incorporated directly into operating systems and end-user programs, while at the same time a whole new class of professional desktop video compression programs will appear—like a *Super MovieShop*—with many more parameters to tweak the video, audio, and data compression process. This happened when desktop publishing exploded; tools simultaneously got simpler, and got more complicated, and went away—depending on how professional a desktop publisher you were.

The areas we're going to explore first are (1) why one would want to compress video, (2) how video compression algorithms work, and (3) what the differences are between major approaches on the market today.

Why Do Compression?

The major reason to compress video is that it consumes enormous amounts of storage. Video data creates not just a storage problem but a transmission problem requiring long transmission times or very high-speed lines; so although disk drive prices are falling 35 percent per year, the cost of transmission channels is not falling nearly as fast. Current CD-ROMs provide a salient example. A CD-ROM stores 650 MB of data. This is enough for only about thirty seconds of uncompressed video (at 27 MB/sec); but even worse, at the 150 KB per second read-rate, it takes seventy-four minutes to read these thirty seconds of video off the drive! The solution to both of these problems is compression, notwithstanding "Bill's Law of Problem Conservation."

Bill's Law of Problem Conservation states: "Problems can neither be created nor destroyed, but may only change form. Any operation to change a problem's form (by ostensibly solving it) will consume time, money, energy and have unintended, unpredictable, and unfortunate consequences. This is otherwise known as the 'You Can't Even Buy a Free Lunch Effect.'"

Compressing and decompressing video very often involves weighing application-dependent trade-offs. The major variables in the video compression process are typically:

(continued)

- Ease (cost) of encode and decode. Is special hardware required?
- Time to compress/decompress. How "asymmetric" are the processes?
- Data rate. Does video come over a telephone line, or will disk arrays be needed?
- Image quality. Is output indistinguishable from input, or is a screen full of static okay?
- Frame rate. Is output indistinguishable from input, or will a picture flip-book quality do as well?
- On what platforms/devices will your digital video file be played?
- What if you have to decompress and recompress the video over and over?
- How prevalent are the production tools related to cost-of-encode?

Strictly speaking, before deciding to do anything to video, you need to understand its eventual use. (See Figure 3.6.) If you're producing an Edit Decision List (EDL) for a video editing suite, then image quality may not be the most important parameter. On the other hand, if you're going to output the digital video directly to tape, then maybe quality is paramount. Then again, if the object is to play video from a standard CD-ROM, perhaps with no additional hardware, then image quality and frame rate may have to suffer for the sake of data rate.

Additional computing power (i.e., extra hardware) allows us to get closer to not having to choose. However, the closer we come to "having it all," the closer we get to "costing too much." On the other hand, if you're the National Security Agency and you want "all three," then there may be no such thing as "costs too much."

Parameters: Actually, for many desktop systems, algorithm choice is the only choice we get; therefore, that's the most important variable in the video compression process. This typically forces many other parameters on us.

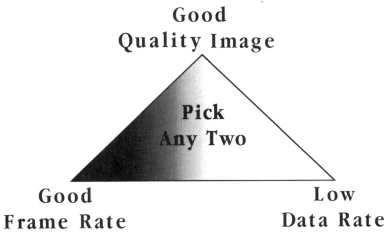

**Figure 3.6
A useful little chart. These are the trade-offs you must consider.**

(continued)

Video Facts of Life

Before algorithms are discussed, there are several video facts of life we should start with. Let's assume our goal is to produce video at CD-ROM data rate for direct use on a Mac or PC platform. Let's start with the source.

Video from a camera is a series of discrete lines of contiguous analog signals. In television there are no "pixels," and the input color scheme is RGB. The actual first step in the video compression process occurs during the conversion of these red, green, and blue lines from the sensors, either CCDs or Vidicon tubes, into an analog video output. NTSC and PAL were designed to encode (actually, compress) video into a form that allows a minimum of transmission spectrum usage without *visible* artifacts. To do this, video is encoded as a black-and-white signal called luminance, luma, or "Y" and two color signals called chrominance or chroma that *loosely* represent how much red (R) and blue (B) is in the signal. There are several different names and formulations for these color signals, variously called color difference signals; Y minus R and Y minus B; Cr and Cb; I and Q; or U and V. We'll use the Y (for luma) and the PAL names, U and V, for the chroma.

Video is encoded this way because the eye's black-and-white receptors are most sensitive to the green-yellow light (like the sun), whereas its color receptors are most sensitive to the differences between the amount of red-green and blue-yellow light. Since the eye has far fewer color receptors per square millimeter than luma receptors, there is no need to represent the color with as much information as luma for the reconstructed picture to be indistinguishable from the original.

An example: We can represent the magnitude of a signal's three color components (in the YUV colorspace) with an 8-bit "sample" at any given time. This will yield 24 bits of data for each pixel or dot on the screen. (I know. We don't know about pixels yet. Bear with me.) Although it is true that the eye has fewer chroma receptors per square millimeter than luma receptors, we still need to represent chroma samples with as much accuracy as Luma, but we do not need *as many* chroma samples as luma for any desired image resolution; that is, every location on the screen has one luma (Y) sample, whereas some locations don't have any chroma (U or V) samples.

Dizzy yet?

In the case of RGB color components, the eye's receptors would not let us get away with this "subsampling" game. With RGB video there is always one red, one green, and one blue sample for every pixel.

"Ah ha! This must be the first step of the video compression process." Correct! In most video systems, the signal is compressed before it even leaves the camera. With high-end professional video gear, this is not always true, but rest assured that before the signal is encoded to be transmitted (by either wire, air, tape, or disc), it is at least compressed in this way.

(continued)

Subsampling the Colorspace

How much compression can this YUV subsampling get us? First, this subsampling can be done in either the horizontal or vertical direction—or both. A professional video studio uses either the unsubsampled (uncompressed) colorspace called 4:4:4— that means that for every four Y samples on a line, there are four V samples and four U samples—or an international standard called CCIR-601. CCIR-601 specifies a 4:2:2 subsampling ratio, in the horizontal direction, where for every four Y samples on a line, there are two V samples and two U samples.

Typically, each sample is 8 bits in size. With 4:2:2 video each full-color pixel takes 16 bits of information (YUV16), computed thus: every 4 pixels has [4 × 8 bits of Y] plus [2 × 8 bits of V] plus [2 × 8 bits of U] for a total of 64 bits. Thus, 64 bits per 4 pixels equals 16 bits per pixel.

Parameters: The first compression decision is the choice of "colorspace" with which to start the compression process—for example, RGB24 (RGB 8:8:8); YUV16 (YUV 4:2:2); YUV12 (YUV 4:1:1); YUV9 (YUV 4:1:1 in horizontal and 4:1:1 in vertical directions). Most standard algorithms specify what colorspace and color depth they start with—for example, MPEG, JPEG, and Px64 compression algorithms use the YUV 16 colorspace, Intel's Indeo starts with YUV9, and Cinepak starts with RGB24.

Digitizing Video into Pixels

The next part of the compression process involves digitizing the video into pixels. Remember that true video is a discrete number of continuously variable analog lines. In NTSC there are 525 lines of video per frame (262.5 per field). and in theory, each line has *infinite resolution*. The process of digitizing measures the voltage (samples) of a line's signal any number of times and transmits those values. The number of samples per line is arbitrary. For NTSC, we might take one sample per line and the resulting digital resolution would be 1 × 480—this would not look good at all! On the other hand, we could take a million samples on every line and the resolution would be 1,000,000 × 480. Although this would look a whole lot better than 1 × 480, it would have a very, very large set of pixel values to deal with (14 gigabytes per second's worth)!

So, as you can see, a major way to compress video is to digitize each line less often. The less you digitize, the less space you consume and the worse it looks. But then, you have to target your audience.

Your TV doesn't have this problem. It uses the analog line directly to control the strength of the electron beam sweeping the faceplate of the screen. The CCIR committee standardized a particular resolution for the digitizing process. CCIR decided that there should be 720 visible pixels per analog line (768 total) and that there are 480 dig-

(continued)

ital lines with 4:2:2 (16-bit) color samples. This is a big problem for computer folks who like screen resolutions to be powers of 2 and to be the same scale in vertical and horizontal directions on 4:3 screens (i.e., "square pixels"—it makes the math easier).

Doing the math, this configuration yields an uncompressed video data rate of 27 MB per second. Also, since television is interlaced, the *even* 262.5 lines of each picture (240 visible) are sent, then the *odd* lines are sent one-sixtieth of a second later. This yields the full CCIR-601 resolution of 480 (visible) lines, but not all the lines on the screen really "happen" at the same time. This becomes a problem when fast moving things whiz across the screen.

Parameters: You often can choose the video sampling rate. With still-image algorithms like JPEG or QuickTime's graphics and animation algorithms, any resolution you wish to choose is fine because these algorithms weren't designed with any particular image resolution for input and output. However, algorithms like "motion JPEG," MPEG, Px64, Indeo, SupeRTV, TrueMotion, and to some extent CinePak were designed with "television resolution" in mind, for both input and output. In these cases, you may be able to adjust the digitizing resolution, but there is a standard that you must adhere to.

The first step before using a formal compression algorithm, assuming we're going to start with the full CCIR-601 video, is to decimate the image data to the correct size—that is, to reduce the video to only a fraction of the image vertically or horizontally. Typically we remove one-half of the horizontal data first. The next step is usually to sample only every other vertical line. This is easily done for interlaced TV input—just skip every other field of video, leaving 240 lines of resolution every thirtieth of a second instead of every sixtieth. The decimation process leaves us with a resolution of between 320 and 360 horizontal pixels. MPEG and Px64 (because they are based on the CCIR-601) use 360 horizontal pixels, whereas Indeo, CinePak, and others (because computer people like square pixels) use 320 or 256 horizontal pixels. The term for the 360(320) × 240 input image resolution is Standard Image Format (SIF). Often you'll see references in sales literature to "Full SIF" resolution versus "QSIF" or Quarter-SIF resolution of 180(160) × 120.

Parameters: One of the parameters that high-end compression systems use is the choice of video filter utilized in this resolution reduction (decimation) process. Filtering applies a mathematical process to an image to yield another image. Filters can reduce noise, enhance edges, smooth skin tones, remove motion blur, and add motion blur, among other things. The choice of filters can have a powerful effect on quality and data rate of compressed video.

Television resolution is one-quarter that of a computer screen! Although 320 horizontal pixels doesn't sound like very good resolution to computer people, most normal home TVs can just barely resolve this much information. Even good TVs are able to show only about 460 lines—and only under perfect viewing and signal conditions! For regular TV, fewer than 300 "pixels" is all the resolution you ever have in one field!

(continued)

So, although a 360 × 240 image would comfortably fill a TV screen, it is only one-quarter of a typical computer screen (which is effectively almost HDTV resolution).

As you can see, we haven't formally compressed any video yet (in the sense that we haven't used one of the "compression algorithms" on it) and it's already been shrunk by about 6:1 in the case of MPEG-input (720 × 480 × 24 bits => 360 × 240 × 16 bits) and 12:1 in the case of Indeo-input. This puts us at a ratio of 6:1 to 12:1 before we even start . . . so why do we need a formal compression algorithm anyway? Well, even at 12:1, a CD-ROM will hold only six minutes of video and it will still take *seventy-four minutes* to get it off the disc.

"But You Got to Know the Algorithm!"—
with apologies to *The Music Man*

When compressing video, unlike compressing data, you're allowed to lose information. Although video might not come back exactly the way it started, it can look just fine. This is because the eye is a poor, easily tricked information receptor.

There are several lossless methods of compressing data used in disk compression programs, such as Lemple-Ziv, Arithmetic Coding, and Huffman Coding. (We will apply these algorithms to our 6:1 subsampled or decimated video data eventually.) "Wouldn't that do the trick?" Well, lossless compression schemes typically yield about a 2:1 data compression. Let's do the math: 2:1 lossless compression on top of the 6:1 to 12:1 that our subsampled and decimated compression yields gives us a 12:1 to 24:1 total compression ratio. A CD-ROM would now hold six to twelve minutes of video, but it *will still take seventy-four minutes* to get it off—not enough compression yet!

The advantage of lossless compression is that one does not have to worry about *any* visual artifacts being introduced—they decompress *exactly* what was compressed. This makes them a useful adjunct to other methods of video compression. MPEG, JPEG, Px64, PLV, TrueMotion, SupeRTV (and early Indeo) algorithms use lossless compression as a final step. CinePak, AppleVideo, Indeo 3, and Microsoft's Video 1 do not use these techniques (because they often need special hardware to be able to be done quickly).

You might be asking yourself, "What's the point?" Remember, for the sake of this article, we're trying to get our 27 MB per second (YUV) video stored on a CD-ROM while keeping the quality as good as possible.

Compression Concepts

Before we get into specifics of particular algorithms, let's discuss some of the common methods involved in compressing video. Understanding these techniques will help us understand the parameters used with these compression algorithms.

(continued)

Redundancy Removal

The goal of compressing video is to find data in an image that communicates no unique or visually useful information. To a first approximation, all actual compression is done by locating this redundant information and coding it in a more compact, nonredundant form. Some "less important" information is just thrown away, usually by a process called quantization, described next. All the major types of compression algorithm are just fancy ways of identifying either redundant information or information that will not be missed when it is tossed.

An example of redundancy removal: Suppose that, in an image, pixels with the value of 22 are always followed by a pixel with a value of 33. You could "compress" this image by noting this fact and not storing the 33s. Your decompressor would just insert a 33 after every 22 it decoded. In this case, since the 33 was always present after the 22, the 33 doesn't contain any "information." One of a compression algorithm's jobs is to analyze a data stream (e.g., image), locate redundant information, and remove it. Some nonredundant information may be removed also in the case of lossy compression, because (in the case of images) the human eye will "fill in the blanks."

Quantization

Another concept in compression is quantization. This is the process of taking some set of information and representing it with a smaller set by "lopping off" some parts of the set. An example would be representing the numbers 0–255 (8 bits) as 5-bit values: numbers between 0 and 7 would be represented as 0, between 8 and 15 by 1, between 16 and 23 by 3, and up to between 248 and 255 by 31. This quantization creates "inaccuracies," but if you can tolerate each number being off by about 4 on the average (either way), then you've just "compressed" a bunch of 8-bit values into 5-bit values—a 37 percent reduction of the data.

Run-Length Encoding (RLE)

The RLE technique examines a pixel value to see if it is essentially the same as the next one (on a line). If it is, RLE continues to look ahead until it finds something different. When it does, it doesn't send all the pixels it looked at; RLE encodes this data as a pixel value with a repetition factor. This is an especially good technique for compressing animation, which typically has large areas of identical color. It is not as good for video, because real-life scenes have many subtle color changes that would keep any potential run of identical colors very short and unproductive. RLE is typically lossless, but if you count "almost-the-same" as "the same," then it can be made more efficient, and becomes "lossy."

Parameters: For RLE compression, typical parameters might include the maximum length of a run as well as how close a pixel's value has to be to another's to still be considered "the same."

(continued)

Frame Differencing (FD)

The concept of frame differencing is that between two video frames typically not much changes. At encode time, you can save a lot of data by effectively transmitting "everything is the same except these *xxx* pixels." For instance, if you're watching a car drive through a frame and the camera is still, most of the image is identical— only the car is changing. If you subtract one frame from the next, DPCM-like (as mentioned below), you get mostly zeroes except where something changed. You can then apply RLE to these zeroes, and send the differences. On the decoder side, since "the previous" frame is available, you can just add back in all these pixels and "Poof," you have your next frame.

Parameters: Frame-differencing controls exist on almost all compression systems. A typical FD parameter is usually called "key frame spacing"—that is, how many difference frames before a key (nondifference or intra-) frame. Another parameter can be a number that represents how much difference between frames should be allowed before the algorithm decides that a key frame should be inserted instead of a difference frame.

Block Truncation Coding (BTC)

The goal of BTC is to simplify the coding of a block of pixels (P) while keeping the statistical properties of the reconstructed pixels (Pr) intact. BTC takes a block of pixels (typically 4×4) and computes statistical properties on it—for example, Mean (M/8-bits) and Standard Deviation (SD/8-bits). The block is then transmitted by sending M and SD plus 1 bit for each pixel to represent which value it should be reconstructed with (vis-à-vis the statistics). For example, a one means Pr = (M+SD) and a zero means Pr=(M-SD). The reconstructed block is statistically correct so the eye still understands the whole image. Typical compression ratios are ([16x8 bits] : [16x1 bits + 8 bits + 8 bits]) = [128 bits : 32 bits] = 4:1.

Parameters: The only parameters usually used in BTC are (1) what are the bit sizes of the statistics (M and SD), and (2) how big is the block in question: 2×2, 3×3, 4×4, and so forth? The higher the block size, the more compression and the worse (more blocky) the video will look. The fewer bits used to represent the mean and especially the standard deviation, the more the compression and the worse (less accurate) the video will look.

Differential Pulse Code Modulation (DPCM)

DPCM video compression is very simple, very old, and quite good for certain things. In DPCM, an image is analyzed pixel by pixel. A property of images (versus random noise) is that if you know some pixel in an image, you might be able predict a pixel you haven't seen yet. The trick for DPCM is to figure out what "formula" is best at "predicting the future" for a given image or set of images. For

(continued)

example, if on one horizontal line you found a green pixel, you could make an educated guess that the pixel next to it might also be green. By assuming it is, you might be able to save the trouble of sending this next pixel. In DPCM, for some pixel *under prediction* you take some other *predictor* pixel(s) in the image, in some relative position (e.g., one to the left or one above), then subtract the predictor from the pixel under prediction. What is sent to the decoder is not the stream of pixels, but the stream of differences. *This in itself does not save any data,* but since the data will tend to zero (with a good predictor), you can represent these new values with a smaller set of numbers by quantizing—pixels from 0 to 255 may have differences from -256 to +256, but cluster between -8 and +8. We can represent these numbers with 4 bits instead of 8. Good DPCM compression means picking good predictors and good quantization schemes. Compression ratios depend on the match between the statistics of the image(s) and the predictors, though "visually lossless" DPCM can be usually done at about 4:1.

Parameters: The pixels chosen as predictors and the quantization schemes are usually fixed for any given implementation so there usually are no variables associated with DPCM compression, though there could be.

Vector Quantization (VQ)

VQ quantizes several (possibly pixel) values as a group instead of quantizing one value at a time. This yields better compression and, because of the way the human visual system works, this creates fewer artifacts as well. Basically, VQ uses a dictionary (called a code-book) lookup scheme. Several values are taken as a group (a vector)—they might be pixels, differences, transform coefficients, or whatever—and they're looked up in a code-book to find the "closest" match for the whole group. It's as if one took groups of ten letters and looked them up in an English dictionary and found the word that most closely matched. Instead of sending the ten letters, you send the page number and word number of this closest match. The decoder would put the sentence back together by using the same dictionary (usually sent with the file). The references are much smaller than the entries in the dictionary itself—hence, compression.

Code-books usually are not more than 1,024 entries and come in a variety of mix-and-match forms. They can be fixed and stored at the encoder and decoder. They can be built or changed "on the fly." They can be transmitted frame-by-frame or created once for a particular sequence of video by a process called *training*—the process of analyzing all the "vectors" in a sequence to find the "best" 1,024 or 512 or 256 to put into the code-book. As you can see, the process of VQ encoding is very, very hard—a closest match for each vector must be found in the code-book. VQ decoding is very, very easy—all you have to do is to jump to the specified coordinates in the code-book and remove a group of values.

(continued)

Parameters: There are too many possible variables with Vector Quantizers to list here. The biggest difference between most VQ schemes is what data constitutes a vector. Vectors can be the individual RGB or YUV content of a single pixel or a small group of pixels (CinePak), or they can be the differences of YUV values between lines of pixels (Indeo), or the transform coefficients of DCT blocks. The most prominent variable in VQ schemes is how many vectors the code-book has. Large code-books give better visual results, but take longer to transmit since both compressor-transmitter and decompressor-receiver need to have the same dictionary to look things up in.

Motion Estimation/Prediction (ME)

Motion estimation is almost like frame differencing (FD), except the goal is not to find the differences between two frames; the goal is to locate moving blocks of pixels. In the car example given previously, ME's goal is to find where in a future frame (maybe ten frames hence) the image of the car will appear. This allows the compressor to encode "car is here in this frame and will be at *xxx* in ten frames" and the decoder fills in all the in-betweens. Typically, the term *motion estimation (ME)* refers to the process of finding moving groups of pixels on the screen and encoding their direction and speed into the data stream; *motion prediction* is the process of decoding this data and moving pixels around on the screen accordingly. Just as in VQ, this technique is very, very hard to do, especially in real time, but the reconstruction of moving pixels from the ME data is very, very easy.

Parameters: The variable in motion estimation is specifying how accurate it should be in searching for a set of moving pixels. In *full search,* the entire picture is searched for a match to the pixels we're tracking. In *partial search,* we look within a limited distance—much easier and likely will be good enough. In *heuristic search,* the amount of searching depends on how what we're tracking has been moving so far—if it's fast moving, look farther away; if not, then stay close. Another parameter is the size of a moving feature (e.g., a 2×2 or a 16×16 or a 256×256 block).

Discrete Cosine Transform (DCT)

DCT is one of many transform-coding techniques whereby the pixels are transformed into something else and this something else is what is compressed. When this something else is decompressed, it's converted back to pixels by an inverse transform function. DCTs are mathematically very cumbersome. Loosely, a block of pixels (typically 8×8) is transformed into an 8×8 block of values where each value represents the frequency information of this block of pixels for each of 64 frequency bands. This process does not remove any information—it only changes its form into something easier to compress. The coefficients in the upper-left part of this 8×8 block represent frequency values relatively important to the eye, whereas values in

(continued)

the lower-right part don't; so next we grab these values in a zig-zag fashion from upper left to lower right and truncate/quantize them from 8 bits to some lesser number of bits. This is where the compression happens. Furthermore, many of the numbers are or become zero, so applying Run-Length Encoding on these strings of zeroes results in more compression.

Parameters: For DCTs there are several possible variables. One is the size of the blocks to be transformed. Another is usually called the *quantization matrix.* Each frequency coefficient can be quantized differently—some not at all because they represent very important information, and some down to just a few bits because they represent information that the eye would hardly notice as being incorrect. The size of the blocks fed to the DCT may be variable but typically aren't for any given algorithm implementation—for example, in MPEG the blocks are 8×8.

Sub-band Coding and Discrete Wavelet Transform Coding (SBC/DWT)

Sub-band coding is very similar to DCT except that it is done on entire images, not just small blocks of images. SBC passes an image through mathematical filters that separate the image into frequency bands. Visually, this yields lower-resolution subsets of the whole image—one for each band or tap on the filter. Once the image is separated into many different other-resolution pictures, you can employ many of the other redundancy removal or quantization operations on these images. Some subimages are good candidates to be compressed out of existence, whereas others contain frequencies that are important to the eye, so these subimages are likely to be redundancy-coded and not quantized (at least, not very much).

Wavelet coding is just a form of sub-band coding that uses a simple mathematical filter over and over again on each successive subimage produced instead of a complicated mathematical filter with many taps. For example: Filter an image down by 2x, save it; filter it again by 2x, save it; and so on. This makes wavelets very simple to implement on general purpose-processors and simple silicon.

Parameters: Sub-band or wavelet coding has a wide variety of parameters possible. The basis of these algorithms is the process of filtering the video into sub-bands. As we discussed earlier, filtering is a mathematical process and each of the many equations used in a sub-band scheme can have many coefficients. The possible kinds of knobs and dials on sub-band systems are usually only for guys in white lab coats with pocket protectors and glasses.

So now that you're drowning in alphabet soup, it's time to put your extensive knowledge to the test. The major compression algorithms on the market today are constructed as follows:

(continued)

MPEG	1) YUV;	2) SIF;	3) ME;	4) DCT;	5) Quantize;	6) RLE;	7) Huffman
PLV	1) YUV;	2) Decimate;	3) ME;	4) VQ;	5) Quantize;	6) RLE;	7) Huffman
Px64	1) YUV;	2) SIF;	3) ME;	4) DCT;	5) Quantize;	6) RLE;	7) Huffman
iMIX	1) YUV;	2) Decimate;	3) DWT;	4) Quantize;	5) RLE;	6) Huffman
JPEG	1) YUV;	2) DCT;	3) Quantize;	4) RLE;	5) Huffman
SupeRTV	1) YUV;	2) Decimate;	3) DPCM;	4) VQ	5) Huffman
Indeo 3	1) YUV;	2) Decimate;	3) DPCM;	4) ME;	5) VQ;	6) RLE
CinePak	1) YUV;	2) Decimate;	3) VQ;	4) FD
AppleVideo	1) BTC;	2) FD
Microsoft Video 1	1) BTC
Animation	1) RLE

As you can see, each algorithm uses a multitude of techniques—some to reduce redundancy (lossless) and some to quantize (lossy), and some use forms of transforms to make data easier to find redundancy and superfluous information within.

Back to the Saga of Video on a CD-ROM

When we last left off, we had managed to "compress" video to about 8:1 (on average)—that is, we can put four minutes of video on a CD and "play it" off in seventy-four minutes (thirty-seven minutes with 2x speed drives and eighteen minutes with 4x drives.) By adding the "formal" compression algorithms from above, we can get to where we need to get—seventy-four minutes on a seventy-four-minute CD. In the case of MPEG, the final 20:1 compression we get is a mix of DCT/quantizing, ME, RLE, and Huffman/arithmetic coding. (The latter two are lossless.) MPEG was designed to be able to do this type of compression without much loss, but it currently requires extra hardware to be used to play back the compressed video.

The goal behind CinePak and Indeo was to make a video compression algorithm that would work well, but wouldn't need any new or extra hardware. As a result, both focused on the Vector Quantization algorithm. This is because, although the process of finding the "best" vector in the codebook is very hard and almost cannot be done in real time (even with special hardware), the decoding of the bitstream is very, very easy and can be done well even on slower and older computers.

One thing that is typically done for CinePak and Indeo, in order to help the algorithm along (remember our little *data rate* ↔ *frame rate* ↔ *image quality* chart—

(continued)

Figure 3.6), is to keep the frame rate that is expected off the CD to 15 fps (versus 30 fps), yielding a 2x reduction in required compression, and the data rate is allowed to move up to 2x CD rated (250 K/sec). This means that the algorithm now needs another 2x less compression.

With these two stipulations, we only need our compression algorithm to deliver about a 5:1 to 8:1 compression. Both of these are pretty "easy" for CinePak and Indeo. Still, the holy grail of desktop compression is to produce something that is "television quality" without extra hardware for encode or decode that can run on many platforms and fit on a 1x CD-ROM. We're getting there.

So Where Are All Parameter Controls?

This is the whole point, I suppose. Desktop systems using standard QuickTime and Video for Windows compression dialogs limit you to only a couple of parameters for any particular algorithm or codec: a quality setting and a key-frame rate (how often a nonframe difference picture is to occur in the data stream). Some programs that use QuickTime (for example, MovieShop) do allow for many more controls over the compression process—though not nearly as many as high-end professional compression systems, where one does MPEG and PLV compression.

One of the most important things desktop compression algorithms should have is source video presented to them as free from noise as possible, especially in the color information. This entails controls on the digitizing processing, especially concerning image jitters, color saturation, noise filtering, and cross-talk elimination.

Next, most algorithms need to be told how often a full or key frame is to be inserted in the bit stream. Key frames are usually much larger than FD or ME frames because they are completely self-contained. Motion JPEG uses all key frames because the algorithm was designed for still images, not video. Too many key frames will cause the data rate to be unacceptably high, whereas too few will cause a phenomenon called video popping—where the video image slowly degrades over the course of a few seconds and then, when a key frame finally comes along, the video suddenly snaps back to perfect.

Selecting the Parameters

In the case of a professional MPEG compression solution, an operator can specify how many macroblocks the DCT will run on, what the quantization matrix for these blocks looks like, and how accurate the Motion Estimation is (that is, how accurately the algorithm tracks pixels around the screen). A good operator will understand how to change these parameters, possibly on a frame-by-frame basis, to get the best-looking video sequence at the lowest possible data rate.

(continued)

For example, if an object moves through the video very quickly, the motion-estimation accuracy can be much lower because the eye will not notice small displacement problems on fast-moving objects. On frames with much high-frequency noise, like brightly lit mist in the air, the quantization matrix must be made so as not to remove most high-frequency information. If the image is animated with large expanses of similar or identical color, the quantization of the 8 × 8 blocks can be done much more coarsely.

Desktop MPEG compression stations use special programs that try to figure out most of these parameters, because there aren't that many people who will know or care about the accuracy of the motion estimation. This is why there will be professional compression artists and why service bureaus are springing up throughout the country. Paramount Pictures will not MPEG-compress *Top Gun* on a $20,000 desktop compression station. They'll use a multimillion-dollar computer in a full-blown post-house with trained operators and compression artists and get the best possible results for VideoCD.

For production of CinePak and Indeo video titles—typically for the desktop computer and corporate or education training markets—most of the tools are standard QuickTime-savvy programs such as Adobe's Premiere or Radius/VideoFusion's Video Fusion. There are not many available parameters for creation of the video using these programs. Strangely enough (as of this writing), the most "control" over the Indeo and CinePak compression process that can be had comes from the venerable "old" program (two years equals an eternity in this business) MovieShop. With this program, you not only can spec the frame rate, key frame rate, and basic quality settings, but you can specify what parameters need to change when some output consideration (such as data rate) is violated and both the intra- and interframe quality parameters are set in full-scale numerical manner instead of a 32-position slide bar (part of the QuickTime standard compression dialog).

Hopefully, this article explains the underlying *technical* issues and trade-offs that a multimedia developer or new media producer must make when deciding a compression methodology for the production. At the lowest level of involvement, the compression artist working for the producer chooses only quality and key frame rate, whereas at the most involved level of production, the compression artist chooses various parameters for various scenes or pieces. These are, of course, the technical choices.

The business choices are entirely another matter.

Well, some of you asked for it. Actually, knowing a bit more about compression can help you make more educated adjustments of your settings within a compressor. And who knows what tools will be available before we get a chance to update this book? Maybe Bill Fulco's vision of a *"Super MovieShop"* will become a reality and the desktop video producer will need to become more of a compression artist.

We hope so, because having limited control over the available settings means that almost every production we create either becomes a victim of the process of averaging the entire presentation and compressing to this average, or becomes more involved in that we must individually compress segments and assemble the final piece from these multiple parts.

We don't profess to understand each and every detail of how every codec works. No, not for the reason you may be assuming . . . it isn't that we aren't technical enough to understand. We know that it is a better use of our time and energies to let the experts understand the fine-grain details while we concentrate on getting the best results from our general understanding and use of the tools. We know that we can turn to the experts on those occasions when we need more detailed information. A working knowledge generally suffices. We will go as far with that analogy as to add that, although both make fine musical instruments, a fiddle maker is not going to turn out an instrument equal to a Stradivarius.

Video Digitizer and Compression Cards

We briefly discussed the characteristics of cards in each of the three price categories in Chapter 1. Although compression cards may be slightly newer, video capture cards have been around as long as QuickTime and have been getting better and better with more features and better capabilities on, it seems, a quarterly basis. Trust us . . . if you looked at a capture card a year or more ago and didn't like the quality, you may be very surprised at what is out there today.

There are several types of cards for capturing and compressing digital video. They range in capabilities and fall into these four basic categories:

- Capture only
- Capture and display
- Compression only
- Capture, compression, and display

Let's talk about each type of card in a bit more detail.

Capture Only

Capture cards do just that: They are designed to capture video from your source, whether tape, disc, or direct, and let you store them as digital files in your computer. There are two subtypes of these capture-only cards; full-screen and quarter-screen. (See Figure 3.7.)

**Figure 3.7
Quarter-screen
display versus
full-screen.**

- *Full-screen:* These are remnants of predigital video products. Originally designed to capture video stills for desktop publishing work, they are still produced today for that specific purpose. They are generally inexpensive but are unsuitable for digital video work for one main reason: They are unable to digitize enough frames per second in real time to be of practical video use.

  The only exception is when these cards are used in conjunction with a frame control card that is designed to control the frame-by-frame play of the source deck (assuming that you have a tape deck that can accept this type of control input). This form, although still in use, is very slow and outdated by a myriad of less-expensive capture and compression systems.

- *Quarter-screen (or less):* Targeted at the entry-level/prosumer category, these are capable of capturing video directly to system RAM or to hard disk at a rate of up to 15 fps at quarter-screen, or as high as 30 fps at much smaller window sizes. They are reasonably priced, but are not generally suited for professional multimedia work as the quality of the digitizer circuitry is rarely good enough for commercial application.

  The exceptions in this category are the AV cards from Apple. which offer very good quality capture; their frame rates vary based upon the performance level of the computer to which they are added.

  Both of these card types—full-screen and quarter-screen—are excellent for the entry-level user and cost under $1,000.

**Capture and
Display**

There are several cards that offer up to full-screen digitizing capabilities *and* function as accelerated display cards at the same time. These cards frequently offer an upgrade path to add on a compression "daughter" card to gain these features. The quality of video capture varies from model to model but generally is very good. The display attributes of these cards (monitor size supported, color depth) also vary. These cards are good starting points for the entry level user who wants to save some money by buying a combo card.

Understand that without compression acceleration, the capture size and frame rates will be limited to the capabilities of the computer you use. Typically this will be quarter-screen or smaller, and 15 fps or less. These cards are capable of full-screen capture but, like the capture-only cards, they are limited to very low frame rates for full-screen capture. They also require a frame control card to control the frame-by-frame play of the source deck, in order to adequately digitize larger frame sizes.

Capture-and-display cards may or may not include audio digitizing capability. Some do not include audio capture simply because the Macintosh they are designed for features some form of audio capture.

The prices for this type of card currently are all over the map, ranging from the moderate hundreds to many thousands of dollars. This wide range is attributable to the display side of the equation. The more display real estate a card must support, the greater the amount of such things as video RAM (VRAM) such a card must contain. Support for very large monitor sizes at 24-bit color can raise the price considerably.

Compression Only

Compression-only cards take precaptured video—meaning that it is already digital—and compress it using various algorithms. Cards of this type fall into two basic subcategories:

- *On-line (real-time):* Generally, these are the add-on or *daughter* cards for the capture-and-display cards just discussed. They most often are JPEG-based, but each has its own distinct flavor of JPEG. They range from 320 × 240, 30fps compression to true 640 × 480, 60 field (broadcast standard) compression. These cards range in price from $1,000 to $2,500.

- *Off-line (post-processors):* There are several cards designed to speed up the very compute-intensive compression algorithms used by codecs such as CinePak, MPEG, Indeo, and others. These are not real-time compressors but compression accelerators that can speed compression up to 300 times. The prices for cards of this type vary, sometimes widely, based on the codec they support.

There is a third card type, but one that is used less frequently. This is the tandem card—a compression card that resides in another bus slot and works directly with a capture card.

**Capture,
Compression,
and Display**

These cards (sometimes sold as card sets) are the most common. They generally offer JPEG compression, but the implementation of the compression varies greatly by product.

They feature accelerated 24-bit display capability and support numerous monitor sizes. These products offer various upgrade paths and a variety of input types. They also digitize audio at most of the standard sampling rates (44.1 MHz, 22.25 MHz, and so forth). These cards form the basis for the midrange Digital Video Studio category.

They include:

- RasterOps MoviePak and MoviePak II
- Truevision (owned by RasterOps) TARGA 2000
- Radius VideoVision Studio and Telecast
- SuperMac (now Radius) DigitalFilm
- New Video (now defunct) Eye-Q
- Products from several PC suppliers

These cards are the staple of the multimedia professional. These are the cards that provide the broadest range of features and capabilities, in the most compact format. We use several of these cards in our Quadra 840AV computers for our video processing work. They may cost more than the cards in the three other categories, but in our opinion provide the best return on investment.

What we are really talking about here is *time*. With all the different clips that even a single multimedia project may require, anything other than real-time capture/compression and accelerated post-compression would be economically disastrous. Multimedia projects would be much more expensive to produce with all the extra production hours required to capture, process, and compress digital video in individual steps.

The prices for this type of combo card set range from $3,000 to $6,000.

Don't discount cards in any of these categories. As long as you understand their best uses and limitations, each of these card types can be a welcome addition to the desktop video studio. For instance, we still use an older capture-only card for some full-screen captures where we need to turn a video frame into a full-screen display.

Understanding more about the different compressors available to you will add to your ability to turn out a first-class product. Understanding what to do during compression to make your videos viable on a single platform is equally as important as understanding how to make your movie playable cross-platform.

Although a few of the same compressors are available on both the Macintosh and the Windows sides, you must be aware that many are not. To learn more about this subject, and to see how to best compress movies for cross-platform use, please see Chapter 5.

"Total" Solutions

Almost everything we have discussed to this point could be classified as a piece-by-piece solution; you buy the correct pieces as you need them to fit your needs. Another approach is to purchase a total solution—an all-in-one package designed to work as a single unit, usually very powerful and almost always at the high end of the cost charts for the desktop studio.

How many of us in the desktop video world need to go directly to a total solution, or can afford one? Very few indeed. But don't discount total solutions. We are looking at one to take us to the next level of services that we can provide—services that take us out of the realm of off-line rendered effects into effects generated in real time.

Yes, it costs money, and we would never have thought of looking into this type of system during our first couple of years in business. It may be just a bit more than we should spend even today, but we *are* looking.

A typical total solution has some or all of the following attributes:

- Large capacity, very fast storage using RAIDs or arrays
- A platform-specific, even model-specific, computer
- Capability for multiple monitors and support
- Custom capture and compression hardware
- Special hardware (usually cards or an intermediate control box) designed to perform special effects
- Special editing software designed to get the most from the hardware
- Single-point support

These nonlinear on- and off-line systems are specifically targeted at the professional video producer. They compete with traditional tape-based linear video production equipment. The output quality of these systems varies, but generally it is in the BetaCam SP range. They were not designed for producing multimedia content, but offer very good import and export capabilities. Some are only remotely QuickTime-compatible.

Typically, you capture all of your raw video onto a large-capacity drive or array. From this "pool" of video, you pick and choose all of your elements, effects, transitions, and so forth, building an edit decision list. Where these total solutions vary wonderfully from traditional tape editing is in their ability to produce previews of your work. If you like a particular transition, you move onto the next one. If you don't, you can try something new—chop out a few frames, stretch a short piece out to fit the narration, add effects for some pieces, set up multiple windows on screen. You can do practically anything, and in any way you wish it.

Your final piece can be assembled, sometimes in real time, and saved back out to tape or kept in storage for future use.

We recently had the opportunity to sit down with one of these solutions—the ImMIX Video Cube—and were amazed at what is possible.

Are these total solutions a flash-in-the-pan, or is a full digital editing system right for you? Following is one viewpoint.

MOVING TO DIGITAL EDITING SYSTEMS
by Roberta Margolis

Ms. Margolis is president of Runway Video, one of the largest providers of nonlinear editing systems to television and feature film productions. She directs the ROUGH CUTS program for LACE in Los Angeles and serves on their video committee. She serves on the program committee for the International Forum for the International Teleproduction Society. She has also served on the screening committees for the International Documentary Association awards. Originally a CPA for an international accounting firm and director of financial affairs for Crossroads School in Santa Monica, Ms. Margolis returned to school and received a Master of Fine Arts from the California Institute of the Arts. Her video, Vessels of the Heart, *was recently chosen for exhibition in a show by the Houston Center for Photography.*

Runway Video provides nonlinear digital editing equipment for television series, movies of the week, feature films, and long-form documentaries. We have watched the availability of nonlinear have a profound effect on the editorial process—but not always in the ways one would expect.

Television networks and film studios are beginning to think of film and video material—picture and sound—as all being elements in a "bit bucket" to be formed into shows at different times. The production process that formerly was chemical and mechanical is now becoming digital from beginning to end. This increases the ability to sell multiple versions of the same material (television shows and films) to different markets (such as home video, foreign, and airline versions) with ease.

But when you say a "bit bucket of images," that is not a familiar concept to an eighty-seven-year old editor of an hour-long television series. When his producer

(continued)

decided to edit the series on a digital editing system, we had to teach the editor to be fast enough on a nonlinear editing system to "keep up to camera."

Many television series are still shot on 35mm film. Each evening, film dailies are developed in the lab. When editing is done digitally, the "dailies" are telecined—a process that transfers the film, scene by scene, to videotape. Early the next morning, the previous day's dailies, now on videotape, are digitized onto the hard disk of the editing system. The editor works to "keep up to camera," editing the previous day's scenes before that day's dailies arrive.

Within just a few weeks, the eighty-seven-year-old editor was able to keep up to camera.

Digital editing has also made it possible to work with less expensive and more accessible technology. Work done with these lower-cost technologies is being integrated into mainstream video broadcasts and films. Material is shot on Hi-8 video and 16mm film, transferred to video, and edited in the wee hours on powerful editing systems being used by day for television and feature films.

Or it is being edited on less expensive desktop video systems. Availability of digital editing at a moderate cost has also allowed videomakers to produce more personal, less commercial work. As video-making programs in schools proliferate, editors are beginning at a younger age.

The nature of the editing process itself is changing. Physical barriers to the editing process are being removed. For example, a feature film editor told me that by the end of a long day editing on film, if he had a bright idea about how to edit a scene, he often was too tired to find the film, lug down the film can, and thread the film or wait for his assistant to do it. Sometimes film would get lost. At some point pieces of film become damaged from handling and being taped and untaped. New film has to be printed. Bits of film (called "trims") get lost in the editing room. He frequently would let his idea wait until the next morning.

With nonlinear editing, he says he often feels "in the groove" and free to try new ideas all the way to the end of his workday.

The quality of the finished film or television show is better because of nonlinear technology. Directors and editors talk about the efficiency of the database management aspects of nonlinear editing. For example, multiple readings of an actor's line can be collected and played successively for the director to mix and match, taking a picture from one reading and bits of dialogue from another.

Being able to group material in several different ways also assists in cutting together action scenes: All the shots of cars of different colors in a car chase can be kept together for access in editing. It allows for good cutting of action scenes with scanty material, making varied types of movies such as action features more accessible to low-budget feature makers.

(continued)

Some things change, allowing film and television makers to think about new possibilities with nonlinear editing. And some things remain the same. Quality material and talent in handling it are still highly valued. Producers continue to hire people for their ideas and ability. Nonlinear editing just gives them more powerful tools to tell stories.

Most editors and directors tell me they would not return to editing on film or linear videotape.

Perhaps even more than filmmaking and television, nonlinear editing dominates the world of commercials. Although we all know the ubiquitousness of special effects in commercials, the real change occurring now is the power of nonlinear editing in the hands of art directors. Many art directors are learning nonlinear editing and are editing rough cuts of their own commercials. The trickling down of technology to ever-lower levels on the desktop enables them even to include special effects in their work.

So the power to create, to integrate material in different forms—videotape, film, still images, and sound—is saturating the center and spreading to the edges of the professional world of television and film.

What's Available in a Total Solution?

There are several packages that fall into this category built around off-the-shelf computers such as Macintosh and PCs, and there are total solutions built around either proprietary systems or less-available computers, such as Sun platforms.

Total solution products include:

- Data Translation Media 100
- Avid Technology Media Suite Pro
- ImMIX Video Cube (Figure 3.8)
- Radius Telecast (includes VideoVision Studio)

Such systems come complete with all the necessary components (although the computer may be sold separately), editing and effects software, appropriate and approved hrd disk subsystems, and the capture and compression hardware. Sometimes these items are sold separately, but each subsystem has been exactly specified for use with that system. The solution suppliers typically do not support any equipment that is not specified for use with their system.

The good news is that a total solution can provide you with practically everything you might ever want. The not-so-good news is that these systems range in price from $12,000 to $40,000 plus.

We mention total solutions in this book, although we do not feel that

**Figure 3.8
ImMIX Video
Cube—a power-
ful, high-end
editing and
effects solution.**

they are designed for the desktop video studio. The average desktop video producer just isn't going to spend that kind of money right out of the bag.

But . . .

As we said before, some of these total solutions provide elegant, real-time editing, effects, and transitions that easily go out to tape with broadcast-quality results. If we had the money lying around today, we might have a hard time resisting.

Where these solutions shine is in the corporate video production world. Generally, a corporate video team or department will service the needs of the entire company, making speed and quality a big issue. Enter the total solution. The cost of one such system can easily be paid for within the development of the first several projects. Corporate departments that also become involved in the production of in-house video and closed-circuit television will want to take note of these products.

The external development of a thirty-minute video can be in the tens or even hundreds of thousands of dollars. A skilled video professional can turn out a similar product using many of these one-stop solutions for considerably less.

We asked Dan DiPaola, who has been involved in the use of computers in the video industry for more than fifteen years, to give us his perspective on the subject of the use of computer solutions in the corporate world.

WHO NEEDS DESKTOP VIDEO IN THE CORPORATE WORLD?

by Dan DiPaola

Mr. DiPaola is the director of Fractal Design's Entertainment Technology Center in Los Angeles and is an internationally renowned expert on desktop computers for motion picture and television production. His film industry experience spans fifteen years. Early in his career he worked for Francis Ford Coppola at the Zoetrope Studios, where he was involved with such films as Apocalypse Now *and* One from the Heart. *His expertise was in the creative end of motion picture and television. His responsibilities ranged from directing to art direction and special effects. For the past seven years, Mr. DiPaola has been devoting his energy to evangelizing and implementing technology into the industry—for four years as the owner-operator of Mac'N'Stein, a high-end desktop consulting firm, and then the next three at Walt Disney Studios running the DeskTop Graphics Lab.*

Who needs desktop video? With over fifteen years of experience in the entertainment industry, I feel confident in answering, "All professionals who would like an edge on the rest of the gang."

Done right, it can save money, time, and nerves, and opens up a whole new universe of inexpensive effects and applications. However, it really depends on thoughtful and decisive implementation, whether the road to success is short and painless or a drawn-out disaster. At Disney we had an eager and resourceful team. We managed quite well, despite the fact that, when we first created the "DeskTop Graphics Lab," desktop video was in its infancy. The studio deserves a lot of credit for trying something so radical.

A lot has changed since then, and the technology has become much less expensive, very reliable, and much more intuitive. Any company deciding to set up a desktop video system can expect gratifying results quickly, if they follow some easy guidelines.

What are some of the things you should think about as you try to get your company started down this exciting road? My main rule is, if you decide to make the jump, don't fool around. Never underfinance your operation. Sure, I understand that a comfortably equipped workstation is still a major investment for some. Whether that will be money well spent, or a loss, depends on the willingness of the decision makers to put full support and weight behind it. You can either spend the money on putting it together right or pay the consequences.

If your workstation is not properly configured, you could end up wasting precious production time trying to jerry-rig it. In larger companies you might have to overcome a reluctance to change because entrenched departments can become set in their ways. A commonly heard phrase is, "If it ain't broke, don't fix it." Don't look at digital video as a fix; look at it as an exciting addition, something that brings a new level of professionalism to your work.

(continued)

Selecting the right ballplayers for the right positions is crucial to the success of the department. This is especially true when it comes to justifying the need for departmental dollars. If at all possible, when demonstrating the capabilities of the system for a client, avoid sending an executive up to bat for the department without a tech on hand. Some of the questions that arise during these demos need a well-polished team of business and technical staff. Because the technology is so new, there are a lot of questions. Although they do exist, it is extremely rare to find a person in an executive position who is also a technologist. Successful presentations depend heavily on a complete team effort. If at all possible, avoid cutting corners by having people wear multiple hats. Many companies have not yet gotten this message.

Once you get the go-ahead, keep the implementation manageable. Depending on the size of your organization, start with a couple of workstations and bring those up to full working speed before you expand. At this time, you can expect to spend anywhere from $25,000 to $35,000 for a comfortably rigged stand-alone station. This will get you a fairly hot-rodded Macintosh with all the trimmings and an abundance of essential applications such as Fractal's Painter 3.0, Adobe's Premiere and PhotoShop, Cosa After Effects, Electric Image, Elastic Reality, and then some.

But wait—don't stop now. Putting all the goodies into a darkly lighted room is only half the game. You need to back your equipment up with professionals. As a very rough index, be prepared to spend approximately $2 on a professional's salary for every dollar you invest in equipment. You're looking for production people gone digital—someone with at least a few years of production experience. This person has then decided to pick up the computer as a tool.

A well-seasoned professional is very important. So again, the last thing you want to do is take a basic Macintosh person and teach them how to do high-end production—not that this hasn't been done successfully. There will be less worry when it comes to making quick decisions that only an experienced pro can make. You do not want to be supervising this person eight hours a day. Once you've found 'em, give them elbow room and some credit.

There will be a number of thankless hours spent learning and streamlining the way your production process happens. When the department is in place and running, having your professionals work directly with the management avoids one very common and dangerous mistake: overselling the technology to the client. Only the people who are familiar with what their equipment is capable of producing in a given amount of time should make deadline commitments.

We all know that the one thing that we give up when working on a desktop system is speed. A snazzy presentation might raise the desire and expectations of a client to unrealistic heights. In such a situation you need your tech to work with the account manager to realistically gauge what's possible. You don't want an account

(continued)

executive coming back to the lab and handing your desktop video manager an assignment of such scope that quality must be compromised to make a deadline.

Know what can be done in a certain amount of time. A good example is a job where we used Fractal Design's Painter to do a previsualization of a before-and-after make-up EFX. After we used Painter, we went in with Morph to do the in-betweens, and it looked great. The first thing somebody said was, "Can we have that head morphing as it turns 180° in front of the camera?" All of a sudden a simple retouching job turns into a 3D monster because the client expected it in the same amount of time. Someday that may become a no-brainer, but as of yet it still takes a little work and a lot of processing time.

I think one of the hottest things to start happening on the Macintosh is painting onto frames. Basically what we have is a baby rotoscoping station. Fractal's Painter, with its highly sophisticated brushes, actually can do things that some of the larger mainframe systems can't.

On that same note, don't be a platform bigot; when the growing pains hit, have an open mind. When it's time to expand, you might not be able to stick exclusively with your desktop system. They are still valuable and you don't want to disregard them, but because of the lab's growth you now may need a larger and more powerful system to complement your Macs and handle the heavy duty jobs, especially 3D.

So far I have discussed only the core elements of a desktop video department, but there are two very important peripherals that absolutely need to be implemented along with the core applications. One is connectivity—the future lies with the telephone companies, not Federal Express. Tomorrow, almost all your resources and points of output will be on-line. Why send a video clip on tape and worry if it will be there in the morning if you can send it over a high bandwidth line and get it running on your client's desktop machine in ten minutes? You can even do it in real time if you want to spend the dollars on bandwidth.

Today's options run the gamut from inexpensive to moderately priced solutions. To find the perfect solution for your needs, consult with a network professional, and don't leave your desktop video system isolated.

Just as important is documentation and archiving of your work—not only to secure thousands of person- and machine-hours against disaster, but more importantly for repurposing your previous work. Initially, archiving creates additional work and cost, without bringing in additional bucks. But down the road it becomes very profitable. I think the new buzz term is *asset management,* as quoted by Doug Dawirs, the author of Fetch, a well-known image archiving package. Quite a bit of work goes into creating these digital graphics.

One of the cool things about your art's being digital is that all of these pieces can be considered objects and may be repurposed any number of times. Get it? Create

(continued)

once; $ell many! The better job you do cataloging these pieces—as in creating descriptions and their organization—the easier it will be to find them at a later date for reuse.

As the director of Fractal Design's Entertainment Technology Center, it is my focus to introduce and share this technology with production professionals throughout Southern California. We currently are conducting three to five demonstrations a day for professionals ranging from motion picture producers to CD-ROM developers.

If all these considerations seem overwhelming, I assure you they are not. If done properly, you can make a smooth transition into the digital future. Once you live in cyberland, it really is a very cool place. Who needs desktop video? Chances are, it's you!

Again the question, Are these total solutions right for most of us? Not today—but look for lots of the capabilities from these systems to find their way into the software and hardware that will be used on the digital desktop in the near future.

4

Video Sources

We have said it before, and we will say it again: The quality of your end product depends greatly on the quality of your original source and how you handle it. The better the source, the higher quality possible for your digital video.

Just because you're working in the digital realm doesn't mean that you always start with, or even end up with, digital video. It is certain that you will work with a variety of sources, including (but not limited to) direct camera feed, videotape in many formats, laserdisc, off-air feeds, and so forth. They all have a lot in common, and they each have special capabilities, requirements, and peccadilloes. We work with a fair number of source types and have discovered some tricks and things to keep in mind.

In the broadest sense, you have only two possible sources of material, analog and digital. Both of these offer delivery variations on the basic theme—tape size and format, type of signal, and so forth—and each one gives you something a little different. Analog is the most common and is probably what you will be using 99.98 percent of the time. Digital video sources are very expensive and generally are found only in high-end production environments.

When you watch television from your cable or antenna, you are looking at an analog signal. When you look at a VHS tape, you are looking at an analog signal. When you listen to an LP or a standard cassette tape, you are listening to an analog signal.

Look at a laserdisc and you are looking at a picture recorded as a digital signal and then converted back into an analog signal for display. Listen to a CD and you are listening to a digital data stream converted back to analog. Why? Because our ears and eyes only understand analog. Sure, we can see

135

a visual representation of the 1s and 0s that make up the digital signal, but we can't interpret it without some sort of analog conversion and display.

If this is true, then why bother with digital? Easy. A digital source does not degrade from original to copy to copy to copy. The data remains pristine; there is no signal loss. Don't confuse this with "compressed" digital video, which may have lost considerable information during the compression process; once compressed, it will remain the same from copy to copy (as long as it is not recompressed in the process of copying). You start with a potentially great source and go on from there. (We say *potentially* because it is entirely possible to have a lousy piece of video with a source that is digital just as you can have a lousy piece of video with an analog source.)

If the better the source the better the end result, then don't you *want* the most pristine source possible? Yes. But is the best source always going to be digital? No. It may not be cost effective, and it may be overkill for the task at hand.

Let's look at each of the sources and talk briefly about their pros and cons, and how to get the best results from each.

Analog Sources

Recorded analog audio goes back to the first Edison Talking Machine, more than 100 years ago. For that, cylinders made of hard wax were used along with a needle that vibrated from the sound of a voice being yelled into a large megaphone attached directly to the needle. The same needle was used to play the cylinder and the vibration/sound sent back through the megaphone. Not very efficient, but damn fascinating.

Recorded analog video began with the first experimental use of videotape in the 1940s. A lot has changed since then, and a lot has remained the same. The analog information is actually a sine wave fluctuating above and below neutral, with the amount of fluctuation determining what that signal represents. This is a temporal stream of information. Any interruption or degradation of the signal will cause the resulting visual representation (once converted into a picture) to suffer.

There are many sources of analog video signals available to the desktop video studio (see Figures 4.1 and 4.2). Among them are video cameras, broadcast television (both through an antenna and cable), and videotape. Some offer better quality than others, and each has it own pros and cons. For instance, taking a direct feed from a video camera into your computer provides you a very clean, strong signal, a signal that has not been greatly affected between the time it leaves the camera and the time it enters the

**Figure 4.1
VHS tape: ana-
log source for
the common
man.**

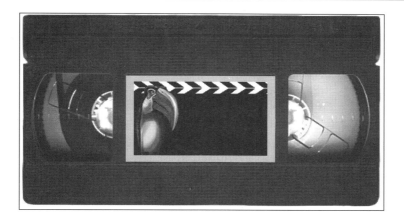

computer. However, a poor-quality camera, or one that provides only a fair signal (consumer-grade VHS, for example), will not provide as good a source as a professional, BetaCam SP camera.

Likewise, broadcast television signals can range from very good to very, very poor. You might think that a signal coming through your cable would be stronger and provide a better source than a signal received from an antenna. In many cases, this is true. Any analog signal coming through the airwaves is subject to all sorts of influences, such as buildings, mountains, electrical power lines, and a poorly aligned antenna, to name a few. But cable is also subject to negative influences. Our local cable hookup always suffers from moisture when it rains. No matter what the potential signal strength, whatever happens to lessen a signal's quality along its path is exactly what you will capture at the receiving end.

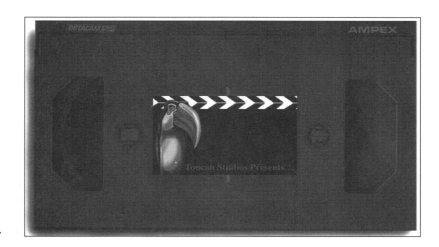

**Figure 4.2
BetaCam SP:
one of the best
analog sources
available today.**

For the purpose of this book, we are assuming that you will work less with these types of sources and more with videotape, today's biggest source of analog video. The quality of the output from these tape formats is also affected by what signal type is used (for example, composite, S-Video [YC], component, or RGB).

The quality of a tape format is generally rated by lines of resolution. Listed next are the approximate maximums for major formats. The equipment used may not be capable of actually recording to that limit or displaying all of the lines of resolution:

VHS	240
8mm	260
3/4 U-Matic	260
3/4 SP U-Matic	320
SVHS	400
Hi-8	400
LaserDisc	420
Professional SVHS	420
BetaCam SP	440

There are other tape formats such as 1-inch C, MII, D1, and so forth, but we've listed the most common. Remember that even though you may use a format with 400 lines of resolution (SVHS, for example) in your edit suite, if the video originally was shot with a recorder that provides only 260 lines (8 mm), once duplicated to your edit equipment it still has only 260 lines of resolution. The rule is, if it wasn't there to start, it will never be there.

Your project quality is only as good as the absolute source and will degrade somewhat with each generation of tape transfer. Minimize the generation loss by digitizing into your computer from the original tape whenever possible.

Analog tape and signals are fine for most desktop digital video production, but you must take precautions to ensure that the best, cleanest, and most complete signal is digitized. This includes, but is not limited to, using the highest-quality equipment you can afford. As we've already mentioned, even little things such as too-long or cheap or damaged cables can spell doom to an analog signal. The farther the signal must travel, or the more "battles" it must face on its way, the more compromised the end result.

Some signal loss is inevitable, but *major* signal loss is almost always avoidable. For starters, use the highest-quality signal output and inputs your equipment offers. If you have S-Video in and out, this is far better than using composite in and out. Component is even better. Dirty tape heads or gunked up connectors can kill you.

Where possible, avoid using adapters that change one type of connector to another, or adding cables to cables because you don't have one set that is long enough. Every additional piece you put in the analog line takes away some of the signal.

Now that we've told you some of the pitfalls and how you can minimize them, here are several things that are good about analog signals:

- The components are much less expensive than those for digital video, so more people can afford them. Some formats, such as Hi-8 and SVHS, offer very good signal strength and resolution for the desktop video studio.

- If you take precautionary measures, the analog source and signal can be kept very clean.

- It is possible to get good-quality cables and tapes for just a bit more money than the inexpensive varieties.

- For most desktop digital video work, a high-quality analog signal will have no noticeable difference from a digital source.

Although we most often end up using analog sources, we just as often combine them with digitally sourced screens, backgrounds, and effects.

Next, let's look at digital signals.

Digital Sources

By far, the least lossy digital video can be achieved by never going through an analog stage. To do this, you must either go directly from a digital camera into your computer using digital cables, or record to digital videotape and transfer that digital signal digitally to your computer—again, using digital cabling. In the case of audio, if your source is a CD (see Figure 4.3), the audio can be converted inside your computer without going through a digital-to-analog and then analog-to-digital capture process.

Just as with analog signals, there are a number of different sources for digital video signals. These include digital cameras (both motion and still), laserdiscs, video CDs, satellite broadcast, and others.

Also, as with analog signal sources, the quality of the picture can vary from source to source. This variance is not so much with the quality of the signal as with the amount of data that can be stored or transmitted to make up each frame of the video. A laserdisc and a video CD both offer digitally encoded signals, but the video on the CD is usually highly compressed, so

**Figure 4.3
CD-ROM: the
most readily
available digital
source.**

that more video can be stored on the disc. If the compression method used removed data from the original, then the signal coming from the CD will have less data. And less data means a lower-quality picture.

Digital signals, no matter what their origin, are made up of a series of 1s and 0s; you already know that. These 1s and 0s are transmitted in a data stream of many thousands or millions per second. At the receiving end, the stream of data is registered "as is," with no interpretation or loss of information. What you start with is what you end up with (Which is a very good thing!)—as long as there has been no compression along the way.

No data loss means no difference between what the digital source captures and what comes out the other end. (Also a very good thing!)

Why is this important? Because one of the biggest criminals in the desktop video studio world is signal loss. Signal loss can manifest itself as noise in the picture or, in severe cases, as a loss of the picture itself. Any signal loss or noise makes eventual compression more difficult and less efficient.

Capturing digital video from a recorded digital source is about as close as you can get to direct capture into your computer.

How often does that happen today? Probably less than 1 percent of the time. If that is so, why devote any book time to the subject? Because digital is the wave of the future. Our HDTVs will use a digital signal to handle all of the data necessary to create that great picture we will come to know and love. On our roofs today are the new 18-inch DSS digital antennas capable of receiving digital transmissions that suffer no signal loss despite being sent from 22,300 miles above the earth. These receivers have high-speed digital signal outputs that someday could be connected directly to our computers, allowing us to take digital information directly from the satellite.

Even with all these advances, there are still some types of digital video signals that need to be compressed, the aforementioned digital satellite being one such example. If the satellite only had to contend with a few channels, it would be able to send all of the data in realtime. But, these satellites must deal with up to one hundred and fifty channels simultaneously. The sheer amount of data needed to represent that many signals is beyond both the capability of the satellite and the equipment that sits next to your television. For this reason, the signals are compressed at the sending end and decompressed at the receiving end. For the DSS satellites, this means using MPEG-2 encoding.

There are several reasons for the extremely low use of digital sources; primary among these is the tremendous cost of equipment that handles uncompressed, or lossless, digital signals. We are not talking about "twice the cost" of analog equipment. We are talking a factor of 10 or more.

The digital source materials that are available to most desktop users have already been compressed so that they can be used with inexpensive playback equipment. (MPEG is the compression method most often used for mass distribution.) Probably the most common digital source that most users will encounter are the graphics and animations that are created on their own computers.

The Upshot of It All?

Is a digital source mandatory? No. Is it better than having analog signals involved somewhere in the path? Sure (if you can afford it). Would you see the difference in most of your multimedia productions? Probably not! Everything depends on what your final results need to be. We have said all along that you should know what your target is before you begin. If you are producing quarter screen QuickTime movies for a multimedia CD-ROM project, chances are that there is no real benefit to a digital video source. There just won't be a noticeable difference.

So, if digital sources are going to change your life, what should you strive for? Just the best source and signal possible, of course.

Don't sweat it if you don't have the ability to utilize digital sources; not many people do. Perhaps by the time you really need the capability, the costs will be down to an affordable level (and pigs might fly).

Signal Quality and Processing

It is important to know your video source and to treat it appropriately. If you have a single source, such as a BetaCam SP tape, you usually set up your equipment and do your video capture with little adjustment necessary. If you produced the original video, you know that you color-balanced the camera and you know the typical picture quality you get with your camera. But most of us don't shoot our own material; we get our tapes from the client.

Let's say that your source video *is* coming from someone else, or your video is coming from many different places, or you have materials from many different types of media. It is vital that you do everything possible to minimize the signal differences between each source so that your final product looks as consistent as possible.

One of the first things you must do is to adjust your playback and recording settings so that each source comes through optimized and with the most consistent signal possible. Before you begin capturing, especially when dealing with multiple tapes or sources, we suggest that you view sample segments from each source to determine, visually, if there are noticeable differences. If you have a vectorscope—and we suggest this as an important piece of equipment—then check the signal levels of your samples.

Take the best source, the one that appears to be the best balanced, and adjust your other sources to that. Or, take a known good signal, preferably color bars, and adjust everything to match that. A video producer acquaintance of ours explains further in the following sidebar:

PREPARING TO DIGITIZE ANALOG VIDEO
by Jerry Huiskens

Mr. Huiskens is the principal of Huiskens Video Productions in San Jose, California. He and his company have provided professional corporate video and media services to Silicon Valley companies since 1981. His experience as a computer programmer, video producer, and graphic artist has gained him corporate clients such as Control Data, Fujitsu, and Sun Microsystems, among others.

If you are in professional video or media production, you already know the importance of time base correctors, processor amps, vectorscopes, and waveform monitors. If not, these devices correct and detect a myriad of video problems—from chroma noise and video levels to sync, saturation, and black levels. This is essential for digitizing analog video signals so they look their best. I want to discuss the basic equipment, setup, and procedures needed to analyze some of the problems in the signal and solve them before the video is digitally captured and compressed.

(continued)

Chroma, Saturation, Noise . . . and Blue Guns and Bars

There are a few inherent problems with analog video signals that, once digitally captured, not only forever remain a part of the clip, but can actually propagate and worsen as compression algorithms are applied. Under ideal conditions in the production and post-production environments, the video, shot and edited on tape, will have been monitored and adjusted to proper specifications. However, this is not always the case. You may find yourself in a position where you need to digitize video footage that is inconsistent in quality between scenes or even from edit to edit. Shadows may lack detail and the light areas may bloom or wash out. Depending on the tape format and generational loss of the video you are about to digitize, the color may be overly saturated as well. There are some quality problems that can never be corrected after the original recording. So, it is important to shoot and edit it correctly in the first place. There are, however, some procedures you can follow to ensure that you digitize the video signal with the best quality possible under your control. Let's start by discussing the basic setup of your equipment.

The ideal setup includes a professional monitor, with a "blue gun" or "blue only" mode, and a waveform monitor, vectorscope, and processing amplifier (proc amp). The minimal equipment needed is a monitor and a processing amplifier, used to correct the color and video levels. This discussion is meant to be at a basic level to get you started. To eliminate confusion, for those without benefit of technical training, some technical terms will not be explained beyond what is needed to understand basic concepts. For a deeper understanding of the test equipment and procedures, consult a video engineer.

Color Bar Types

The color bars used today are of three types: full-field, split-field, and SMPTE. They all display the same basic colors, divided equally in vertical bars, left to right in order of luminance. The vertical colors are, from left to right: white, yellow, cyan, green, magenta, red, blue. They should look somewhat close to those colors on your monitor. Full-field color bars have an extra black bar at the right and the vertical bars extend from top to bottom of the screen. SMPTE color bars have more capability for setup purposes. If your monitor has presets (factory-set positions, usually in the middle of the range) for each setting—color, hue, brightness, contrast, and picture—try setting these controls to their detent or reset positions.

A good color bar signal needs to be fed to the monitor, from either a camera or some other device that generates color bars, such as a SEG (Special Effects Generator) or color bar generator. If bars are recorded on the videotape you are about to digitize, you can use these as reference. If these are not available, record color bars

(continued)

on your VCR from a good broadcast TV station after hours. Some still broadcast bars. The FCC requires these signals to be within certain specifications. If not, try cable channels. These are certainly not ideal ways to get a color bar reference signal, but you need to start somewhere. Without proper test equipment, it's just a guess. We need to show you how to make it a good guess.

Monitor Setup—Visually with a Nonprofessional Monitor

At the very least, you need a reference monitor so you can see any problem areas in the video signal. It is best to have a professional monitor, but if you don't, you can use a consumer monitor that is properly adjusted. First, we need to discuss how to basically adjust the monitor being used for reference. If the monitor is not adjusted, you run the risk of having bad quality color bars that may have been dubbed incorrectly. This could cause more problems than you're trying to correct. If it isn't adjusted correctly, you cannot detect problems with the signal.

Since brightness and contrast can affect the look of the color picture, they should be adjusted first by turning down the color level all the way, to a black and white picture. Then adjust these controls so it looks pleasing as a grayscale signal—white and yellow not too bright, and dark colors so they aren't too dark and muddy looking. They should have some definition between them. If you do not have color bars, adjust the brightness so the blacks can just begin to lighten up the image. If you have SMPTE color bars, adjust the brightness so that the lightest of the three black boxes is slightly visible. The darker two will appear blackest. With full-field color bars, the black bar will also appear very black.

Next, adjust the color level up to a nice color level, but not oversaturated, especially red and magenta. We also don't want them to be undersaturated—too washed out looking, having too little color in the signal. If the hue doesn't show the proper colors for cyan (light blue with a slight amount of green in it, maybe like a light turquoise blue) and magenta (sort of a hot pink with a little purple in it), adjust the hue left or right a bit so they look as close as possible to cyan and magenta.

Finally, a good rule of thumb is to display a signal with a person's face in it. It should be a known good signal. If the face looks orange or too red, check another source. If it's still bad, the hue is probably adjusted incorrectly. Adjust for natural facial skin tones and return to the color bar signal. It should be fairly close to correct.

Monitor Setup—Visually with a Professional Monitor

For more accurate adjustments, you can use a monitor that has a "blue gun" or "blue only" mode. Very basically, this type of monitor gives you the ability to turn off the

(continued)

red and green guns, leaving only the blue one. (All three guns, when combined, provide the composite color image on your monitor.) The effect is a blue-only picture, which allows you to see the luminance level of the picture without the chroma (color). Some monitors display a grayscale image rather than a bluescale one. The result of both is to turn off the chroma. An alternative trick is to use a dark blue lighting gel held in front of the screen.

You can experiment with that. The brightness, contrast, and color levels can be adjusted with the monitor in this mode. The basic adjustment is to try to get the vertical bars to look equal in luminance intensity. Adjust the color so the blue bar at the left and the blue bar at the right are equal in intensity. Adjust the hue control so the two blue bars in the center are equal (the cyan and magenta bars). The other bars appear as either blue or black. The earlier adjustments of contrast, brightness, and color level can also affect their appearance.

Monitor Adjustment Completed

Now that the monitor is adjusted with this "good guess," don't touch it for the rest of the session. This is your only reference to the real world. Our objective is to reduce that noise in the video signal to an acceptable level before it is digitized, and to keep the color saturation, luminance, and black levels adjusted so they look best when displayed on the computer. The next question is how to adjust the levels.

Out of Control . . . Why You Need a Proc Amp

Processing amplifiers are used to correct errors in the video signal. Generally, they allow you to adjust the video level, color level, black level, and hue. Most time base correctors and frame synchronizers have proc amp controls built into them. If you're not careful, you can create a fairly bad looking picture any time you start adjusting levels. The idea here is to use them only when necessary. If the video signal is already correct, don't use it. Later in the discussion on scopes, I'll cover how to determine if it is a correct signal relative to digital capture.

If your analog signal has too much saturation, turn the color level down a bit (or up, if it looks too washed or pale). Assuming you're using a standalone VCR to play from, you correct the hue with the hue control. If the VCR is timed into a larger system—synchronized with a common house sync—first check that the subcarrier phase adjustment is correct. If that is the case, you may not need to read this because you probably already have the knowledge of correction techniques and system timing. (Timing is beyond the scope of these basic techniques.)

The black level, or pedestal, can be corrected with its proc amp control. If the

(continued)

overall blacks in the signal are too light or too dark, this control can adjust it. Be careful—without a waveform monitor it is difficult to tell if it needs adjusting. The proper level is 7.5 IRE.

Visual Guessing versus Waveforms, Vectors, and TBCs

You cannot always tell if the luminance level of the picture is too high or too low by simply looking at the video monitor. If the peaks are really hot and bright—or the opposite, the blacks really dark with loss of detail—you probably can tell visually, but a waveform monitor makes it easier.

The waveform monitor is basically an oscilloscope designed to monitor composite video signals and is essential in analyzing the analog video signal for sync and video levels. Whether you use a traditional waveform monitor in a separate enclosure, or one built to go into a PC slot, it is used to get the best digital look from the analog signal.

A standard 1-volt peak-to-peak (p-p) signal from VCRs, switchers, cameras, and other video equipment, which is terminated at 75 Ohms, is measured on the waveform monitor as a graph of voltage and time. The voltage is measured vertically and time is measured from left to right. The levels are measured in IRE units. The 1v p-p voltage measurement extends from –40 to 100 IRE, for a total of 140 IRE units. The graduation scale has lines that indicate reference points every 10 IRE units from –40 to 120 IREs.

For our purposes, the settings used are 2H Sweep (two horizontal TV lines are displayed), and the response is either Flat or the IRE filter is on. With a color bar signal connected to the waveform monitor, set the vertical position so that the horizontal blanking level of the signal is at the zero IRE reference point. (The blanking level looks like a solid horizontal line when these settings are used.) This line has little time graduations running horizontally. This reference point divides the scale between sync, which extends down to –40, and video, which rises to 100 IRE units. The setup or pedestal level (or black level) is at 7.5 IRE units. The pedestal from cameras is set at 7.5 so televisions will show the proper amount of black levels when displayed and won't lose detail in those areas. The brightest part of the picture is at the top of the scale. Peak whites are at 100 IRE units. The color burst is 40 IRE units from top to bottom, extending from +20 to –20 IRE.

The auto-exposure systems on cameras are usually set to 100 IRE. They automatically adjust the iris to maintain that level so the brightest parts of the picture will not exceed the peak white limit. Auto black levels can also be used to keep the blacks black. Auto controls are useful when lighting conditions vary, keeping gross errors under control by opening the iris when lighting becomes dark and closing, or stopping down, the iris when light becomes too bright. But automatic compensation can also cause problems. If you're shooting a scene in which there is a very bright,

(continued)

uncontrollable area, the iris will stop down and the rest of the scene can become too dark; most of the picture has little detail. Use caution under various lighting conditions and test your equipment accordingly. What you shoot is usually final, and only some problems are correctable later.

Some highly saturated colors can register values above 100 IRE. This can be a little confusing when viewing the waveform monitor. The color or subcarrier part of the picture stretches above and below the luminance value. In order to separate color from the signal, so that only the black-and-white part of the image is displayed, turn on the IRE filter on the waveform monitor. Now, brightness can be seen by itself, and highly saturated color doesn't skew your view of the luminance that is really in the picture.

When using full-field color bars displayed on the waveform monitor, the chroma should be at the proper upper and lower limits. The top of the white bar to the left is at 77 IRE. (The other type of color bars contain 100 IRE peak white bars.) The top of the yellow and cyan bars are at 100 IRE. The bottom of the green bar extends down to 7.5 IRE, and the bottom of the red and blue bars should be at −16 IRE. The relative color phase and saturation signal affects the size of the bars as displayed on the waveform monitor.

The color phase and burst should be checked on a vectorscope. When bars are displayed on the vectorscope, six small boxes with cross-hairs in them are registered on the vector display. If the phase is correct, the vector from each color bar—displayed as six small dots representing each color bar—will fit inside its relative box. If the vectors are rotated clockwise or counterclockwise, the colors are out of phase. If they are above or below the boxes, they are oversaturated or undersaturated. If you don't have a vectorscope, a "blue gun" monitor can be used as described previously in "Monitor Setup—Visually with a Professional Monitor."

A time base corrector (TBC) is used whenever VCRs are used in the editing suite. Stable sources, such as cameras, do not need TBCs. The general purpose of the TBC is to strip the sync from the video signal and regenerate it. Video tape recorders are mechanical devices. When they play back video, the motors and transports built into the machine can vary in speed and timing. The proper operation of the editing system, for frame-accurate editing and switcher effects, depends on the exact timing of all components of the system at the edit point. If the sync signal, horizontal phase, and subcarrier phase are incorrect, the picture will tear or jump when the edit is performed. When a VCR fluctuates on playback, it causes unstable sync. Since the sync timing is a critical component of the system, the edit cannot be performed accurately. The TBC removes the original sync from the video signal, digitally regenerates it into a clean, stable signal, and outputs it to the video out connectors. Then, you route it to the switcher, computer, or other desired device as input. As a bonus,

(continued)

many TBCs feature digital effects within the TBC before it is output, like freeze frame and strobe.

Most time base correctors have proc amps built in. Using a TBC is best for digitally capturing the video clips because they provide the clean, stable signal you need, plus control over the signal levels. Although you can use a non–time-base-corrected VCR for playback into your capture board, it may not provide the best results.

Digital Capture

Most of the work is in the setup and preparation of the equipment. Now that you are familiar with some of the procedures, connect the VCR output to the digitizing board in your computer. Set up the software per the manual for that device. You'll probably want to adjust settings in the software you are using with the board, so you have a reference point to begin with on the digitizer side. If you have a known good color bar image file in your computer, use it to check your computer screen adjustment. Usually, the only adjustments to these, if any, are in the software.

Input your color bar signal to the digitizer to see what it looks like on the RGB computer monitor. It should look like the bars on your reference monitor. Whatever software adjustments you make to the computer monitor display will affect your visual judgment of the material you are digitizing, so make sure you start from a known reference point and leave it there. Remember, you can also use the blue gel trick when checking your computer screen color bars.

If you can afford to use lots of disk space for your clips, the best quality will be achieved when the original clip is captured at the highest possible level. Once your digitizer is set up to your required specifications, you can begin.

First play the segment through the capture board. Compare how it looks on the RGB screen to the original on the reference monitor. Much of what you do to capture at the best quality is subjective. Clips that contain a lot of black can be the biggest file space savers. The various compression algorithms compare changes from frame to frame. Depending on the compression method, if there is no change in the image, or if there is a lot of black (no color data, less storage required), the data space per frame is smaller; therefore, it takes up less space on the hard disk. All areas in the video clip can contain noise, which can show up as random dots of color sprinkled all over the image. It can be most noticeable in the black areas.

Computer-generated black typically is absolutely black (R-G-B values of 0-0-0) and video black or pedestal is at 7.5 IRE, which really is "almost" black. Most of the time, depending on the type of clip, the captured video will look better with black levels a little closer to computer black. When the black level (pedestal) is lowered in the analog video, those areas of the clip tend to capture with less digital noise. Try

(continued)

lowering the pedestal (with the proc amp) somewhere between 7.5 IRE and 0 IRE (the baseline on the waveform monitor). If you don't have a waveform monitor, take a good guess for this test, but always remember where your proc amp controls are for future reference.

Next, compare the white peaks in the picture on both monitors and the waveform monitor, if you have one. The video level on your proc amp will control this level. If it looks too hot, lower it slightly; conversely, if too dark, raise it. Remember, however, that certain colors such as yellow are highly saturated and may show up on the waveform monitor above 100 IRE. Use the IRE filter to eliminate the chroma from the picture, so you are viewing only luminance or brightness. The idea is to adjust the signal so the peak whites are between 80 and 100 IRE. Some clips can have spikes above 100 IRE and below 80. Use your judgment.

Check the color level of the incoming clip. If it looks oversaturated with a lot of color bleeding—too much chroma in the reds, for example—turn it down a bit. This can also save space in your files. Besides, it doesn't look very good once your clip is finally compressed. If the signal is too pale or washed out looking, try raising the chroma level. In the final compressed clip, the color should be as vibrant and natural as possible.

It All Comes Down to This . . .

You cannot correct for all the problems found in the video source, especially if it wasn't recorded with the proper equipment and production procedures in mind. However, knowing a little more about the principles behind the analog video signal should give you a better idea of how best to try to capture it digitally. Remember, the better the signal going in, the higher the quality when you capture and play it back.

Sometimes, the standards of the original video must be higher than you have available to you. You may need to consult professionals in the video production industry in order to produce the results you require.

Try some trial captures, compress the clips to make the movies, and play them back to see if they meet your requirements.

The nice thing about digital video is that once you've spent the time to get it to look the best possible, it can stay that way forever.

Summary

To briefly review, you need to know your video (and audio, for that matter) source. Take the time to get to know the strengths and weaknesses of as many types of media as you can. If you ever get the chance, try to do a side-by-side comparison of a known subject using analog and then digital signals. Depending on the subject and the way you handle the source, you may not see that big a difference.

Finally, be sure to handle your sources with as much care as possible, starting with the little stuff like cables, through proper signal balance and processing. Taking care takes a little more time, but the end results are worth it.

Part Two

TECHNIQUES

5

DIGITAL VIDEO TECHNIQUES

Over the years, we have created everything from horribly jerky, improperly processed trash up through digital video masterpieces that have pushed the envelope in their quality and playability. During all this time, we have either discovered on our own, or borrowed from others, techniques that helped us achieve and now maintain a high-quality standard.

These run the range from techniques on shooting our own videos through the proper massaging of digital video for the best possible results. This chapter covers many of these techniques, and also includes articles by several other professionals.

If you are looking for pages and pages with hundreds of hints or things to remember and do for each desktop video production you produce, then you've come to the wrong place. And you're in the wrong business. Certainly there are many things to keep in mind, especially when you are just starting, but the real truth is this: If there were hundreds of things we had to remember, then we wouldn't be in this business.

Creating a good product is fairly straightforward. Creating a superior product requires a bit more from each of us. The following pages contain information on how you can positively affect your productions. Do we guarantee that by following each of our steps you will create nothing but masterpieces?

Of course not. In this business, the only guarantee is that everything changes as the technology gets more advanced and the costs come down. What we can tell you is that we use everything in this chapter.

We cover:

- Shooting your own video
- Basic steps for creating good digital video
- Audio processing for your digital video
- Editing techniques
- Effects techniques
- Polishing your production

Shooting It Yourself

There comes a time in the life of a young (or old) digital video producer when your thoughts turn lightly to the subject of shooting your own video. There are great benefits to being in control of what is included in the source video and how it is shot.

For starters, you can control movement, both of the camera and of the subject matter. One of the big offenders in a video source is lots of movement or quick camera pans and zooms. Digital video played at 15 fps does not like lots of movement.

Another benefit is that you can shoot to your own visualization (the good, the bad, and the downright ugly). If you are the type who can sit in a movie or watch television *without* once saying "I would have done *that* differently," then shooting it yourself may not be for you. If you *have* thought something like that, then you might want to look into taking the reins once in a while.

To be fair, there are drawbacks. First, you need to own or rent all of the appropriate video equipment. Second, not everyone is cut out to be a cameraperson or director. Third, you may not have the luxury of the time it often takes to do it yourself.

We're not suggesting that you don't give it a try. Just don't expect to create a Hollywood-style epic the first time.

Among the things we have learned are some "slap yourself up the side of the head" commonsense things, as well as some hard reality lessons. In the first category are little things like:

- Know the camera(s)—We covered a special outdoor sporting event during 1994. Toucan Studios took a camera crew of five and a support crew of four to this multiday event. The cameras used were one SVHS and four Hi-8 cameras. Everyone was aware that frequent color balancing of the camera is mandatory when shooting outside. That we did. Everyone used tripods to get the steadiest shots possible. Everyone set the proper shutter speeds for the lighting conditions. Almost everyone did everything right. What tripped us up was that one person forgot to turn off the camera's built-in time/date stamp. We ended up with eight hours of unusable footage from that camera—some of it vital to the proper coverage of the event. Because of the loss of vital footage, this also fits into the *hard lessons* category.

- Avoid cheap tapes—Earlier in the book we talked about this. This is a lesson that usually must be learned to be believed. "Oh, I've always used this tape on my VCR and the picture looks pretty good" is something that each of us has said at some point. The problem with tape that provides a "pretty good" picture is that any dropouts on the tape translate into noise in the picture, and that means a less than optimum compression.

- Setup—In a few pages, one of our guest authors discusses some of the types of set-ups in which you may find yourself involved. Setting up your shots properly is very important. You must visually balance everything that will appear on camera. You want the main subject of the shot to be prominent, but you also don't want that subject to be the only thing visible. Anything that might be distracting to the viewer should be either removed or made less visible. This is always tricky when dealing with onsite videotaping at a client's location. You can't always remove that picture of Elvis bullfighting on black velvet from behind the Managing Director's desk.

- Light everything professionally—If you are going to shoot it yourself, get yourself a good set of lights. Get enough lights, or know where to rent them, to cover everything from talking heads to full-stage productions with props. The first project an acquaintance of ours did on his own was a one-camera shoot featuring a spokeperson demonstrating a table full of computer products. He only had a pair of low-power lights, so he aimed one at the face of the spokesperson and one down at the products. The results were a five-minute video so full of shadows and harsh shiny spots that the video was scrapped.

Proper Lighting

Proper lighting depends on many things. The lighting professional must take into consideration everything that will appear in the shot. Decisions must be made about what to light.

As you begin shooting your own video, you can experiment with different techniques. Since videotape is inexpensive, you want to experiment. Start by lighting everything from in front. You will notice shadows that can be distracting. Move the lights around. Try putting lights that brighten the shadows of the subject. You can even try techniques of lighting only the main subject and leaving everything else in the shadows.

There are dozens of very good books on lighting techniques. They discuss all of the different types of lights, positioning, the use of filters, and how to create special lighting effects. We strongly suggest that you either purchase books on professional lighting techniques or that you take them out from your local library.

Finally, if in doubt about your own ability to light properly, try contacting a local college. We have found several in our area with film study programs that offer their students as unpaid interns. They already have learned the techniques. What they want is experience.

SHOOTING FOR THE EDIT
by Tam T. Fraser, TAM Communications

Tam Fraser is a veteran executive producer, director, and cameraman, and is the co-founder of Tam Communications, a video production company located in San Jose, California. In his more than fifteen years of experience, he has produced and directed hundreds of television commercials for national and local broadcast, private satellite broadcasts, and corporate communication programs, as well as several music videos. Tam's lengthy awards list includes two Houston International Film Festival Top Honors, a CINE Golden Eagle, two IABC Gold Quills, several Silver Tellys, and a host of others. He has created work for ABC, NASA Ames Research, and Silicon Graphics, and for musicians such as David Grisman. He is currently working as creator and producer of a television series for The Health Channel.

There's probably nothing more frustrating than being in an edit session and realizing that your director forgot to, or didn't, give you enough cover. Cover is referred to as "having enough video with which to edit." It is especially frustrating if you *were* the director and *now* you are the editor.

I believe "shooting for the edit" is about having as many options as possible. It is vitally important when you are editing your video together that you have as many good takes as possible to choose from. The question arises, of course, as to how to keep the raw footage organized. This had always been a daunting task until the

(continued)

advent of nonlinear digital editing. The trick here is to digitize the takes and the material that you need, and nothing more.

Some people get *shooting for the edit* confused with *in-camera editing.* The latter means that you are shooting and the camera is doing your editing. Just so that we are all on the same page, in this brief sidebar I will try to give you a glimpse of what you should consider when shooting for the edit. But realize that an entire book could be written on this subject alone.

Preplanning your video shoot is extremely important in shooting for the edit. And different types of video projects require slightly different processes. A few hints to keep in mind are:

- Once the script is complete, you must begin developing a shot list. The script may come in standard AV format—meaning that the visuals are in the left column and the audio is in the right—or it may be in screenplay format, which is more typical for dialog-oriented productions. Needless to say, both should include a list of all the foreseeable shots that must go into the production.

- Storyboards—picture representations of the proposed action and dialog—may be utilized in place of a shot list. However, I rarely use storyboards in shows that are over five minutes. For short-format productions or "spots," storyboards are good to work with. You are able to visually communicate everything to everyone concerning your vision of the flow and sequence, and how each shot or scene will impact the next.

- Camera techniques: Don't be afraid to experiment a little with different angles. For instance, dutch tilts (any camera tilt off of level, best when performed from a tripod) are very acceptable for interviews and give a refreshing look to interview-based shows. Other camera movements work in this type of production as well. Try using slow pans up to the subjects' faces. (The operative word here is s-l-o-w. Remember, your production eventually will be digital and fast motion means jerky results!)

  The shaky camera technique (cinéma vérité) has become an acceptable look, but I would stay away from this until you perfect the technique. There really *is* a technique to this style of shooting. Needless to say it is *not* one of the best styles to use if your production is going digital.

  Be creative in your composition. If used properly, unusual framing and dutch angles (another name for dutch tilts) can add a whole new dimension to your presentations.

- Always record several minutes of ambient sounds. If your production takes place in several different locations, be sure to record ambient sounds for each. This allows the editor to make smoother sound edits between scenes.

(continued)

You may be responsible for the following types of videos:

1. One person to the camera
2. Several people speaking to the camera
3. Narrator-driven show
4. Interview-based show
5. Roleplay with actors or real people

One Person to the Camera

The simple "one person to the camera" presentation may actually be anything but simple. There are a number of things to consider: Is the on-camera presenter scripted? Are you using a TelePrompTer? What is the experience level of the on-camera presenter?

Suppose that a sales manager needs to do a video that provides direction to the sales force. He says that he works best without a script. He says that he does this a hundred times in front of people with no problem.

It never seems to fail that when these people get in front of a camera, they tend to become stressed and come off less than stellar. There are some people who have a natural video presence and are very good, but for the most part the majority usually lose it. This can be a nightmare for directors and editors alike. Unscripted presentations or outlined presentations tend to be difficult because the presenter becomes too occupied thinking about what is being presented rather than just presenting the information. This in itself requires the utmost concentration.

Basic Considerations When Shooting

- Choose a large conference room if you are not shooting in a studio. It's always preferable to be in a larger room than a smaller. Framing and composition considerations come into effect here, such as having the camera far enough back so that you can get a good wide shot.

- This type of presentation is best shot utilizing two focal lengths: a wide shot and a tight shot. Make sure your wide-shot frame is at least down to the belt level—if not wider. Framing looks a little awkward unless you have something else in the scene with your subject—for example, a large computer and monitor, a video monitor, or an easel. By adding one of these onto your "set" you will be forced to get wide enough to allow for a pleasing shot. Also, it makes for a good cut to close-up. Your close-up should be framed to include the top line of the shoulders.

    By intercutting between the wide and the tight shots, you break up the presentation and keep the viewer interested. You also help the on-camera presenter get

(continued)

through the presentation in a timely manner. As you shoot and the "sales manager" makes his presentation, you are able to stop at any time if he goes off track. Have him gather his thoughts, then back up and repeat what he said just before the mistake occurred. Change to a wide shot or punch in to the close-up and continue moving forward.

- If your presenter is utilizing a TelePrompTer, you can approach the shoot using the same basic technique. However, if a mistake occurs, have the talent read "into the cut." This means having him go back a couple sentences or a paragraph before the "problem" so that the eventual cut you make as the editor looks and *sounds* natural.

If you want more editing options, then have the presenter read the entire presentation from start to finish in a wide shot. Then, move in to the close-up and have him read it all again.

Multiple People Speaking to the Camera

The same techniques just discussed can be utilized for presentations where you have more then one presenter and you want it to appear that you are using more than one camera.

The Narrator-Driven Show

One of the more difficult scenarios when shooting for the edit is a narrator-driven show. By and large, this constitutes a video presentation that is visually driven by the narration, and utilizes images edited together to tell a story. Shooting efficiency in this type of presentation varies on your knowledge of how the edited show should look and feel. For instance, are you cutting from one scene that zooms in to another that is zooming out?

Shooting for this type of edit requires that you overshoot (shoot far more than you need using as many possible setups as possible) unless you know how the show will finally flow together. In my earlier years when I did all of my own editing, I knew as the director/cameraman how I was going to tell the story when I was editing it.

Now that I hand off the editing to an off-line editor, it is really my job to shoot each scene in combinations: a static wide shot, a static close-up, slow zoom-in, medium zoom-in, faster zoom-in, and then the same for the zoom-outs. Of course if you are incorporating dolly shots, this adds yet another dimension.

Not to mention pan shots, which I will caution you to *not* use since pans are not aesthetically pleasing when used in a digital format.

(continued)

The Interview-Based Show

When shooting for an interview-based show, you should consider "talk room" as well as which side the interviewee is looking at. Talk room is aligning the person in your shots off-center with the extra space kept to the side the person is looking toward. For instance, if your interviewer is looking to camera right, frame your shot so the interviewer is in the camera left area; the extra room is between the interviewer and the off-camera interview subject. The same goes for setting up the shots of the responding interview subject. Simply reverse this setup.

I tend to break interview shots up if I'm utilizing more than one interview subject. Doing this tends to even things out and helps keep the edits from jump cutting. This is still kind of tricky because when you're shooting you really may not know how the interviews will be cut together.

It goes without saying that sometimes you get people looking in the same direction back to back as well as at the same focal length. That means it looks a little jumpy or as if someone has just changed into another person. This is one place where a good shot list can be a real saver. If nothing else, write down each shot as you take it and check to see that you don't get confused.

Suggest to the interviewer and the subject that they pause for about a second between the end of a question and the answer, and again between the end of an answer and the asking of the next question. This leaves enough quiet space to perform proper edits and keeps everyone from "stepping on" each other's words.

Another hint for this type of production is to remind the interviewer to alternate between verbal and physical acknowledgments to the interview subject. This keeps the interviewer's responses more interesting.

Roleplay

For a scripted roleplay with actors, again you want to have as many choices as possible. I tend to make sure that I cover these scenarios in the classic wide shot–medium shot–close-up scenario. By shooting these presentations in this style, you can save yourself invaluable time and provide yourself with the best product.

There are many considerations to make from the point of view of technicality, lighting, sound, and continuity. Basic rules of editing apply in these situations—such as not crossing the line, making sure you have good ambient noise to cover over some edits. I can't stress enough here that you need to make sure that you get your talent to repeat everything for each angle shot. Time and again I have edited work for other directors who, for whatever reason, didn't get full coverage and, ultimately, the final product suffered because it wasn't fully covered.

(continued)

Conclusion

As I said earlier, an entire book could be dedicated to this subject alone. Just remember that as you're shooting, you will make life much easier for yourself or your editor if you go into the shoot knowing what you need and end up having options to choose from.

Acquiring Equipment

As with anything associated with the desktop video studio, shooting your own video takes time and practice. It is not always the smartest or the most cost-effective thing to do, but there are times when creating everything from scratch can give you a superior product. If you have a creative nature, you may even surprise yourself with the results you can achieve by "letting yourself go."

It also doesn't hurt to do it yourself a few times so you better understand what is going on in other video shoots. This really helps you speak intelligently with the people creating the video and can lead to better source materials for your desktop video productions.

Just don't fall into the category of people who know just enough to be either dangerous or annoying!

The type of equipment used when shooting your own video is usually based upon two things:

- The project requirements
- Your budget

Of course, you want to use the best possible equipment so you can get the best possible source materials. But you don't want to go into hock just to pay for the equipment. This is a balancing act. If your project will be delivered ultimately as quarter-screen, 15-fps CinePak-compressed video, then you may notice no difference between a BetaCam SP source and a SVHS source. However, if your project is to be edited on computer and saved back out to tape as full-screen, 30-fps video, almost anything less than BetaCam SP or ¾-inch (Hi-8 in a pinch) will not be adequate. Of course, there are exceptions. If your full-screen project doesn't need to have a broadcast-quality look to it, Hi-8 may be more than sufficient. It all comes down to knowing what the end result will be.

Do you need to run out and purchase all this equipment? Must you have an entire set of lights, filters, and stands? Should you invest in a full suite of BetaCam SP equipment? No, not if you live in or near a city with a video rental company. Most fair-sized cities have at least one. We use BetaCam SP for most of our corporate projects. For the rest of our projects we use source materials in almost equal amounts from ¾-inch, Hi-8, and SVHS sources. Although we do own ¾-inch and Hi-8 equipment, we don't own a BetaCam SP camera or tape deck. We rent them for the exact days they are required. This saves a large up-front cost and allows us to spread out the cost of using it over just those days when it is necessary.

The interpretation? We have spent only about one-third the cost of ownership on rental fees during the past two years. This way, we get to use the most recent equipment, spend less, and are not burdened with maintenance. And we think that is a winning combination.

Capturing and Producing Digital Video

Given many months and at least a dozen projects, you begin to hit upon little techniques that give you better end results, that make your work go more smoothly and quickly, and that help you avoid many of the petty little annoyances that seem to crop up as you create and process digital video.

That's fine. That is exactly how we did it and what's good enough for us . . .

Actually, we rely on shared information and hints from others in this business all the time. This sharing generally happens spontaneously as others discover something great and then tell us, or we discover it and tell them. We don't mind sharing tips and techniques, so this section features many of our hints for producing better digital video.

This section also discusses the general steps we use every day in our business.

Digitizing Tips and Techniques

There are literally hundreds of tips that might be categorized here, but we have chosen to list and discuss the top twenty or so that seem applicable across the broadest range of software and hardware.

Once you have your equipment set up and adjusted correctly, you are ready to perform the actual capture and processing. The software and techniques you employ here will, and should, vary depending on the requirements of the finished product—and how many times have we said *that* before?

No matter what software you decide to use, there are certain techniques you can try to get the best capture possible. Since the act of capturing digital video to a digital storage medium (your hard drive) almost always involves compression—or you don't get very many second of video per gigabyte—there is always a level of data loss. By carefully selecting the appropriate compressor and adjusting its settings, the end results of such data loss can be minimal.

Of course, the more data you capture (full-screen versus quarter-screen; 30 frames versus 15 frames; unlimited data rate versus restrained data rate), the better the source you will work with in the editing stage. Don't go hog-wild, but try to capture at the highest data rate possible.

System hints and tips. Following, in no particular order, but all important in some manner to successful digital video creation, are some of the system-based hints that we keep listed in our studio. Lots of these are common sense, but some of them may surprise you if you are new to this field. Since we do all of our capture, processing, and editing on Macintosh 840AV computers, all of these hints are applicable specifically for the Macintosh, but many of them are applicable if you are performing your work on a PC.

- The 32-bit addressing mode must be on. To function properly, most digital video applications require 32-bit addressing to be on.

- Put 32 MB or more of RAM in your system. You can never have too much RAM. If you are digitizing very short clips (and have slower hard drives), digitizing directly to your system's RAM can give you the best performance.

- Upgrade your VRAM to the maximum for your system. It is nearly impossible to do accurate work on a 256-color system when everything you work with is in thousands or millions of colors.

- Many digital video applications are actually memory hogs, but their manufacturers set their suggested memory low enough for most systems to use. Set each application's memory allocation (from the Get Info box) to a point several megabytes higher than its "suggested" size. This allows for larger files to be processed, and makes many smaller jobs run faster. Some applications will try to use all available memory in your system. If you encounter this, set the memory allocation to about 1 megabyte less than your available RAM. These same memory-intensive applications usually do not work well with other applications running at the same time.

- DO NOT use the Virtual Memory feature or RAM disks! Many programs suffer conflicts with virtual memory because this is actually a cache scheme going out to the hard disk. VM and RAM disks take away both processing time and access time to the disk. This same caution is applicable for the use of memory-doubling utilities.

- Use as few extensions in your system as possible. The greater the number of extensions loaded in your system, the greater the performance degradation. Use only what is minimally required to complete the tasks at hand (QuickTime, Sound Manager, and so forth, plus any extensions created by your digital video applications). The use of Apple's Extension Manager makes shutting off extensions a breeze.

- Turn File Sharing off (in the Control Panel) and turn AppleTalk off (in the Chooser). Because of their requirements for processing cycles, these have a big impact on system performance while capturing video. Be sure to restart your computer before using your software.

  If you are creating a CD-ROM, *be very sure* to have File Sharing and AppleTalk turned off, and reboot your system prior to saving anything to the disk on which you are mastering your project. If you break this rule, you will most likely end up with a CD-ROM that contains invisible alias information requiring that all or some of your original drives be mounted on each and every computer before those computers can access the CD-ROMs files. This is particularly bad if you press hundreds of CD-ROMs and give them to people who don't have all of your drives mounted to their systems. We have seen even the best companies make this mistake.

- If you will be making a CD-ROM from your work, always master your final work on a freshly formatted hard drive. This is a good idea even if you are not going to CD; the more contiguous your digital video files, the smoother they will play and the less chance of skipping frames while the drive searches for the next piece of information.

- If you have a Macintosh Quadra 605, 610, 630, 650, 700, 800, 900, or 950, use Apple's SCSI Manager 4.3 extension. You should have formatted your drives with a SCSI Manager 4.3–compliant utility software program such as *Hard Disk Toolkit* or *Silver Lining.* We don't mention the Macintosh 660AV and 840AV because they already have SCSI Manager 4.3 built into their ROMs.

- Before recording video clips, defragment your hard disk. Use an empty hard disk if possible for your captures. Frames of captured video can be lost when the hard-disk heads have to jump around to find empty space to write to.

- Do not have any other applications running in the background. This rule goes for everything, including "invisible" applications such as scheduling/meeting apps and print spoolers. They all steal valuable processor time. Applications that run "in the background" have a major impact on your capture performance.

- If you use external amplified speakers on your capture station, disconnect them and use the computer's built-in speaker when you set the audio capture level. If you set audio levels based on the external speaker volume, you probably will set it far too low for the end users. We have made that mistake far too many times.

The results are usually fine when the target computers all have amplified speaker systems, but when using a computer with just a built-in speaker, people will think they just went deaf. The quality and positioning of the speakers in many computer models leaves a lot to be desired, which is why there is such a wide variety of external powered speakers for PCs. But you can't expect that your audience will have them.

If the audio is set to the proper level for the internal (low power) speaker, then amplified speakers will be fine.

- The Cache control in the Memory Control Panel must be set to 32 K. QuickTime requires this setting. Playback and recording of movies will be impaired with any other cache setting.

- In MovieShop (a utility application supplied to developers with earlier QuickTime releases), the application seems to assume that you are going to have a minimum audio track of 11 KHz 8-bit attached to your video. This normally requires about 10 K per second of data. Should you not have audio attached to your video, you will want to set your requested data rate at least 10 K higher than your required end results so that you take advantage of this unused data space. (For double-speed CDs in this case, set the data to 190 for Windows and 250 for the Macintosh.)

- If you create QuickTime movies on your Macintosh, and your work will be used on Windows-capable PCs, be sure to save them as self-contained movies, selecting to save them as "cross-platform" (or as "playable on non-Apple computers," depending on your application). This generates a "single data fork" movie that will play on both Macintosh and Windows-based PCs. Be sure to use a name that contains the PC-standard "8.3" character naming convention.

- If you play a QuickTime movie partway through prior to saving it, be sure to move the slider control all the way back to the beginning of the movie before you save. This ensures that the movie will always start at the beginning.

- If you change the screen size of a QuickTime movie (such as viewing a quarter-screen movie in a doubled mode or a half-size mode), be sure to return it to its correct (normal) size prior to saving it again. Otherwise, it will save out in the larger (or smaller) size. This is usually okay for going to a smaller size, but your file will lack enough data to make up for the increased requirements of a larger than normal size.

- You can import PICT files directly into MoviePlayer (a part of Quick-Time) and then select your preferred compression scheme, bit depth, and quality under the Options setting. They may then be saved out as QuickTime movies. A single PICT image is saved out as a QuickTime movie of about one second.

- Likewise, you *may* export any frame from a movie into a picture file. However, we recommend that you use the Copy and Paste features to make such a still frame into a picture. Just locate the frame you want, select Copy and then open a good graphics program such as Photoshop and paste the frame into a new document. If you want to perform any processing on that image, do so. Then, save it as the file type of your choice.

- You may wish to set the poster frame of some QuickTime movies to a frame other than the first one (the default frame). To do so, open your movie in MoviePlayer, locate a preferred frame, then select Set Poster Frame from the Movie menu.

- Use your highest-performance computer to do your movie digitizing. The higher the performance, the less likely there will be any skipped frames during the record process. This is also true for digitizer cards that have hardware compression.

- Test samples of your final compressed movies on the lowest-performance computer system that will be using them. This will let you know if you are compressing the movies appropriately. If you or your client do not have ready access to such a computer, you may want to see if a local school or library will allow you to use one of theirs.

Toucan's Steps to Better Digital Movies

We've come up with the following generic tips to help you use digital video to create movies that play well. It doesn't matter what your final compressor will be, as these simple steps are accomplished before the compression.

These are our guiding blueprint for whatever we do. Some of what is listed next has been talked about elsewhere in the book. Bear with us if you think you've heard it before. As we have said all along, we realize that your specific projects are different from ours and that the techniques and tools that you use depend on the requirements of that project.

Begin with the best possible source. To achieve the best digitization and compression, you need to capture your video from the highest possible quality source, with the least amount of "noise." If you have any say so in the creation of the source video, request that pans and zooms be kept to a minimum and that quick action or sudden moves on the part of the actors be reduced. Remember that solid colors compress the best.

Use the highest-quality video format you can and always try to use first-generation sources (no duplicates of duplicates of duplicates). In descending order of their quality and favorability, the most frequently used sources are:

- BetaCam SP
- ¾-inch or Hi-8
- Laserdisc or S-VHS
- VHS

Use quality equipment; use it right. You don't have to use a poor-grade source to get poor results; just throw in a set of lousy or damaged cables between your source and your computer. If you want quality results, use good equipment—and use it to its best advantage. For instance, if you have an option between composite video and S-Video, use S-Video. Use the shortest possible cable runs and use shielded cables.

Keep your equipment adjusted. No two monitors are exactly alike, but you can alleviate grave differences by adjusting yours to a known good color bar source. (See the sidebar in Chapter 4 on signal quality and processing.)

The following adjustments can be made on most video digitizer cards:

- Saturation
- Hue
- Contrast
- Sharpness
- Brightness
- White level
- Black level

This is another area in which experimentation is necessary. You will also want to make adjustments each time you change video sources, and even each time the scenes on a single source vary noticeably. One scene may have a lot of light and the next be a bit dark. You can help equalize them by adjusting the picture settings.

You can make these adjustments through QuickTime's Video Settings, accessible from any video digitizing application. The defaults are okay, but you are much better off making changes to these settings that specifically match your video. Black level is especially important, as any noise in what you believe to be black does not allow for the most complete compression.

Grab using JPEG or RAW. If you have enough RAM and hard disk space, and can control the source deck, capturing your video frame-by-frame in the raw RGB format will give you the best source possible with which to work. The problem is that this is exceedingly slow, and you need a lot of RAM and hard-disk space, both of which are very expensive. The best compromise is to use a real-time JPEG hardware digitizer card. Even if your final results will not be JPEG-compressed, capturing at JPEG's highest quality gives you the best digitized source from which to work.

Although it uses less disk space than RAW captures, high-quality JPEG requires a bit more hard-disk space than capturing with some other codecs, but it usually means a superior end product even if you will eventually use a codec such as CinePak or Indeo. If you can't afford one of these cards, or don't have 64+ MB of RAM, use Apple's Video codec at its highest setting with your digitizer card. Your frame rate and window size will be limited, but you'll get good results.

Capture sound at 22 KHz. Unless you are creating an audio CD, chances are that your playback device has only moderate fidelity. It isn't necessary to capture sound at CD sampling rates (44.1 KHz); 22 KHz is the standard sound rate for Macintosh computers and will give you the best overall quality sound. Capture in 16-bit stereo for the best sound quality. If you need to save space, capture or process your sounds from stereo to mono (a 50 percent savings) or downsample to 11.127 KHz, 16-bit to save even more space.

We don't suggest using 11 KHz, 8-bit mono if your audio contains anything other than voices.

Select the appropriate frame size. The rule of thumb here is that the larger the frame size, the more information that must be stored and used for each frame. Although not rare, it is unlikely that you will do the majority of your digital video work in full-screen, unless tape is your final destination. Although your choices are almost unlimited, some popular standards are:

- 160 × 120 (good for use with the Video codec)
- 240 × 180 (good for use with the Video or CinePak codec)
- 320 × 240 (good for use with the CinePak codec)

In order for your video to function properly, it is very important that your frame size be set up in multiples of 4 pixels. You would not use 225 × 193, for instance; QuickTime just doesn't handle odd dimensions well.

If you are inserting a non-full-size movie into a full-size screen, you will also gain better playability if the left edge of your movie begins on a pixel that is also a multiple of 4.

Select the appropriate frame rate. Setting the most appropriate frame rate depends a lot on your source video. If it comes to you at full-screen, 30 frames per second, your choices run from 5 fps (very nasty!) up to 30 fps. Generally, the smaller the window size the higher the frame rate you can have. (Refer back to the rubber band analogy in Chapter 1.) In the low- to midrange computers (anything with a 68030 or 86386 running at 25 MHz or faster) 15 fps, quarter-screen movies can play very successfully using only CinePak or Indeo compression. High-performance computers can give you acceptable quarter-screen, 24–30 fps playback using CinePak.

If your source was shot on film (24 frames per second) and then transferred to videotape, your best choices is 12 fps—which gives you about the same quality as reducing 30 fps video to 15 fps.

One thing you should understand is that when 24 fps film is transferred to 30 fps video, six additional frames are added to the source frames for each second of video. Usually, new frames are created by adding two adjacent film frames, which gives a blurred appearance to those frames. Sometimes this slight blurring is noticeable, sometimes not.

Edit and create effects without compressing. Most editors and effects applications allow you to perform your editing and effects steps and compress your video all at the same time. If all you are doing is a simple edit and compression, this is okay. However, if you are going to do more to your video, or if you are unsure if this will be the final version, don't lose source quality by compressing now, and possibly compressing again later. Use no compression or highest-quality JPEG for your intermediate versions of movies.

If you have performed all of your edits, transitions, effects, and so forth, and find that it is time to compress your final movie into the end product, now is the time to use the codec that is needed for playback. If you have many movies to do, you may want to take a look at a tool we frequently use—MovieShop—for batch compressing the movie clips. Other editors such as Premiere also offer batch services.

Use the appropriate codec for final compression. Regardless of your source, using the wrong compression scheme can seriously damage a digital video project. Use JPEG for CD-ROM playback, and you are doomed to have movies that play about one frame out of every ten, and seem to take forever to draw each frame. Even assuming that you use the appropriate compressor, such as CinePak for your CD-ROM–based movies, there are several setting that can help or hinder proper compression and playback. Following are four things to consider.

Understand the data rate required. For Macintosh computers, single-speed CD-ROM drives have an effective data transfer rate of about 150 kps, with double-speed drives offering about 300 kps. This is not, however, the sustainable data rate. Various processing overheads cause the actual throughput to be less than the drive's maximum. Windows computers with CD-ROM drives have sustained data rates that are at least 25 percent slower than those on Macintosh computers. For instance, a PC with a 486/33 MHz processor and a double-speed CD-ROM drive may only be able to sustain an effective data rate of 95 to 110 kps.

After importing a movie to compress, you must set the *data rate* to be compatible with the sustainable rate of the playback system. Even though QuickTime 2.0 has greatly improved CD-ROM playback performance, we have found that a data rate of 240 kps for double-speed CD playback on the Macintosh or a rate 180 kps for double-speed CD playback on a PC provides the broadest compatibility.

Adjust the video settings. To optimize the compression and playback of your movies, you need to adjust the video compression settings. Depending on the compression codec you choose, you may have all or only some of the following choices:

- The *Video Quality* should be set appropriately for the functionality of the codec. This is not always 100 percent. For instance, selecting 100 percent (or "highest quality" for JPEG) may be overkill. Most times, a setting of about 75 percent is quite sufficient. This keeps the quality up and the data per frame down. But you would not use a setting of anything but 100 percent for a CinePak-compressed movie. Anything less and the quality drops off a cliff. This is because CinePak quality is set by using the *Data Rate* settings. When using CinePak, always have the Quality setting set to 100 percent, or "highest."

- The *Frame Rate* depends on both your edited master material and your final use. Keeping the frame rate up—preferably at 15 fps—gives you fairly smooth motion with little noticeable jumping. If, however, you captured your video at a rate of, say, 10 fps, then upping to 15 fps will only increase the data rate and give you no beneficial results.

- The *Key Frames* setting should be related to the frame rate of your video. Generally, you will select one key frame per second. (If your video is at 15 fps, then you set to have a key frame every fifteen frames.) Depending on the content in your video, and the codec used, the key frame rate may need to be more or less frequent than one per second. For instance, Indeo works best with a key frame every four frames. Through testing your content and making many movies over time, you will be able to judge the appropriate key frame rates more easily.

- Restraining the *Data Rate* is mandatory when dealing with a final delivery medium such as CD-ROM. Remember: 240 kps for Macintosh double-speed drive playback and 180 kps for Windows systems.

  These numbers include the data rate for the movie's audio. We discuss audio considerations later in this chapter, but the rule of thumb is to expect to use between 10 and 40 kps for the audio portion of the movie.

Sound settings. If your compression application allows you to select alternate settings for your audio, be careful. Keeping the audio clean means keeping the level of data up. There isn't a lot that sounds good at low sampling rates. Because the standard Macintosh sound rate is 22 KHz, you get the highest-quality audio by resampling to 22 KHz. Be aware that with higher audio rates, less "room" remains for the data rate of the video; the lower the video data rate, the less detail. This is a balancing act.

As discussed earlier, you can resample your audio from stereo to mono, and from 22 KHz to 11 KHz, but you should keep it in 16-bit format whenever possible. Voice-only tracks *may* be resampled to 11 KHz, 8-bit mono, but don't expect perfect sound. In most cases, the less audio data and more video data, the better your end movies look.

If your application doesn't let you change audio settings, don't worry; chances are that it simply defaults to whatever the source rate is.

Cropping and scaling your movies. You may need to crop or scale your movies. One reason is that some video sources have a horizontal phase shift that can't be adjusted. This results in a black band, several pixels wide, running along the right or left side of the movie window. This occurs because the digitizer hardware sees the whole video signal and it digitizes exactly what it sees. You won't see the band watching a TV because the TV overscans the video by about 5 percent, and that extra video is "off the screen."

If you can't adjust this *before* digitizing, you need to crop it away after you have digitized the clip. If the movie was captured at 320 × 240 and you've cropped 4 pixels off the right side, you could leave it that way. If the final movie must be exactly 320 × 240 (for instance, if it must fit into and fill a window in a background), you will need to scale the movie back up to the appropriate size.

If your compression application lets you resize your movies, do so with the following caveat:

Make sure the new numbers you select for your movies have horizontal and vertical dimensions in multiples of 4, or the compression and playback may not be optimal. (Some applications will even notify you if they detect a nonoptimal window size.)

Once your settings are registered, all that remains is to click OK and sit back. Most compression schemes require a bit of time; some take up to a minute or more per second of final movie.

One last suggestion: If you are working with a large movie, and you aren't absolutely sure that your settings are the optimum ones, try copying a small sample (5–10 seconds) into a separate file and experimenting on that.

Now that you have heard from us about some of our tips and hints, let's hear from someone in the industry about her hints and techniques for getting better digital video.

MAKING GREAT CINEPAK MOVIES
by Karen Dillon

Ms. Dillon presently is the director of video marketing at Radius. For the past five years, she has been a marketing manager for Macintosh video hardware and has been involved with such award-winning products as Video Spigot and Thunder/24. Before becoming involved with the Macintosh, Karen was an engineering manager at Hewlett-Packard in their networking product lines. She has an MBA from Stanford and a BSEE from the Massachusetts Institute of Technology.

Digitizing video is part art and part science. As with any creative endeavor, the key is not only to understand the particulars of the media—in this case, digital data—but to understand how it will be viewed.

Before any editing can be done, the video must first be digitized. The process of digitization converts the information from the tape format, which is "analog" information, to a form that the computer can understand and manipulate—digital information. During digitization, you can make a big difference in the quality of your final product.

Before the digital video can be utilized in the majority of instances, especially on CD-ROMs, it must be compressed. Compression is the process of reducing the amount of storage space that a digitized video clip requires, with minimal impact upon image quality. This is another place where you can make or break a digital video.

(continued)

Making CinePak Movies

The CD-ROM market is booming; the installed base of drives is growing at an unprecedented rate. Yet, until SuperMac developed the CinePak technology, video was scarce on CD-ROMs. It was difficult to compress the enormous files small enough to fit more than a few minutes on a disc. It was even more difficult to create smooth-motion video because of the slow data rates of the CD media.

The CinePak video compression of SuperMac's software lets each video frame occupy a fraction of its original size while retaining image quality. CinePak is scalable, taking advantage of whatever processing power is available from its host system, running at the highest performance possible.

Because CinePak compression is software-based, it does not require that the viewing system contain any special hardware. It is possible to compress full-length movies into CinePak's 320 × 240 pixel (quarter-screen) format and record them on CD-ROMs.

Following are some helpful hints in making CinePak movies.

Keep the Video Source as Pristine as Possible

Compression is possible because of spatial and temporal redundancy between video frames. The biggest issue is in keeping the source signal as free from noise as possible. The very random nature of noise drastically reduces the redundancy between frames and can inhibit its detection. As a result, frame-to-frame compression rates drop.

The light-sensitive receptors in today's video cameras generate noise in low-light conditions. If possible, use good lighting. If not, expect that your compressed video will not be as small as it could be.

The quality of the recording medium is also a factor. When possible, Hi-8 or better should be used, with BetaCamSP being preferred. The lower the video standard (consumer VHS is about the worst), the more likely you are to have noisy video.

Adjust the Decoder for Proper White/Black Levels

The CinePak compressor performs well with signals that contain an even distribution of luminance and chrominance levels. Adjusting the DigitalFilm decoder (in Adobe Premiere, under the *Movie Capture→Video Input→Image* menu) to the following levels improves this distribution for a higher-quality CinePak encoding:

Hue	50%
Saturation	60%
Brightness	60%
Contrast	60%
Sharpness	0%
Black level	100%
White level	0%

(continued)

For the perfectionist, distribution can be checked by capturing a single frame from your source, loading it into Adobe Photoshop, and performing a *histogram*. Adjusting the input parameters of the DigitalFilm card for a wider distribution and *iterating* this process yields improved image quality.

Capture Using the Highest-Quality JPEG Your System Allows

At higher compression ratios, JPEG can introduce artifacts that add correlated noise to the video stream upon decompression. This noise reduces not only the quality of the video but also the CinePak compressibility. Increasing the quality of the JPEG capture reduces these artifacts. Using fast drives, and an add-in fast SCSI-II controller, enables capture at the highest rates.

If cost or availability prohibits the use of faster, larger hard drives, reduce the capture rate from 30 fps to the target rate of the CinePak movie. Since capturing at 640 × 480 allows a higher-quality resize in the preprocessing (explained following), it is preferred to reduce the frame rate before you consider reducing the capture size.

Resize and Filter with CoSA AfterEffects

Once a video has been captured, CoSA AfterEffects can be used to maintain the quality of the source during resizing operations. Additionally, CoSA offers some preprocessing of the video that can improve the quality of the CinePak compressor.

If the target size of the CinePak video is to be different from the capture size, use CoSA AfterEffects for the resizing. CoSA AfterEffects resizes using a bi-cubic spline that maintains the linearity of the video images. Adobe Premiere uses a nearest-neighbor method that introduces aliasing artifacts. Capturing with DigitalFilm at 640 × 480 and resizing with CoSA AfterEffects prevents these artifacts.

The method for processing the video is simple. First, in CoSA AfterEffects, open your video source file. Create a new Composition. Select the video source in the project window and drag its window into the composition window. In the properties window, select "scale" and resize to the target size. Then, select the Gaussian filter (Effect→Gaussian Blur) and slide the control to "0.4." Finally, make your movie, making sure "PhotoJPEG" is selected as the compression method and the quality slider is set to "Most." To conserve disk space, you may also select the target frame rate. Click "OK" and wait for the process to complete.

Residual noise and JPEG-transition ringing adversely affect the CinePak compression quality. During the resizing, the application of a Gaussian Blur filter (set at 0.4) smooths out JPEG ringing and reduces noise without adversely affecting the video.

Know Your Application

You probably work with four main types of shots. By understanding your application, you can determine the suitability of changing the window size and frame rate to suit

(continued)

the performance limitations of your system. Following are some common examples of digital video applications and how they are affected by performance issues:

- *Talking heads:* The most important issue with talking heads is audio/video synchronization—the lips must be sync'ed with the audio for best performance. A full 30 fps is not always needed. Many training clips use 15 fps for tight talking head shots with satisfactory results. Fifteen fps is half the normal frame rate, and therefore requires half the storage space and transfer rate of comparably sized full motion (or 30 fps) video. Since a talking head typically fills the frame, a smaller than full-screen size (i.e., 240 × 180) can be used without sacrificing view ability. You also may want to cut the frame rate to 15 fps if your delivery platform doesn't have the speed to support full 30 fps playback.

- *Panning shots:* Long, slow pans require the highest frame rate for the smoothest performance. If you can't achieve a full 60 fields per second, then evaluate your real need for them in the final production. If your system is at all prone to dropped frames, long, slow pans will show them. If you must have such pans, consider lowering the quality (increasing the compression ratio) to reduce the overall data rate in order to avoid dropped frames. Most viewers find dropped frames more objectionable than increased JPEG artifacts.

- *Action scenes:* Short, fast action scenes hide many digitizing problems. These are ideal if you want to add "demo appeal" or if you have performance problems. One thing to keep in mind, however, is the faster the motion of objects and characters on the screen, the more likely you are to notice "jumping" at slower frame rates.

- *Panoramic scenes:* Beautiful, large-scale scenes require full-screen video. If you reduce them to a quarter or smaller screen, your shot of the Grand Canyon will look like a postage stamp. So use them at full-screen or find something else!

Conclusion

Making high-quality CinePak movies is easy when you remember to:

- Keep video pristine.
    - —Hi-8 or better recording medium
    - —Good lighting to reduce noise
- Set up decoder for proper white and black levels.

Hue	50%
Saturation	60%
Brightness	60%

(continued)

Contrast	60%
Sharpness	0%
Black level	100%
White level	0%

(These parameters are for DigitalFilm, but they're also a good place to start for other digital video capture cards.)

- Capture using the highest-quality JPEG your system allows.
- Resize and filter with CoSA AfterEffects.
  —Resize from 640 × 480 using CoSA AfterEffects.
  —Filter using Gaussian Blur 0.4%.
- Know your application.

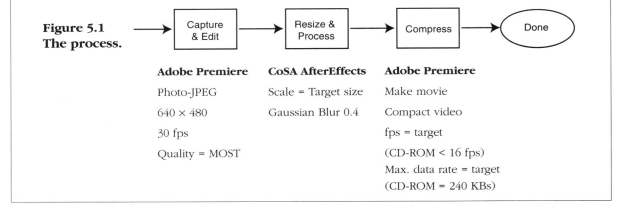

**Figure 5.1
The process.**

Adobe Premiere	**CoSA AfterEffects**	**Adobe Premiere**
Photo-JPEG	Scale = Target size	Make movie
640 × 480	Gaussian Blur 0.4	Compact video
30 fps		fps = target
Quality = MOST		(CD-ROM < 16 fps)
		Max. data rate = target
		(CD-ROM = 240 KBs)

We continue to say throughout this book that your best course is to experiment. What we have just discussed, and what Ms. Dillon mentions, is fine for many digital video applications, but nothing is right for everything.

Audio for Digital Video

A big component of many digital video projects is audio. If you have ever heard a compact disc, you know how good digital audio can sound. Just as with digital video, good digital audio begins with the source. From there, it usually must go through processing in order to be used successfully with video.

When using audio in your video—and we are the first to admit that we rarely *don't* have audio—you need to be aware of a couple things. You need to understand that audio takes up both space and processing bandwidth, and that audio can be adjusted—within limits—to accommodate almost any playback scenario.

Digital audio is saved in exactly the same manner as digital video. It is saved as samples of the original. In audio CDs, the sampling rate is 44.1 KHz (44,100 samples per second). Digital audiotape (DAT) uses 48 KHz sampling. Each sample has a number of bits of data, generally 8 or 16 bits per sample, and then there are the two tracks for stereo, one sample per track. This equates to a data rate of 172 K per second for 44.1 KHz, 16-bit stereo!

If the audio is going to be processed, mixed, or "sweetened" by an audio editing application, then we suggest that you digitize the audio at a data rate that is higher than your eventual output. This will maintain fidelity throughout the editing process and give you cleaner-sounding audio when you finally subsample the audio to its delivery sample rate.

That brings up the trade-offs. Different sampling rates offer different fidelity. Since you probably don't need CD-quality audio for your digital video productions, you can get by on lower sampling rates. Just don't go too low or the fidelity gets pretty awful. Our ears are much more sensitive to bad audio than our eyes are to video. Our eyes are very forgiving in that dropped frames can go by unnoticed—our brains tend to fill in missing information—but our ears can pick up even the slightest of aural imperfections. Great audio can make mediocre video very watchable; mediocre audio can kill a great video.

Here is a quick list of some of the different sampling rates and their corresponding data and storage requirements:

- Stereo, 16-bit, sampled at 48 KHz (great stereo sound; DAT quality); requires 187.5 KB per second, 11.25 MB per minute of audio.

- Stereo, 16-bit, sampled at 44.1 KHz (great stereo sound; may be overkill); requires 176 KB per second, 10.5 MB per minute of audio.

- Stereo, 16-bit, sampled at 22 KHz (good stereo sound for most projects); requires 86 KB per second, 5.25 MB per minute of audio.

- Monaural, 16-bit, sampled at 22 KHz (good for almost everything); requires 44 KB per second, 2.6 MB per minute of audio.*

- Monaural, 8-bit, sampled at 11 KHz (good for voice-only audio); requires 11 KB per second, 660 KB per minute of audio.*

*These two audio sample rates are the most common ones used for final QuickTime movies. They offer the best trade-offs on performance versus fidelity. The 22 KHz rate is used when music is part of the audio content. 11 KHz is used when only vocals are involved or the playback systems are entry level and if video quality is more important.

Almost everything we do uses either 22 KHz stereo, 16-bit, or 22 KHz mono, 16-bit. On those occasions where we need to save a short presentation to a floppy diskette, we have gone down to 11 KHz mono, 8-bit, but the result is usually a bit disappointing.

One thing to note is that dropping down from stereo to mono has the same data rate results as dropping your sampling rate by half. For instance, a minute of 44.1 KHz 16-bit mono has the same data rate (and file size) as a minute of 22 KHz 16-bit stereo.

Having music in the background of a video, even one with a narration or other sounds, can greatly add to the overall experience. You should think about investing in a music library. These usually come in sets of CD-ROMs, and range from acid rock to country to classical. There are also libraries that specialize in certain types of music.

For your first investment, we suggest one of the general-purpose libraries. Look for something with a reasonable number of different tracks—something with at least 100 different pieces. Read the labels carefully. Some libraries consist of a few different pieces of music, but with up to a dozen cuts of each piece in varying lengths, from a few seconds up to a minute or more. Although it is nice to have the ability to pick a 15-second music clip for a 15-second video, we prefer to have more variety than more versions. We frequently cut down longer tracks using audio-processing software such as Alaska Software's DigiTrax.

Using music effectively requires you to match the action or theme of a video to appropriate music. Watch your video, then load in a music CD. Play a few tracks, picturing the video in your mind. We suggest that you not play more than three or four tracks before you go back to the video to remind yourself of what you are trying to match. This will keep you "centered."

Once you find a good piece of music, load it and any other audio track(s) into your audio software and adjust the balance of each element. You don't want the music to be too loud when compared to other audio; likewise, you want to set the volume high enough so that it can be heard. Sometimes music works best when you set it at a medium volume to start, then back it down so that it is almost subliminal, then back it up to end the video.

You may not want to use music throughout a presentation. You may want to use it only as lead-in and exit music for an entire video, or just between segments. No matter how you use audio, be sure to treat it with as much care as your video.

We asked an audio expert for his opinion on the use of digital audio.

AUDIO FOR DESKTOP VIDEO
by Jeff Boone

Mr. Boone is the founder and president of Alaska Software, which publishes audio-production software tools for the Macintosh. Before starting Alaska Software, Mr. Boone worked for Apple Computer, Inc., where he contributed to the design and implementation of the Apple Real Time Architecture (ARTA).

What makes a good sound track?

Physical Factors

Sampling Rate

When an audio signal is recorded digitally (digitized), it is recorded as a sequence of numbers that closely represent the original signal. The number of times per second the audio signal is measured (sampled) is called the *sampling rate.* The higher the sampling rate, the more closely the digitized signal resembles the original audio.

Theoretically, the selection of the sampling rate only limits the highest frequency that can be recorded. The highest frequency that can be reproduced is roughly one-half of the sampling rate. So if you digitize audio at a 44.1 KHz sample rate (or measure and record the signal 44,100 times per second), the maximum frequency that you can accurately record is approximately 22 KHz. Although it varies from person to person, the highest frequency a human can hear is around 20 KHz.

In practice, selecting the sampling rate will sometimes add noise due to the fact that the given hardware or software does not filter out the high frequencies that cannot be accurately recorded. For example, if you are recording at 22.05 KHz, a filter must be applied to the input to eliminate all frequencies above 11KHz *before* the signal is digitized. If this is not handled properly, artifacts in the recorded signal, called *aliasing,* occur. This can also occur when converting a file from one sample rate to a lower one—a process called *sample rate conversion.* Make sure the hardware and software you use filters the signal appropriately when performing a sample rate conversion.

Bits per Sample

Another physical factor that determines sonic quality is the resolution of each of the measurements (samples) of the audio signal. This is referred to as bits per sample, or simply *bits.*

The bits per sample determines the theoretical maximum signal-to-noise ratio of the digitized signal. The formula for determining the maximum signal to noise ratio is:

$$S/N \approx 6 \text{ dB} * \text{number of bits}$$

So for an 8-bit recording, the theoretical maximum S/N ratio is about 48 dB. A 16 bit recording has a theoretical maximum S/N ratio of about 96 dB (6*16=96).

(continued)

Audio Codec

The audio codec is the piece of hardware that handles all the "measuring" of the audio signal when it is recorded. The actual specifications are often overlooked in the current marketing blitz of "CD-quality audio." Having a 16-bit codec that can sample at 44.1 KHz does *not* mean you will necessarily have CD-quality audio. One of the most important specifications is the S/N ratio. (CD players typically have an S/N ratio around 92–95 dB.) One worthwhile "reality check" when you are shopping for audio hardware is to find the S/N ratio for all of the existing components in your studio. The component with the lowest S/N ratio will be your "weak link." If the S/N ratio of the audio hardware that you are considering is lower than the weak link, it will limit the quality of your recordings.

Digital Signal Clipping

Signal clipping occurs when the strength of the signal you are recording exceeds the range of the converter. The converter will simply record the maximum value that it can. This has the effect of "clipping" off the top (or bottom) of the signal. Digital clipping sounds horrible and must be avoided at all costs! Most audio recording software packages include clipping indicators on the input meters. These will tell you if the signal was clipped when it was recorded.

Emotional Factors

Achieving Balance in the Mix

Balancing all the elements of a sound track (music, dialog, sound effects, and so forth) to achieve the desired emotional effect is an art in itself. I would encourage you to watch a few of your favorite films and concentrate on the sound track to see how it enhances the film.

Audio Editing Tools

Waveform Editors

Waveform editors allow you to perform "micro surgery" on your digitized audio. You can cut, copy, and paste chunks of audio and even use a pencil tool to remove clicks or pops that were inadvertently recorded with the audio. These tools are great for manipulating audio files, but they generally are not suited to production-oriented tasks. Examples of waveform editing tools are SoundEdit 16 from Macromedia and SoundTools from Digidesign.

(continued)

Multitrack Editors

Multitrack editors let you mix together various elements of audio such as music, dialog, and effects. They generally have the screen appearance of a traditional tape deck and mixer for simplicity. These tools are geared toward production as they can provide real-time mixing of multiple channels of audio. Examples of multitrack editors are DigiTrax from Alaska Software and ProTools from Digidesign.

Optimizing for CD-ROM Delivery

Create a High-Quality Master

When creating the audio for a CD-ROM, generally you want to create a master of the highest possible quality even if you have to scale it down for the CD-ROM. The reason is simple: If you re-release the material, the CD-ROM technology might be far enough along for you to release a higher-quality version.

Quality/Data Rate Trade-offs

The sustained data rate of CD-ROM drives generally forces you to compromise on the audio to obtain the best frame rate for your video. Figure 5.2 summarizes the data rate for various sample rates, bit rates, and number of channels.

In general, the perceived increase in audio quality going from 8 bits to 16 bits is much greater than going from 22.05 KHz to 44.1 KHz. If you are considering limiting the audio to stereo 8-bit at 22.05 KHz, I encourage you to use *mono* 16-bit at 22.05 KHz instead. The data rate is the same and the increased dynamic range and S/N ratio are worth the sacrifice of mono versus stereo.

Sample Rate Converting the Master

As mentioned earlier, care must be taken when downsampling (or sample-rate-converting to a lower sample rate than the original) a file. You generally will have to downsample the master audio file because of the limited data rate of CD-ROM drives.

Figure 5.2 Quality versus data rate chart.

Sample Bits	Channels	Sample Rate	Date Rate
8	1	22.05 kHz	22 KB/Sec
8	2	22.05 kHz	43 KB/Sec
8	1	44.1 kHz	43 KB/Sec
8	2	44.1 kHz	86 KB/Sec
16	1	22.05 kHz	43 KB/Sec
16	2	22.05 kHz	86 KB/Sec
16	1	44.1 kHz	86 KB/Sec
16	2	44.1 kHz	172 KB/Sec

Most QuickTime editor applications offer some form of audio editing, but this level of capability is generally the simplest "cuts-only" editing with a few such applications allowing gain and fade controls. If you want to edit or mix audio with more flexibility than that, we suggest that you use a specific audio editing application. This will provide you with a broad range of controls over the audio portion of your movies.

A caveat of traveling down this path is that you may have to separate your audio from your video during the editing process, requiring a simple "extraction" process to start with. It is during the reassembly process that things can become complicated, especially when vocal lip sync is an issue. Higher end audio editors can handle this by providing preview windows for the QuickTime video and the ability to "nudge" the audio forward or back to sync it to the video.

A final note: Although audio usually requires far less than video in the way of processing, be sure to take the time to listen to the entire audio and clean up or equalize those portions that fall below the norm. Even a visually stunning video presentation can become a poor overall presentation if the audio is "muddy" or poorly processed.

Techniques for Editing

If there was only one editing application, there would be only one complete set of techniques. But there are many applications and many individual techniques. This is not to say, however, that there aren't some basic, seat-of-the-pants techniques that go across all or most of the applications. There are.

We've developed and borrowed a number of them, and have also asked some people in the industry for their favorite application-specific techniques. First, let's go over some of the editing techniques that are going to be the same, from application to application.

For openers, with projects that include more than three or four scenes to be edited together, create an *edit decision list* (EDL). An EDL is basically a list of all the scenes to be edited together, in the order they are to appear. Traditionally, an EDL is used by a videotape operator to assemble the final edit of a video. An EDL can also be used to keep track of the individual clips to be used in a production (our suggested use). This list usually contains the starting, ending, and duration timecode. Optionally, it may contain some other reference information such as frame numbers (if used on laserdiscs, for example). Each item in the EDL also has a shot name and/or description.

EDLs can be generated manually (you watch the videotape and write down or type up the information) or automatically. Some applications, like Premiere, can generate an EDL log from the edits that are made. This is true only if the timecode information was recorded at the same time that the video was digitized. Your EDL doesn't have to be as exact or as detailed as those used in traditional film or tape editing; just create a rough guide, in a format that makes sense to you, that lists the location, the start and stop times, and a description of the clip.

If your next question is, "So, what's timecode?" then we have a short answer for that. Timecode is basically a clock or counter. The numbers on the front of your VCR that change as the tape is played are a rough form of timecode. Timecode is a way to find a specific spot of frame of video on a tape. Each frame has a unique timecode number. Timecode typically looks like 00:00:00:00. That means (left to right) HOURS:MINUTES:SECONDS:FRAMES. The industry standard form of timecode is known as SMPTE Timecode. All professional video decks have timecode generators, and their editing is done using timecode as the reference.

Once you know what you will be editing, the next steps for creating a finished product run along the following lines. Of course, the order and number of your steps may vary.

- Capture the raw material.

- Perform a rough edit to get rid of unwanted material.

- Import the rough edit material into your video editor application.

- Identify the in point (beginning) and out point (end) of each clip, and place them in the proper order.

- Identify and place any transitions or effects to be used (make sure to properly adjust their individual settings where appropriate).

- Import additional materials such as music or other audio tracks, and position them.

- Preview several small sections of your work, especially transitions and effects.

- Make all appropriate output settings (codec to be used, frame rate, key frames, and so forth).

- Process your video.

Of course, these are the general steps. Your project may require a variation or shuffling of these steps. Let's discuss some things to consider when accomplishing these general steps, beginning with the capture of your video.

Fire up your capture application and begin the capture process (being sure to do all of the balancing we've discussed elsewhere). Although they follow similar patterns, the exact steps necessary to capture video vary from application to application. Some applications that allow you to capture also have effective editing capabilities. Be sure to read up on your application or video capture card.

Don't worry if you get a bit more video than you need—you actually should capture more frames at the start and finish. We generally try to get about one second extra at the head and at the tail of each clip. This lets us make fine adjustments in our final editing processes.

Be sure to have all of your elements ready as you begin the editing process. This includes any audio you may wish to use that is not already part of video clips (music background track, narration, and so forth). The more preparation work you do to ensure that each element is ready, the smoother the actual edit session.

If you will be using effects, try a few of them using samples of the project to see how they work. We go into more detail about effects in the next section of this chapter.

We will assume that the particular editing and effects application you have decided upon offers the ability to set in and out points on each element used. Import each of your captured clips. As an alternative, you can import each of your clips into a utility such as MoviePlayer 2.0 and perform your edits. It is not necessary to save these new clips as self-contained movies at this point. Import each of these clips into your editing or effects application.

As an aside, we sometimes do a rough copy-and-paste edit in MoviePlayer just to see how the final product is going to look and flow. This is also a good step to take if your client wants to see some intermediate examples of the project. This has helped us avoid wasted time (read: *costly*) where the clients *actually* wanted a different clip or two than they had originally specified. Had we gone all the way through the editing process, we would have spent several additional hours making the fix. As it is, these quick "edit for approval" movies we create take very little time.

Once you have all of your elements ready and imported into the editor, and you have arranged them in the appropriate order, it is time to add your transitions and effects. Effects are not always necessary or appropriate for a video. One hint we can pass along is to put together a sampler with all sorts of strange effects. Watch it several times. You should begin to see some that really don't work! If you don't like them, chances are that a lot of other people won't also. You can use this later as a demo piece for prospective clients so they can see what various transitions look like.

This whole test runs into trouble should you be among the few who like everything. In that case, ask a friend or associate to check your selection of effects. This is a good idea, anyway. It never hurts to get a second opinion.

**Figure 5.3
Settings menus
from Premiere,
VideoShop, and
VideoFusion.**

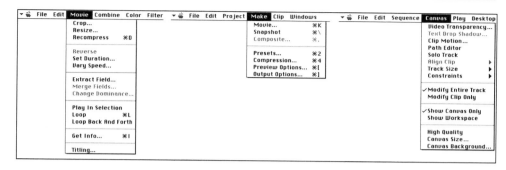

As soon as you have things ready to go, double-check all of your settings. Make sure that you will be saving your work to contiguous disk space on a drive with enough capacity to handle the entire piece. If disk space is in question, you can always create your edits in several shorter pieces. These can later be edited together into the final program.

If you are sure that this edit is the final version, you can perform your compression along with the edits and effects. If you are not sure, then don't compress at this point. You don't want to compress now and have to compress again later. That will lead to some loss in quality.

Different applications have different settings (often found under the heading of Preferences) that need to be set before you begin processing. They will also feature different functions under their menus. Indeed, we doubt that you will find any two applications that even use the same menu names. Figure 5.3 shows sample menu selections from three of the applications we frequently use: Adobe Premiere, Avid VideoShop, and VideoFusion VideoFusion.

Check all the settings in your application. Make sure they are where you believe them to be. We have been caught up short several times by applications that save some settings but not others. Now, we never take it for granted that the settings we saved last week are going to be there the next time we open the application.

Once you are sure of your settings, and you have all of your elements in the editor, push Start and sit back.

There are many good editing applications, each one with special techniques that can be used to get the most from the software. We currently use four main editing applications, depending on the project. There are others that you may use, or may want to use, that we don't. Try many and select those that meet the needs of your desktop video studio.

We asked an experienced multimedia designer to provide us with his tips for working with his favorite editor. Here they are:

TOP TEN TIPS AND TRICKS FOR VIDEOSHOP 3.0
by Steve Demirjian

Mr. Demirjian received a BA in film and TV production from Loyola Marymount University in Los Angeles. He worked in all forms of production at various independent film companies before moving to Paramount Studios as part of Henry Winkler's production team for the television series MacGyver. Mr. Demirjian, Avid New Media's in-house video and multimedia designer, has compiled his top ten secrets for getting the most out of VideoShop 3.0.

VideoShop 3.0 is the video editing software anyone can use. A demo of VideoShop is on the accompanying CD-ROM. With Avid VideoShop, you can mix video, text, graphics, effects, CD-quality audio, and pictures to create high-quality videotapes and digital movies. VideoShop is the perfect tool for business communicators, educators, and media professionals who need to create compelling messages.

1. Quality Effects

To get the absolute best-quality video when you render effects, follow these steps to change your compression settings. Select Special Effects from the Preferences submenu under the File menu heading. Choose Add Custom from the Default Compression pop-up menu. A dialog box opens. (See Figure 5.4.)

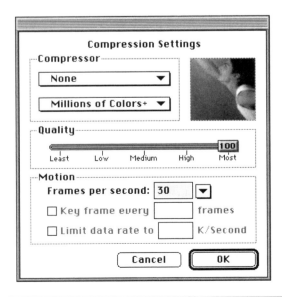

**Figure 5.4
Setting the
Effects prefer-
ences.**

(continued)

In the dialog box, select None for compressor, select Most for quality, and set the FPS to 30. Make sure you have a lot of drive space available wherever your recording folder is located.

2. Field Rendering

VideoShop 3.0 allows you to capture and render effects for 60-field video. If you are using a capture card with a 60-field option, don't forget to select Full Frame (Two-Field) in the Special Effects Preferences (Figure 5.5).

3. 3D Titles with Alpha Channels

With Specular LogoMotion 1.5 (provided with VideoShop 3.0), it's easy to make great 3D titles for VideoShop movies. Simply design your title using LogoMotion, then save it as a QuickTime movie. Be sure to save the title using the Animation compressor (Most quality, Millions + colors) rather than None. It saves *greatly* on drive space and does not significantly degrade the quality of the title. (This *only* applies to titles.)

If you will want to key out the black background of the title in VideoShop later, be sure to check the Create Alpha Channel checkbox in the Save dialog of LogoMotion.

4. Alpha Map

This feature uses an alpha channel to give an exciting multitrack composition effect. It can be used to create a video in a title while moving over a video background. Experiment for yourself!

To make a video in a title with motion control scrolling from right to left, make

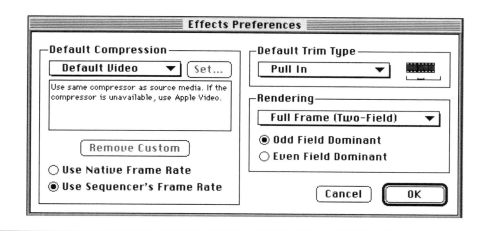

**Figure 5.5
Choose Full
Frame.**

(continued)

**Figure 5.6
Use Most as
the desired
video quality.**

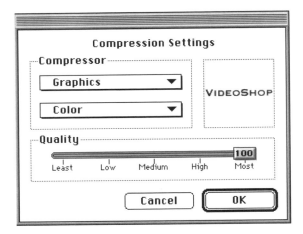

and save a title *exactly* the same height as the movie, in either Fractal Design Painter
or any other paint package. (That is, if the movie is 240 pixels high, then create a
title 240 pixels high.) *The title must be black; the background must be white.* Save the
title as a PICT file.

Launch VideoShop and drop the title (the PICT file) into the video track of a new
sequencer in VideoShop. A dialog box appears. Choose Graphics for the processor
and select Most from the Quality pop-up menu for the best results (Figure 5.6).

Make sure the sequencer is in time view, and select the Stretch tool from the
sequencer tool palette. Click and drag the title to change its length to the span of the
duration of the movie it will scroll through (Figure 5.7).

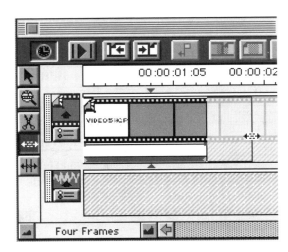

**Figure 5.7
Stretching the
title to change
the duration.**

(continued)

**Figure 5.8
Moving the
canvas
window.**

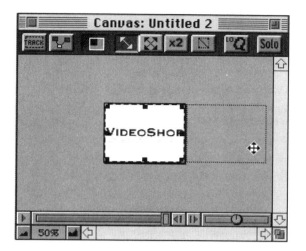

Select the Canvas Background command from the Canvas menu. A dialog box appears. Click the Solid Color button to display the color wheel; choose White.

Next, click the canvas window Zoom button to zoom to 50 percent or 25 percent. This will help you see the entire workspace for easier manipulation of your clips. Click the title in the canvas window and move it off the canvas to the right, so the left edge of the title is aligned with the right edge of the canvas (Figure 5.8).

Click the Motion Control button and click where you want the center of the title to end on the opposite (left) side (Figure 5.9).

Select Save as Movie from the Edit menu. Be sure to check the Mixdown Movie

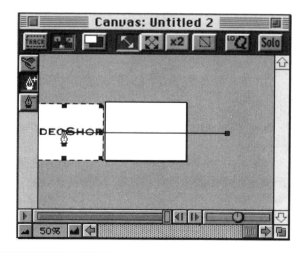

**Figure 5.9
Centering the
title.**

(continued)

**Figure 5.10
Optimizing.**

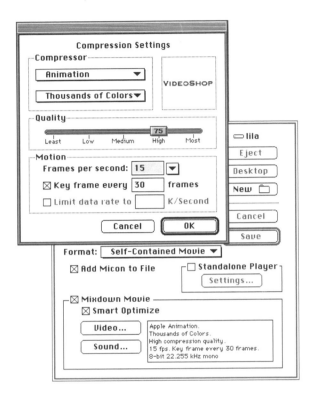

option, then click the Video button. Optimize with the Animation compressor on High quality. (See Figure 5.10.)

Once the title is saved, open a new sequencer and add two more video tracks (to make a total of three video tracks). Put the optimized title movie in the middle track. Put the movie that you want to be in the title in the top track, and put the movie that you want to be the background in the bottom track. Make a selection across *all* tracks and choose Alpha Map from the Sequencer menu and the Apply Filter submenu.

When the Alpha Map filter has been built, a layered composition title will be incorporated into your movie.

5. Motion Control

The key to getting great motion control results is in keeping organized. If you want to apply motion control to a number of tracks, work on one at a time. (Use the **Solo** button (Figure 5.11) on the canvas window toolstrip so you won't accidentally select the wrong track.

(continued)

**Figure 5.11
The Solo
button.**

To isolate a track, drop a clip into a video track. Select it in the canvas window, and press the Solo button. Now when you apply motion, only the selected track will be affected. It helps to zoom the canvas window to 50 percent or 25 percent—it's much easier to move large titles or movies around the canvas. When you're finished, check the motion with the Frame Advance arrow keys to make sure you got it just the way you want it.

6. Magnifying Glass

To zoom in for a frame-by-frame view of a particular section, select the Magnifying Glass from the sequencer tool palette and click the section of video you want to see more closely. (See Figure 5.12.) The more you click, the higher the degree of the zoom.

While clicking, watch the display factor change in the bottom left corner of the sequencer.

To zoom back out, hold down the Option key and click.

7. Arrow Keys

To advance or backtrack a single frame, use the left and right arrow keys. This single-frame technique is great for checking the "match" or "cut" between two joining clips.

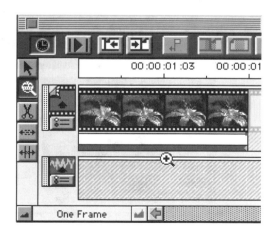

**Figure 5.12
Frame-by-
frame view
using Magnify-
ing Glass.**

(continued)

8. Chroma Key

These simple tips help obtain smoother and more exact chroma keys:

- Use a solid background color. A "studio" blue or green works best.
- Use plenty of light. Good lighting eliminates shadows and makes cleaner edges.
- Don't let the subject wear a color that matches or reflects the background.

9. Digital Scrub

The scrub feature is a great tool for synchronizing dialog, music, or sound effects. Click and drag the dial on the lower right side of the canvas window right or left to slowly advance or reverse the movie. Check your cuts by slowly dragging the dial and watching the canvas window to see if the cut matches the beat. If not, you can tell right away where to move the video.

If you hear the beat *before* the cut, move the video to the left. If it's *after,* move the video to the right.

10. Titling

When creating titles in VideoShop, always use the Safe Titles option under the Title menu. Now you can type in this area and know that your title will not be cut off when you print to videotape. (See Figure 5.13.)

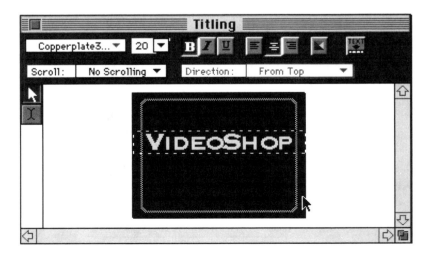

**Figure 5.13
Titling.**

Another expert in his field gave us some inside information on how to get more from Adobe's Premiere:

PREMIERE TIPS

by Greg Roach

Mr. Roach is the art director and multimedia artist for Hyperbole Studios. Before going to Hyperbole, his radio play Horse Arms *won the Midwest Radio Theater national script competition. He wrote, directed, and designed the world's first narrative interactive film,* The Wrong Side of Town, *which was the best-of-show winner at the first QuickTime Film Festival. Since then, his films have garnered more than a dozen awards at festivals and shows around the world, including the full length* Quantum Gate, *nominated for two interactive awards by the Academy of Interactive Arts and Sciences. He recently completed* The Vortex: Quantum Gate II, *which incorporates his Virtual Cinema engine.*

Premiere 4.0 and QuickTime 2.0, both included on the accompanying CD-ROM, represent an incredibly powerful combination for the creation and manipulation of digital video, rivaling features found on high-end dedicated systems. Almost all of the digital video work done at Hyperbole Studios is delivered to the end user on CD-ROM, as part of a VirtualCinema interactive movie.

Although we use software-only codecs for delivery to the end user on CD-ROM (CinePak and Indeo), all of our capture and editing is done at broadcast resolution using Radius VideoVision Studio. This has three advantages:

1. Higher-quality delivery on CD-ROM. By using "interpolated scaling" while transcoding (from VideoVision Studio to CinePak/Indeo) we can achieve better, sharper results than by doing "1:1" scaling. Our tool of choice is Apple's ConvertToMovie 2.0. By scaling from 640×480 to 320×240, ConvertToMovie automatically uses interpolated scaling and you get higher-quality output. The results are quite dramatic, and the difference is visible to the naked eye. You can use this technique to create movies with a nonstandard-aspect ratio—just be sure your source file is exactly twice the dimensions of the desired output.

   Note: Be certain that the dimensions of each side (horizontal and vertical) are equally divisible by four; both CinePak and Indeo are optimized to deal with material of this size and will be able to function at maximum efficiency, producing sharper results.

2. We automatically have promotional and EPK (electronic press kit) materials available at the resolution needed by television stations and broadcast journalists with no additional effort—a big plus when deadlines are tight and the marketing effort needs to be closely integrated with a product release schedule.

(continued)

3. By archiving all of our finished output at full resolution, we help to ensure that our products won't be rendered obsolete by advances in technology. We can upgrade a product to take advantage of full-screen or full-motion video with relatively little effort.

Because VideoVision Studio requires the most horsepower available for good capture and print-to-tape results, we have one station where all of these activities occur. We use a Power Mac 8100 equipped with 64 MB of RAM and a super-fast Studio Array. Once we capture the source material at the highest quality possible (4+ MB per second), we then move it to slightly slower platforms (Quadra 840 AVs) with less robust drive subsystems (3 MB per second) for editing and manipulation.

Although these systems can't play the clip back smoothly in real time, they work fine for basic editing chores and save a lot of money. (With over a dozen editing stations working simultaneously, hardware costs can add up quickly.) We create output tests (using the "Test Delete" approach described later) at "1.5 MB/sec - 15fps - Field one only" to check our work in progress. Once the edit is completed, we create a high-quality output file (4+ MB/sec - 30fps - 60 fields - 640 × 480) and migrate the material back to the Power Mac station for print to tape output (if it's needed).

In addition to rock-solid capture quality, the Power Mac platform offers two other big advantages over older Macintosh models

1. Radically increased processing speed. If you're doing just basic editing, then this is less of an issue than if you're doing processor-intensive operations that involve heavy use of filters, transitions, or output that involves many layers.

2. When transcoding material from VideoVision Studio to CinePak, the Power PC native version of QuickTime offers a significant speed improvement (300 percent faster!) over Quadra class machines. If you've got a lot of movies to convert, the time savings can be substantial. Be sure the QuickTime Powerplug extension is installed in your system in order to see the benefits.

If your intended delivery mode is CinePak or Indeo, you can get sharper results by shooting against a blue or green screen and "keying" the background out to a graphic background or scene. This eliminates the video noise that exists in a non-keyed background—allowing the compressor to concentrate on your actors' image, rather than giving up important bandwidth to nonessentials such as wood paneling.

Often, when keying out blue screen material, you'll hit problem footage that just doesn't want to cooperate. We have two techniques for dealing with these situations:

1. Use Premiere's "Color Replace" filter to "pre-key" the troublesome spots to a true blue (or green). This usually goes a long way toward allowing the transparency module to do its job properly.

(continued)

2. Create multiple pass copies of the clip using Premiere's very powerful Virtual Clip feature. This allows you to gradually work your way into the darker or noisier (read: *problem*) sections of the clip until you can get good, clean results. Adjust key subsequent iterations to a pure color background until you reach the desired results, then key the last pass onto your final background.

Speaking of Virtual Clips: What a time and space saver! In previous versions of Premiere, creating the preceding effect would have required multiple output movies—one at each step along the way—but Virtual Clips allow us to achieve the same results without having to fill up our hard drive with each iteration. Watch out, though; there's a very subtle bug that causes the "Image Pan" filter to malfunction if applied to a Virtual Clip. Interesting if you're expecting it and disappointing if you're not.

Powerful as this feature is, there are still times when you need to create a test file that will run in real time in order to check your work. We like to create a medium-resolution (1.5 MB/sec - 15fps - Field one only) output movie that we name "Test Delete." This lets us see the movie run with full effects, filters, and transitions at full speed. (Even with Premiere's beefed-up new preview feature, this is hard to do.)

Each new test simply overwrites the previous version, and every so often we use the Finder's Search command to catch (and delete) any strays.

The piece of software you use for editing will have its special capabilities; some will be well documented and some you will just "happen on" some day. We still find things that amaze us in many applications. Most of those things are good.

Techniques for Effects

Not every effect works between any two given pieces of video. Some effects are obtrusive (whirling boxes, rotating knives, and other gimicky effects), and some just won't work the way you want them to because of their need for higher frame rates. For instance, a half-second A→B dissolve in 30 fps is smooth and works very well because you are using an entire fifteen frames for the dissolve. The same dissolve in a 15 fps movie uses only about seven frames (still acceptable). But such a dissolve in a 10 fps movie will have only five frames to do its work. For our eye and taste, that just is not enough frames to make for a smooth transition between clips. And just think how sudden a dissolve would be in a quarter-second dissolve at 10 fps!

If you will be using different effects between clips, or even within a clip, you should have already practiced and know what will work. It is not necessary to have a dissolve or a wipe or a windowshade effect between each clip. After awhile, they begin to detract from the viewability of the movie rather than adding to it.

When going from one clip to another where the basic action or actors on screen remain the same, use simple cuts. If you have the luxury of different camera angles, this is a very effective method of editing.

When going from one clip to another where the action changes, or the subject matter changes, and especially when dealing with a "Now let's go to section 2 . . ." situation, a good effect really sets the two pieces apart. For this last example, you may wish to try a fade to black and back up to the next scene (or add a slide with the name of the next section).

It is *almost* always nice to fade to black at the end of a movie. This is not mandatory, but it helps the viewer ease out of the "watch me" mode and back to the real world. Sometimes an abrupt snap to black can effectively punctuate the end of a piece.

One of the techniques used extensively in Hollywood and for television is the blue screen, or ultimatte, technique for superimposing people over artwork or scenes that are elsewhere. The most frequent example of this on TV is "Your TV Weatherman, Snowy Driffts." Snowy does not stand in outer space next to the satellite, or out in the middle of the raging river or the hurricane. Snowy stands, snug and warm, in the studio in front of a large blue screen.

Through the magic of the camera, all of the blue behind him is replaced with a second picture—any picture or video. When done correctly, matting can look very real. When done poorly, the background scene can bleed through the foreground characters or you can see a visible blue line around them, or worse.

Matte capabilities are available to the desktop video studio. Again, you can do good matting and you can do bad matting. Read the sidebar by Lynn Ackler, who is deeply involved in this technique, for his point of view.

We would like to close this part of the chapter with a friendly word of advice: *Get effects and transitions out of your blood early, before you land that big account.* Overuse of effects, like bad visitors and old fish, begins to annoy the senses after awhile.

Effects and transitions are like fonts. When desktop publishing became the rage, everyone and his sister was creating newsletters that often looked like ransom notes. The same is even more true of effects. Professional editors will tell you that they rarely use more than three or four transition types in a given project (often only one or two). Dissolves, cuts, and wipes are by far the most commonly used. Special effects should be used judiciously and appropriately; otherwise, they will completely distract the viewer from the content.

Of course, if you are creating your next music video award winner, you *may* be excluded from what we just said. Often, the effects *are* the content!

THE ART AND SCIENCE OF MAKING DANCING VIDEO CELS
by Lynn Ackler

Until very recently Mr. Ackler managed the video and audio production labs at the 3DO Company. His specialty was in green screen and blue screen technologies. He was trained as a mathematician, receiving his bachelor's and master's degrees from Ohio State and his doctorate from Lehigh University. He has worked in the image processing and enhancement world for over twelve years. Prior to that, he taught at the college level for almost fifteen years. After several years with the 3DO Company, he has just moved into private consulting practice.

Lights, Camera, Action . . . Now Get Rid of That Blue!

We all know that full-screen video takes up a lot of room. But full-screen video is so effective. One workaround is through the use of smaller videos overlaid on static backgrounds, doing what the movie and television industry refer to as ultimatting, or using a blue screen. Such video sprites or cels can contribute significantly to great multimedia titles. With careful planning and the right tools, video sprites can be a very effective element of your titles.

This sidebar explains how to make video sprites or cels dance, under user control, over a background. There are four steps to successful cels:

1. *Shoot video:* Plan and execute the video shoot very carefully.
2. *Digitize video:* Capture and process the video accurately.
3. *Background extraction:* Remove the background completely.
4. *Plan, plan, plan:* And pray for time.

I will discuss each step, techniques, and tools as well as the equipment needed. But first, some technical goals and some real problems. The result of quality blue screen removal is a piece of video that can be played over any art background with the background art showing everywhere *except* where covered by the foreground video image. The desired effect is video cels whose edges don't crawl or jump (anti-aliased edges), no blue spill around the edges (chroma spill), and no blue reflected in the foreground image, as in bluish faces (chroma reflection).

And, of course, we want all of this done as cheaply as possible. The greatest expense is manpower, so careful use of the proper techniques can greatly reduce your final costs as well as keeping the total time spent to a minimum.

What Is a Video Sprite?

A video sprite or cel is a sequence of video frames whose foreground is high-quality video and background is transparent pixels. When displayed over static art, the

(continued)

video appears to float or dance over the background image. Usually these videos are represented as sequences of 32-bit bitmaps; 24 bits are for the RGB foreground color and 8 bits are the *alpha channel.*

The alpha channel is often called the matte channel. Black (0) in the alpha channel represents complete transparency, or 0 percent opacity. White (255) represents 100 percent opacity. Depending on the capabilities of the target platform, the pixel values in the alpha channel around the edge of the foreground image can vary between 0 and 255. Using these values to vary the opacity of the foreground, unwanted aliasing of the foreground edges can be prevented.

Shoot Video!

The video shoot should be planned very carefully. The script and title design must be very detailed. About the most expensive place to edit script or design your sets is in front of the camera.

The background (the walls, the floor, and all invisible props) should be painted with a chroma paint. Whether this is blue or green is a matter of past successes and failures. You may need to experiment. The background paint should be a pure blue or pure green. Avoid paper backdrops; blue or green paper reflects a lot of light and consequently is difficult to extract. Sharp corners in the background usually cause problems; it is difficult to light both sides of the corner equally. Where the wall meets the floor should be rounded to ease the background extraction.

Costumes and makeup should have colors that are complementary to the background, and not identical to it. For example, blue jeans cause problems if shot against blue screen, and green eye shadow causes problems when shooting against green screen.

Getting good lighting from your engineer is of critical importance. The background must be lighted separately from the foreground and should be lighted as evenly as possible. The background lights should also use blue or green filters as appropriate. Foreground lights must be set so they do not cast unwanted shadows across the background. Backlights with 25 percent gels of a color complementary to the background color should be used to light the *back* of the foreground characters. These lights reduce a lot of the chroma spill around the edges. Your video crew needs to have a very strong stomach for living in a blue or green world for the duration of the shoot.

The camera you use and the director of photography are very important and can reduce the amount of touchup work required later. Since the type of video signal recorded will affect the final product, I highly recommend using BetaCam SP equipment if your budget allows. The three-color component signal of BetaCam makes

(continued)

the background and foreground character separation very clear. Both composite and S-Video signals from other camera types can produce a blurred edge, usually on the right side of the foreground characters, and especially when shot against a blue screen.

Another way that the character edges can be come blurred is during motion. Again, if the edge from the foreground to the background is at all blurred, the extraction of the background will be difficult and likely to cause a blue edge to appear around the foreground character. A cure for motion blur is shooting the video using a shutter speed of 1/250 or 1/500. With this fast shutter speed, however, more lights are required. Using more lights during the shoot is cheaper than more "hand" work later.

It is also important to have the foreground character in exact focus and the background in as good focus as the lens permits. The depth of field of the lens will also affect the quality of the video shoot.

If motion blur or out-of-focus effects are desired, they should be added later, after the background has been extracted.

Digitize Video!

Great care must be exercised when the video is captured. Remember, any process that blurs the edges between the background and the foreground will be difficult to extract. The video capture hardware should use component video (RGB or Yuv) as its input. Every frame or every other frame should be captured in full-color, 24-bit and at full resolution, 640 × 480 pixels.

Since the captured video is interlaced 30 frames per second, it has to be deinterlaced. This process can be accomplished in any number of video processing products—for example, Adobe Photoshop and Premiere, or Equilibrium's DeBabelizer. At this time, the background should be extracted and the alpha channel created.

Extract Background!

It is my experience that After Effects does the best job of background removal. Other packages such as Photoshop or Photomatic can do *some* background removal, but both the ease of use and the quality of the end result are better using AfterEffects.

In AfterEffects, a composition should be created with the raw deinterlaced footage. Under the Effects menu choose "Keying," and a number of choices are possible. The easiest method is the "Linear 3 Color." This technique allows you to pick a color to remove, either with an eyedropper or the color wheel.

(continued)

- The Matching Tolerance slider lets you choose how close a pixel has to be to the chosen color. The default of 15 percent is a good place to start.
- The Choke Matte slider expands and shrinks the matte geometrically. Expanding the matte (negative value) by 1 or 2 pixels creates a good matte for anti-aliased edges. A value of 0 is good for crisp clean edge when composited on a background. There are many settings and different keying effects.

What has been described is a very basic technique that results in good clean video clips with a matte channel.

AfterEffects supports "garbage matting." By outlining a portion of the image, After-Effects processes the outlined region only. Often in a video shoot, the microphone boom shows up. The microphone can be eliminated through the use of garbage matting.

Make It a Title!

After all the parameters are set, a QuickTime movie is made. The foreground is composited on black or any other color you choose. The matte channel is in the alpha channel of the QuickTime movie. If you have done all the steps correctly, you will have a high-quality image.

Polishing for Best Results

There are any number of things you can do to "polish" your final digital video product. Our definition of "polishing" is not limited to cosmetic changes and enhancements. To us, polishing a digital video product means doing anything that is beyond the ordinary, beyond what your typical editor or utility does.

This section includes:

- Flattening movies
- Creating custom palettes for 8-bit displays
- Converting QuickTime to AVI and AVI to QuickTime
- Creating full-screen movies where you don't have full-screen movies

We have a few sets of steps and techniques to cover each of these. To begin, let's talk about flattening movies.

Flattening: Making Sure You Have Single Video and Audio Tracks in a Movie

For every clip you place into an edited QuickTime movie, you effectively add an additional video or audio track. These are "cued" so that they play in the proper order, almost always without a noticeable pause between tracks. Although QuickTime for Macintosh can handle these multiple track movies during playback, QuickTime for Windows cannot!

Some earlier applications running under early versions of QuickTime that claimed to be able to "flatten" a movie (making a single data track for each of video and audio) did not actually do that. They only knew how to flatten the first two tracks into one; if you had more than two audio or video tracks, the application would "grab" only the first two. The rest would remain as separate tracks. This is not good!

In order to make your movies as playable as possible, whether they are playing on Macintosh or on Windows, you should flatten them totally. With the advent of QuickTime 2.0 and MoviePlayer 2.0, checking a movie and flattening it if needed is a simple task.

You need to:

1. Open MoviePlayer 2.0.

2. From the File menu, select and open your movie.

3. Once the movie player window appears, pull down the Movie menu and select Get Info (Figure 5.14).

4. Click and hold the Movie pop-up (the left pop-up). You should see only a single video track and a single audio track (or just video or just audio if that is all the movie contains). (See Figure 5.15.)

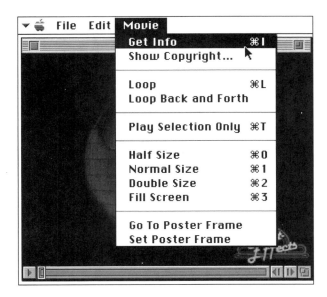

Figure 5.14 Get Info about your movie.

**Figure 5.15
Looking for a
single track.**

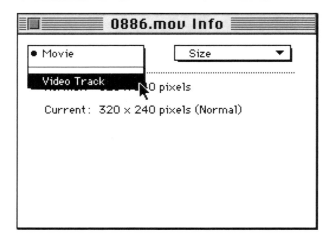

If you see only a single video track or a single audio track, your movie is flattened. There is no need to do anything else. You can Quit the application.

If, however, you see multiple video tracks or audio tracks, your movie must be flattened before you proceed. To do this:

1. Close the Get Info dialog box.

2. Select Save As . . . from the File menu. Click on Make movie self-contained, and then click on Playable on non-Apple computers. (See Figure 5.16.)

Your movie should now be flattened properly.

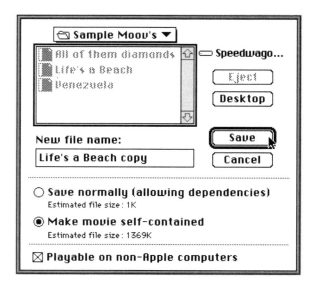

**Figure 5.16
Making a self-
contained
movie.**

Creating a 256-Color Custom Palette

There are going to be times when you must develop movies that will be played on systems with only 8-bit (256 colors) capability. Even in cases where movies may also be played on higher bit-depth platforms, having a custom color palette will greatly assist in the playability on the lower bit-depth machines. For the best color and playback, you should create and use a custom color palette.

This is a fairly simple task (albeit a time-consuming one containing more than two dozen steps). You can accomplish this in two ways: either using the MakeMovieColorTable utility (faster, but not as accurate with an end result that is nowhere as good), or using DeBabelizer (lengthier, but the results are worth it!). DeBabelizer demos are included on the accompanying CD-ROM. We are going to assume that you believe your movies are worth the extra time, so this covers only the DeBabelizer solution.

For this, you will need:

- DeBabelizer 1.5.5 or greater
- ResEdit
- SetMovieColorTable or MoviePlayer 2.0

If creating for Windows/Macintosh 256-colors display, perform all 26 of the following steps. If creating for Macintosh-only 256-color display, skip steps 13 through 23. Here are the basic steps:

1. Launch DeBabelizer.
2. From the File menu, select Batch→Super Palette.
3. Click New; make sure New Batch List Name is selected. (See Figure 5.17.)

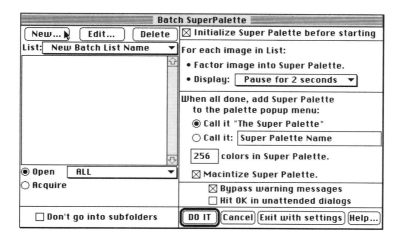

Figure 5.17 The Batch SuperPalette dialog box.

**Figure 5.18
The Batch List
dialog box.**

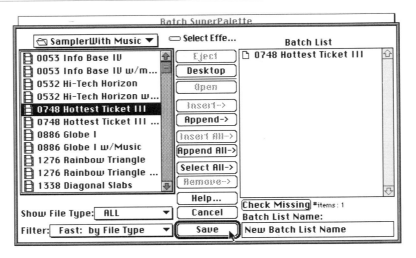

4. Locate and select your movie. (See Figure 5.18.)

5. Select Append; click Save.

6. Click Replace to replace the existing batch name.

7. When you return to the Batch SuperPalette dialog box, make sure of the following settings (Figure 5.19):

   • Initialize Super Palette . . . is checked

   • Display Off is selected.

   • Call it is selected and you type in a unique name.

   • Set 240 colors in Super Palette.

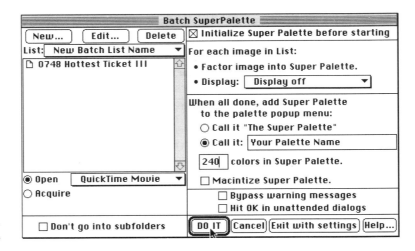

**Figure 5.19
The Batch
SuperPalette
dialog box with
proper settings.**

**Figure 5.20
The QuickTime
Movie Open dia-
log box.**

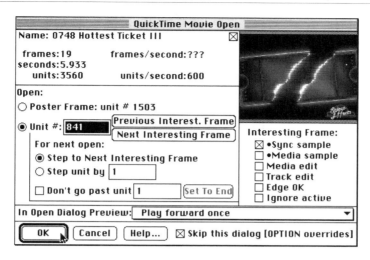

- *Do not* select Macintize Super Palette unless you are only creating a Macintosh 256-color palette.

- Click and hold the Open button; make sure QuickTime Movie is selected.

8. Click DO IT; the QuickTime Movie Open dialog box appears. (See Figure 5.20.)

9. Select Step to Next Interesting Frame. *Note:* You can have DeBabelizer look at every frame to build your palette (very accurate), or have it build a palette by looking at only key frames (faster but not as accurate).

10. Select Sync sample (for key frame checking) or Media sample (to check all frames). *Note:* if your content does not radically change over time, we recommend trying the Sync sample selection; if yours has fast-moving images or contains lots of scene changes, you are better off selecting Media sample.

11. Click on Skip this dialog . . . to disable returning to this dialog after each frame. Click OK. DeBabelizer is now performing all the processing to find the proper palette based on your selections. Depending on how long your movie is, you have time for a soda or a short nap.

12. When done, the Create Super Palette dialog box appears (Figure 5.21). Verify that the name you gave this palette appears in the Call it box; click Create It.

You now have a custom palette in DeBabelizer, but it must be massaged for use in a Windows environment. To continue:

**Figure 5.21
The Create
Super Palette
dialog box.**

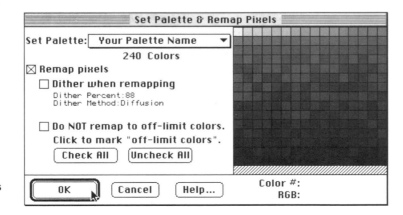

Create Super Palette

Pictures factored in so far: 0   Colors used so far: 0   (View)

Create a Super Palette &
add it to the palette popup menu:

Number of colors in Super Palette: [240]

☐ On creation of Super Palette, Macintize it.

○ Call it "The Super Palette"
◉ Call it: [Your Palette Name]

(Create It)   (Cancel)   (Help...)   ☐ Skip this box next time
                                                      (OPTION cancels)

13. Open the actual movie you just used from the DeBabelizer File menu.

14. From the Palette menu select Set Palette & Remap Pixels (Figure 5.22).

15. Click and hold the Set Palette pop-up; select the custom palette you just created from the list. (They appear alphabetically.)

16. Make sure that only the Remap Pixels box is checked. *Note:* You are not changing your movie even though the frame you see may change; you are just registering a palette within DeBabelizer.

17. Click OK. DeBabelizer now maps and displays the 256-color palette.

18. From the Palette menu, select Merge Palettes (Figure 5.23).

19. Click and hold the From pop-up; select Windows Paintbrush 16. Be sure that the Copy Colors box is set to 16, Start at is set to 0, and Show to is set to 240.

Set Palette & Remap Pixels

Set Palette: [Your Palette Name   ▼]
240 Colors
☒ Remap pixels
    ☐ Dither when remapping
        Dither Percent:88
        Dither Method:Diffusion

    ☐ Do NOT remap to off-limit colors.
    Click to mark "off-limit colors".
    (Check All) (Uncheck All)

(OK)   (Cancel)   (Help...)   Color #:
                                              RGB:

**Figure 5.22
The Set Palette
& Remap Pixels
dialog box.**

**Figure 5.23
The Merge
Palettes dialog
box.**

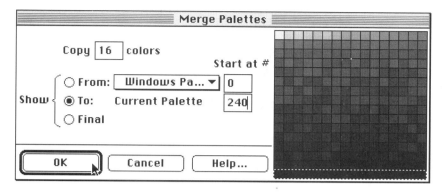

20. Click OK. The palette window is updated to include sixteen colors at the bottom.

21. From the Palette menu select Rearrange . . . (Figure 5.24) to place the Windows colors in the proper palette positions for use in a PC.

22. Make sure the Palette radial button is selected in the Rearrange dialog box. Select the first eight colors from bottom row (positions 240–247) by clicking and dragging across them until they are all highlighted. Click and drag this entire group up to position 0. (Make sure the left side of position 0 is flashing before you let go.)

23. Click OK. The palette is now rearranged properly. The small palette display shows the new arrangement. (See Figure 5.25.)

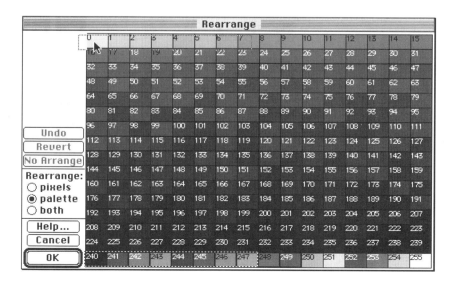

**Figure 5.24
The Rearrange
dialog box.**

**Figure 5.25
The new palette.**

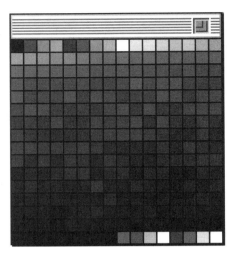

24. From the Palette menu select Palette→Save; give it a new name and click Add.

25. From the Misc menu select Scripts-Palette-Etc→Export . . . ; name it, make sure only the Palettes box is checked (Figure 5.26); select where you want it to be saved; click Save.

26. Quit DeBabelizer. It will ask about saving changes to the current picture—select Discard.

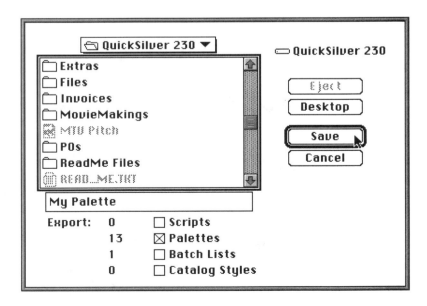

**Figure 5.26
Proper Quit
selections.**

**Figure 5.27
The CLUT when
viewed from
ResEdit.**

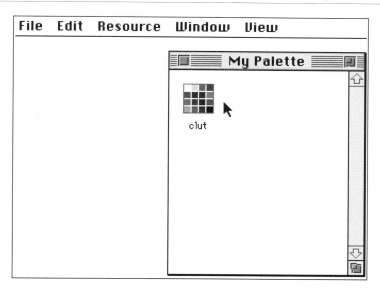

You have now created a ResEdit file with the custom palette saved inside it. (If you had any other custom palettes created in DeBabelizer, they also have been exported into this file.)

To make sure that you are going to embed only the proper palette, you need to check the ResEdit document. To do so:

1. Open ResEdit. Open the file you just created. You will see the ResEdit file window with the CLUT icon. (See Figure 5.27.)

2. Double-click the CLUT icon. A list of all the palettes contained in this file appears.

3. Select all of the palettes in the list *except* the one you just created. Select CUT from the Edit menu to delete the unwanted palettes. (See Figure 5.28.)

4. Close the CLUT dialog box. Select Save from the File menu.

5. Quit ResEdit.

Your custom 256-color palette is finally ready to be embedded into your movie. If you have the developer tool SetMovieColorTable, this is the final set of steps:

1. Launch the SetMovieColorTable application. You are presented with an Open File dialog box. Select the movie you just made your custom palette for and click Open.

2. The Open File dialog box appears again. Locate the ResEdit file you just completed and select it; click Open.

**Figure 5.28
Deleting
unwanted
palettes.**

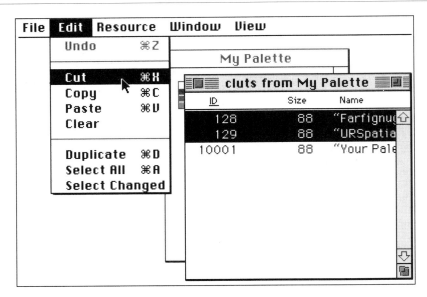

3. A Verify dialog box appears. If you have gone through all of the pre-ceding processes, you should see only the name of your custom color palette in the pop-up box. Assuming this is correct, click OK. The application automatically Quits.

If you do not have SetMovieColorTable, you can still attach your new 256-color palette by using MoviePlayer 2.0. Here are the steps to take:

1. Launch MoviePlayer 2.0.

2. Open the target movie from the File Menu.

3. From the Movie menu, select Get Info. This new feature in MoviePlayer gives you the ability to set and clear colors, allows access to the copyright information, and offers the option to adjust the audio, among others. In the dialog box, select and hold the right-hand pop-up menu; scroll down and select Colors (Figure 5.29). Click the Set button (Figure 5.30).

4. From the Open dialog box, locate and select the palette file you cre-ated using DeBabelizer; click Open. You will see your 256-color palette in the Colors dialog box.

5. Close the Get Info dialog box and save the movie.

The movie is now complete and ready for use in the 256-color mode on your Windows or Macintosh machine. Test it!

Having gone through all of those steps, we should also tell you that the latest version of Indeo (2.2) comes with two special palettes: (1) A 236-

**Figure 5.29
Selecting colors.**

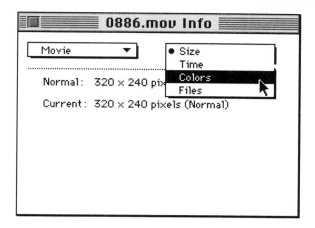

**Figure 5.30
Set the color
palette.**

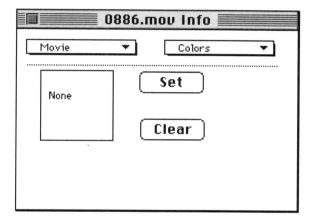

color palette for Windows and (2) a 256-color palette for Macintosh. Although these may not be right in every case, we see this as a trend that will spread to other codec authors.

**Converting
QuickTime to
AVI and AVI
to QuickTime**

You may someday find yourself with the need to create cross-platform movies from existing movies that do not end up or start as QuickTime. The most probable scenario is that you will need to create AVI files for some Video for Windows application.

Conversely, you may be given an AVI movie that needs to be translated into a QuickTime movie for playback on a Macintosh. The process, assuming you have the tools, couldn't be much easier (unless someone else does it for you—at no charge).

If the eventual need is to go from QuickTime to AVI, you must be sure to use a video compressor that is also available for playback in Video for

Windows. The only two that truly fall into this category are Indeo and CinePak.

These are not your only choices, but these are the two readily available in the Macintosh world. By using a Macintosh-based Video for Windows compressor extension (these are available from Microsoft), you can get the following additional codecs:

- Microsoft RLE
- Microsoft Video 1
- Microsoft Full Frame

You can compress your movie as a QuickTime file using one of the Microsoft formats by using your favorite Macintosh compressor application or utility. (And for that matter, you can view movies previously saved in that format—but performance will suffer because those codecs have not been optimized for QuickTime playback.) To add these codecs to your system for use with your favorite compression utility, simply place the new Windows compressor's extension file in your system folder's extension folders.

You will want to use the Microsoft codecs on the Macintosh *only* as a trans-coding mechanism. As we just mentioned, these have not been optimized for QuickTime playback. When the movie is played on a Windows PC, using these codecs, the movies will play appropriately.

QuickTime to AVI. If the target is to create AVI files in CinePak or Indeo, you will need your favorite Macintosh-based utility and the Video for Windows Converter utility from Microsoft, included in the accompanying CD-ROM. The basic steps are:

1. Complete and compress your movie, using your favorite Macintosh utility, selecting either Indeo or CinePak. Be sure to set the appropriate data rate for playback on the final Windows media.

2. Put the Windows compression extension into your Macintosh system folder. Reboot the system.

3. Launch the Video for Windows Converter utility.

4. Click the Open Source . . . button in the dialog box. (See Figure 5.31.) Locate the file or folder containing your movie(s) and select the movie (or the first movie in your list if you are converting multiple movies); click Open.

5. The list of your movies appears in the Source Folder within the dialog box (Figure 5.32). This is a batch utility. If more than one movie appears and you wish to convert a single movie, just click on that movie. Otherwise, click Select All.

**Figure 5.31
Video for Win-
dows Converter
main dialog
box.**

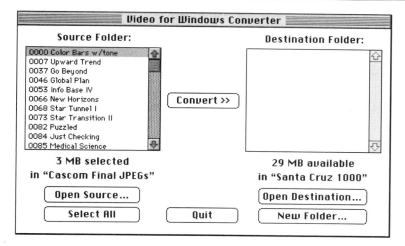

6. Select your destination by clicking on the Open Destination . . . or New Folder . . . button. Indicate your new folder or destination.

7. Click Convert. The Convert Settings dialog box appears (Figure 5.33). At this point, you need to make a few choices. The application will try to pick the best compression method by checking the compression, data rate, and size settings of all your movies. These appear in the middle of the dialog box.

   If the movie is already compressed in CinePak or Indeo, then select Direct Transfer from the pop-up box (Figure 5.34).

   Normally you will already have processed your audio to the proper sampling rate and bit depth; if so, leave the audio settings alone. If

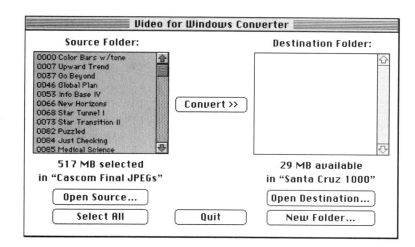

**Figure 5.32
Making your
selection from
the Source
Folder list.**

**Figure 5.33
The Convert Set-
tings dialog box.**

Source File Name:

0007 Upward Trend

Destination File Name:

0007PWRD.AVI

Video:

Source : 24 bit Photo – JPEG
Dest : 16 bit Microsoft Video 1

Compressed ▼

Settings...

Frame Rate: 15 ▲▼

Audio:

No audio in source

☐ Convert Audio

Settings...

Batch Formatting

◉ Bring up dialog   ○ Scan for best format
○ Use this format

[?]   [Scan]   [Cancel]   [OK]

you require different audio settings, or if your multiple movies all
have different settings and you wish to make them all the same, click
the Convert Audio . . . button. Adjust the audio settings as needed.
(See Figure 5.35.) Make sure Use this format is selected in the Batch
Formatting box.

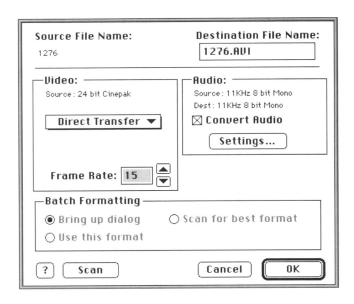

Source File Name:

1276

Destination File Name:

1276.AVI

Video:

Source : 24 bit Cinepak

Direct Transfer ▼

Frame Rate: 15 ▲▼

Audio:

Source : 11KHz 8 bit Mono
Dest : 11KHz 8 bit Mono

☒ Convert Audio

Settings...

Batch Formatting

◉ Bring up dialog   ○ Scan for best format
○ Use this format

[?]   [Scan]   [Cancel]   [OK]

**Figure 5.34
Select Direct
Transfer.**

**Figure 5.35
The Audio Set-
tings dialog box.**

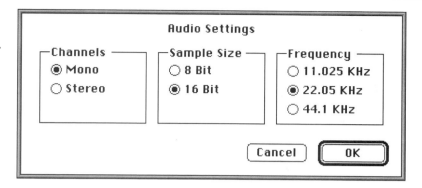

If one or more of your movies are in some other source compressor (Apple Video, Animation, and so forth), then select Bring up dialog from the Batch Formatting box (Figure 5.34). This will give you the opportunity to make choices for each movie in your batch before it is processed.

Once these settings are complete, press OK. You may now make your compression adjustments (see Figure 5.36).

NOTE: This utility modifies all files to a Windows 8.3 naming convention.

**Figure 5.36
Making your
choices from
the Compres-
sion Settings
dialog box.**

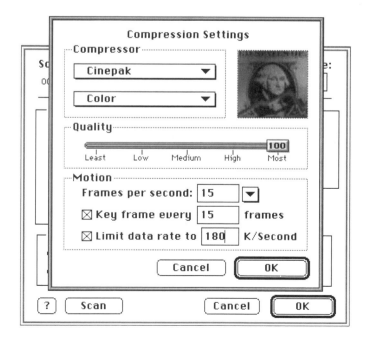

Figure 5.37
The progress
bar.

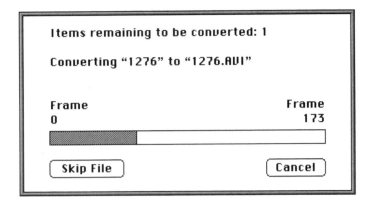

8. Click OK. The Conversion box appears showing the conversion(s) happening. (See Figure 5.37.) When the Conversion box changes back to the original dialog box, your movies have been converted to AVI files. You may either Quit or elect to convert other movies.

If the target is one of the Microsoft compressors, you will follow the same steps 1–7 just noted. You will need to select Compressed from the Video pop-up menu, then click on the Settings button in the video box. You will see the standard Compression settings dialog box (Figure 5.38). From there you select the new Microsoft compressor and other settings of your choice. Click OK. You can now proceed to step 8 and complete the movie conversion process.

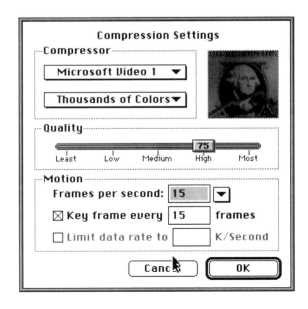

Figure 5.38
Using a
Microsoft com-
pressor.

**Figure 5.39
The AVI to
QuickTime util-
ity Open File
dialog bos.**

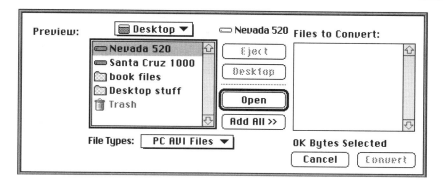

NOTE: Video for Windows normally interleave audio with every frame of
video. Files converted to the AVI format with the Video for Windows Converter
utility are not interleaved. To improve playback of these movies, especially for
eventual CD-ROM use, you will want to interleave the audio and video in
these files on the PC using VidEdit or some other PC-based editing tool.

AVI to QuickTime. If the target is to create QuickTime movies from AVI
files, you will need the Video for Windows Converter utility from Microsoft,
included on the accompanying CD-ROM. The basic steps are:

1. Launch the AVI to QT utility application. Select the source folder that
   contains the AVI files from the Open folder pop-up control and window. (See Figure 5.39.)

2. When the AVI files are displayed on the left side of the dialog box,
   you can select one or more files; then click Add, or you can select
   Add All. The selected files will appear in the Files to Convert window
   on the right side of the dialog box. (See Figure 5.40.)

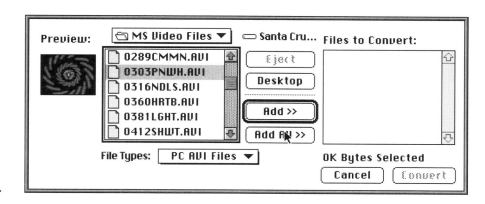

**Figure 5.40
Selecting the
files to convert.**

Figure 5.41
Setting the desti-
nation folder.

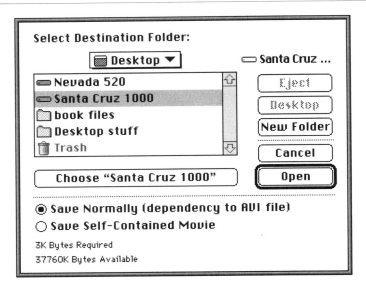

3. Click the Convert button in the lower-right corner of the window. A modified Save dialog box appears.

4. Select either Save Normally or Save Self-Contained Movie. (See Figure 5.41.)

   Saving as a self-contained file means that all of the data that makes up that movie becomes part of the new QuickTime file. Saving "normally" creates a QuickTime alias to the original AVI movie information. It is a pointer file that allows QuickTime to locate and play back the actual data (in this case, AVI data). Unlike a standard Macintosh alias, a QuickTime alias does not appear with italicized text. If you will always want to save your files a particular way, you can set the default from the File→Preferences menu (Figure 5.42).

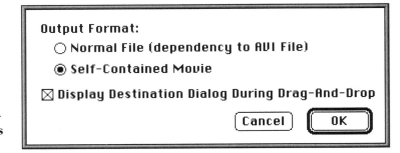

Figure 5.42
The Output For-
mat Preferences
selection box.

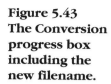

**Figure 5.43
The Conversion
progress box
including the
new filename.**

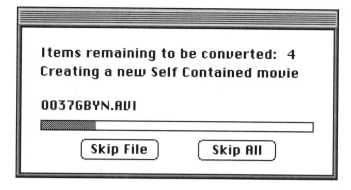

Items remaining to be converted: 4
Creating a new Self Contained movie

0037GBYN.AVI

Skip File   Skip All

Two issues need to be understood when saving an AVI file "normally": (1) If you ever change or trash the original AVI file, your QuickTime alias will no longer function; (2) if you do save "normally" and later decide you want your movie to be self-contained, you only need to open the alias in some utility such as MoviePlayer and use the Save As function from the File menu.

You will then choose Save Self-Contained Movie. This will transfer all of the AVI movie data into your QuickTime movie.

5. Select the destination folder or hard-disk drive. The files will now convert automatically. A progress dialog box shows the progress of the file conversions (Figure 5.43).

This converts the container file format, but it does not convert the digital video or audio data or the type of compression used. If the AVI source file contained video compressed with a VfW codec, it will still be in that format. You now need to use a utility such as ConvertTo-Movie, or your favorite QuickTime editor, to open the movie and select a QuickTime codec.

NOTE: Converting between different codecs can cause additional temporal and spatial quality loss. This can be true for any two codecs or even multiple recompressions in the same codec.

One of the codecs that operates cross platform is Indeo, developed by Intel. As we have mentioned earlier, it is similar to CinePak in the quality of its final output, but it takes a slightly different approach to how it compresses your video.

We asked Intel's Garry Weil to talk more about the use of Indeo, especially as it relates to cross-platform development. His essay follows.

CROSS-PLATFORM DEVELOPMENT USING INDEO VIDEO
by Garry Weil

Mr. Weil has been with Intel since 1988. He has worked on various software develop-ment tools teams, most recently tools for the i750 digital video processor. He currently is working for Intel's Developer Relations Group supporting Indeo technology with an emphasis on QuickTime environments. Garry co-authored a white paper titled "Cross-platform Development Using Indeo Video" from which this is excerpted. This and other Indeo video white papers, as well as Indeo video codec updates, can be down-loaded from the following electronic distribution sites:

- AppleLink: Third Parties, Third Party Demos/Updates, Software Updates, Compa-nies E-J, Intel Corporation
- Internet FTP: ftp.intel.com:/pub/IAL/Indeo_video
- Compuserve: Intel Architecture Labs forum (Go INTELA), Library 9
- Intel BBS: (916) 356-3600, Multimedia file area

Indeo video is Intel's digital video software technology for compression and play-back of video on personal desktop computers. It is a key ingredient for creating application assets that are usable on multiple platforms. There are two primary plat-forms for Indeo video development—namely, the Macintosh and Windows-based PCs. The three most common multimedia software environments that support Indeo video are Apple's QuickTime and QuickTime for Windows (QTW), and Microsoft's Video for Windows (VfW). Since QuickTime for the Macintosh (QTM) and Quick-Time for Windows use the same MooV file format, it is possible to play the same exact Indeo video file on both platforms from a single hybrid CD-ROM. (QTW sup-ports playback of MooV files only.)

Creating cross-platform Indeo video-compressed files entails much more than sim-ply converting a Macintosh formatted file to be readable on the PC. For example, there are several ways in which to assert palettes from a single Indeo video file under QTM, QTW, and VfW. In addition, audio sampling rates and audio interleav-ing are slightly different on the PC and the Macintosh and can degrade playback per-formance when not addressed properly.

Parameters should be set for capturing a movie richer in audio and video data than required for the final compressed file. For example, setting the video parame-ters to 320 × 240 @ 30 fps uncompressed allows for final Indeo video compression to a target movie of 240 × 180 @ 10 fps. This approach also provides for final com-pression with the original 320 × 240 @ 15 fps attributes later without recapturing. When down-sampling the captured frame rate, it is best to use integer fractions of the original frame rate. For example, if your target frame rate is 12, then the original

(continued)

capture should be at 24. Using a frame rate of 30 gives you the most flexibility for the final compressed file. From 30 frames per second, you can get 15 and 10 with one-half and one-third fractions, respectively.

If you are using the Intel Smart Video Recorder or Intel Smart Video Recorder Pro, direct capturing using Indeo video real-time compression capability is an option where Intel Raw capture is not possible with Macintosh capture boards. In one step, you capture and compress a file suitable for CD ROM playback. This can significantly reduce development time. Be careful not to off-line compress a real-time captured movie; this will result in double-compressed video, which may exhibit quality degradation. In fact, when real-time compressed video is recompressed using the off-line compression, any visual artifacts created by the real-time compressor can be amplified. This is analogous to the generation loss (degraded video quality) that occurs when making a videotape copy of an existing videotape.

To make an Indeo video movie file captured on one platform playable on another requires a file conversion step. An AVI movie will not play on the QTM or QTW until it has been converted to the QuickTime MooV file format. Similarly, a Quick-Time movie will not play under Video for Windows unless it has been converted to the AVI format.

Converting QuickTime to Video for Windows

There are two fundamental differences in the way in which QuickTime files can be stored on the Mac versus on the PC:

1. On the Mac, data can be split between files and between forks.
2. On the PC file system, all data must be contained in a single file.

The PC can only create the equivalent of Mac self-contained and single-fork files. Therefore, no further manipulations for Mac playback are required. QuickTime files created on the Mac must be made *self-contained* and *single-forked* before they are played back or compressed on the PC. These issues are discussed in detail next and are followed by procedures to perform these conversions. This conversion process begins on the Mac and is finished on the PC.

A MooV file on the Mac contains the actual video and audio streams in the data fork and all of the organizing information (headers, indices, sizes, media information, etc.) in the Resource fork. For portability, Apple defined a *single-fork* form of the MooV format in which the resource information is stored immediately after the audio and video data in the Data fork. The Resource fork may be empty. There is no playback penalty associated with a single-fork MooV format file. This process may be called single-forking, or "making files playable on non-Apple platforms."

(continued)

Mac-Based Conversion Steps

Start the conversion process by flattening the MooV format files.

- *Using video editing application software*—This conversion capability is a part of most video editing applications (e.g., VideoFusion, Premiere). With VideoFusion 1.5 or later, use the File Save As dialog box selecting "QuickTime self-contained format" and checking the "Cross-Platform" box. Premiere on the Mac offers this capability when using the File Export Flatten Movie command.

- *Conversion with playback utilities*— Both MoviePlayer 2.0 and Movie Converter 1.0 allow for self-containment and single forking. This is achieved by opening the movie file, selecting Save As from the File menu, and selecting the "Make movie self-contained" and "Playable on non-Apple computers" options. A new filename must be used or the conversion steps will not be performed by these utilities.

    The current VfW Converter utility from Microsoft poses this conversion capability but does not support Indeo video and Intel Raw compressed MooV files. These utilities can be patched using ResEdit to overcome this limitation. Microsoft support personnel have stated that an update to these utilities is being planned. Contact Microsoft or Indeo Technology Support for the latest information on these utilities.

Windows-Based Conversion Steps

Complete the conversion process by changing the file format from MooV to AVI.
    Currently, there are two choices for converting between AVI and MooV formats. These two utilities perform conversion with recompression.

- *TrMooV*—To convert a MooV format file, start TrMooV from within Windows. Select the source file using the Browse button. Select the target AVI format file by using the other Browse button. Make sure the new filename you select has a .AVI extension. After selecting the source and target filenames, select the Start button to perform the conversion.

    Conversion is accomplished without recompression, and interleaving of audio and video is correctly converted as well. At this time, TrMooV does not support conversion of Intel Raw compressed files. TrMooV converts Indeo video AVI files (Indeo video R3.1, Indeo video R3.2), but Intel Raw is not supported. Version 1.20 of TrMooV will not convert a palette that is attached to a MooV format file. A subsequent version of this utility should correctly translate palette information for optimal 8-bit color playback of Indeo video MooV format files (under QTW). TrMooV will not convert the audio sampling rate from Mac to VfW.

(continued)

- *SmartCap*—To convert a MooV format file, start SmartCap and select Playback Open File for the source MooV format file. Select the Playback Save As menu item, check AVI as the file type, and specify a target filename. When you select OK in the file dialog box, conversion will start. After the conversion is complete, SmartCap opens the converted AVI format file.

   When converting to QuickTime format, SmartCap, does *not* convert the audio interleaving. The interleaving can be converted by opening the converted file with VidEdit and selecting File Save As. The resulting file will have proper VfW interleaving. SmartCap will convert only Indeo video compressed AVI files (Indeo video R3.1, Indeo video R3.2, and Intel Raw). SmartCap will not convert the audio sampling rate from Mac to VfW. If a custom palette is attached to the MooV format file, it will be removed from the converted output AVI format file.

Converting Video for Windows to QuickTime

Converting AVI format files to MooV format requires both file format and audio transformations. It is essentially a copy process and does not take into account the differences in audio interleaving and sampling rates. Because PC files are single-forked by definition and AVI format files are self-contained by definition, self-containment and single-forking file issues are not relevant when converting from PC file structures to Mac. However, the differences that exist for audio sampling rates between the two platforms create certain issues.

Cross-Platform Development Scenarios

The following scenarios describe typical cross-platform environments and detail the steps by which Indeo video files can be created and manipulated for cross-platform playback.

Scenario 1: Macintosh Capture/Macintosh Compress

Typical Application: Produce Indeo video files in QuickTime format immediately playable on the Macintosh. Additional steps are provided if those files require playback under QuickTime for Windows on the PC.

1. Capture in lossless mode with an appropriate video capture board (assuming real-time capture). Proprietary JPEG compression boards, such as the Radius Video Vision Studio and RasterOps MoviePak II, are commonly used for this purpose.

(continued)

2. Compress into Indeo video using a compression application. Once properly compressed and self-contained, an Indeo video file is suitable for pressing onto a CD-ROM. At this stage, the MooV file is playable on a Macintosh only.

3. To make this file playable under QTW, flatten/convert the Macintosh MooV file to a single fork file. Remember that the audio sampling must be changed to MPC rates for optimal playback under QTW or VfW. The Indeo video file is suitable for playing on a Windows machine that has QuickTime for Windows installed. It is ready to be pressed onto a *hybrid* CD-ROM playable on either a Mac or a PC.

Scenario 2: Macintosh Capture/PC Compress

Two important advantages of the Mac Capture/PC Compress scenario are:

- The Mac capture station is free to perform other work.
- Fast, low-cost PCs can be utilized for compression.

Typical Application: Utilize low-cost PCs for time-consuming off-line compression. This scenario produces Indeo video files in both QuickTime and VfW formats.

1. Capture in lossless mode with an appropriate video capture board (assuming real-time capture).
2. Recompress the MooV to Intel Raw.
3. To make this file playable under QTW, convert the Macintosh MooV format file to a self-contained and single-fork file. Remember that the audio sampling must be changed to MPC rates for optimal playback under QTW or VfW.
4. Transport the Intel Raw MooV file to a PC.
5. Convert the MooV format file to AVI format.
6. Compress the Intel Raw file into an Indeo video AVI file using the recommended compression settings discussed previously.
7. Convert the Indeo video compressed AVI file back to MooV format using a conversion program.
8. Transport the Indeo video compressed MOV file back to the Mac.
9. Use MakeItMooV to set the file creator and type to TVOD and MooV respectively.
10. Check for proper audio interleaving for QuickTime using MovieAnalyzerMac. At this point, there are two separate Indeo video files ready to be pressed onto CD-ROM: an AVI format and a MooV format.

(continued)

Scenario 3: PC Capture/Macintosh Compress

Two important advantages of the PC Capture/Mac Compress scenario are:

- The PC capture station is free to perform other work.
- Stable editing and post-production software tools available on the Mac can be utilized.

Typical Application: Produce Indeo video files in AVI format playable on the PC. QuickTime versions of those files will be produced in the process.

1. Capture in Intel Raw using the Intel Smart Video Recorder or Intel Smart Video Recorder Pro capture board.
2. Convert the AVI format file to MooV format.
3. Transport the Intel Raw MooV format file to a Mac.
4. Use MakeItMooV to set the file creator and type to TVOD and MooV respectively.
5. Compress the Intel Raw file into Indeo video using a compression application with the recommended settings. At this point, the movie is a finished Indeo video QuickTime file, ready to be pressed onto a Mac-only CD-ROM.
6. To make this file playable under QTW, convert the Macintosh MooV to a self-contained and single-fork file.
7. Convert the audio sampling rate to MPC standards for optimal QTW playback. At this point, the Indeo video MooV format file may be played under QuickTime for Windows on the PC, and is ready to be pressed onto a hybrid CD-ROM.
8. Convert the file back to AVI format using a conversion program. Remember that whenever converting from MooV format to AVI, audio needs to be re-interleaved one to one for VfW (one frame to one audio sample). At this point, the Indeo video AVI file is ready to be played under Video for Windows.

Creating Full-Screen Movies Where You Don't Have Them

Think of the sleight-of-hand magician or the illusionist. By using the art of misdirection, he or she makes you think you are seeing something in the hand or on the stage that isn't there, or he or she disguises the fact that something *is* there by making you look elsewhere.

Although a quarter-screen movie may look good and play well, it may be lost if just thrown onto the full-screen stage. Other things in the background—folders, drive icons, and so forth—divert the viewer's attention and take away some level of effectiveness of the video. The best thing to do is to create a full-screen display, thereby covering up everything you don't want the viewer to see. One technique for making a full-screen movie from something smaller—for example, a quarter-screen movie—is to simply blow it up (pixel-double) using something like MoviePlayer. The general result is a highly pixelated movie that doesn't play very well.

Let's assume that this is not acceptable.

You could go back and recapture and reprocess the movie in the larger format, but there are far too many trade-offs to make that practical in most cases.

This is where illusion comes in. The best technique we have found is to create a full-screen background and drop the quarter-screen movie into a window. To which you are going to say, "Of course! I planned to do that anyway. What's the big deal?" There is no big deal, but there are a few things you can do to create a better full-screen background—one that complements rather than interferes with your video.

What we typically do is this:

Our staff artist, Gordon, sits in on our meetings with the client so he knows what they are hoping to get as a final product. He watches over our shoulders as we edit the materials to see what the final theme and composition of the video will be. He also looks for some seemingly little things that can make a difference in the final product.

Things that he looks for include:

- The main colors used in the video. This is so he can create a backdrop with colors that are complementary to the main action without being overpowering or obviously clashing. He does this with an artist's eye, but there are a number of books at local libraries that can help you determine what colors go with each other. Another thing to do is to pick up a PMS color set. (They generally sell for around $40 at art supply stores.) By holding up the different color chips to your video, you can get a pretty good idea of what to aim toward and what to avoid. Another benefit of having a PMS set is in case you take on more than just digital video work. We have clients who want us to do the entire package, from video to packaging to CD-ROM labels to instruction books. With our PMS guide, we can go to any printer and order the exact colors we want, not just "sort of a reddish brown . . . you know?"

- The location with the frames where the majority of the action occurs. This can assist in the proper positioning of the video window within the overall screen. The human eye tends to look just slightly above and to the right of the center point on a page, or the screen. A trick that advertisers have used for many, many years is to place information or images they want the viewer to see near that position on the page and anything they don't really want you to look at in the lower-left part of the page. If you take a lesson from this, it is to position your video window near the center of the screen, but just a bit off center so that the main part of the action occurs in this prime viewing location.

Once it is determined what colors, theme, and location will be used, the artist goes away and creates the backdrop, usually in Adobe Photoshop (3.0) or Fractal Design Painter (3.0). This is saved out as a PICT file using Photo JPEG compression. The level of compression we use depends on two things: the delivery media and the intricacy of the background.

The more restrictive the delivery medium (CD-ROM is considerably more restrictive than running a production directly from a hard-disk drive) the greater the level of compression we use. For most applications, we save the background in 8-bit mode at either high quality or highest quality. If the background is fairly simple (and this is a trick that only works with a limited number of cases) you can create a blurred background; then it is easy to get by with medium quality when compressing your backdrop.

As with everything, experiment. You may even find that a solid black background provides a striking backdrop for some productions. If you do, might we suggest one final thing? For a black, static backdrop, where you either have multiple segments of video to show or where you can "chop" your large video into several segments, vary the location on the screen where the different segments appear. This adds a bit of variety and visual excitement to your production.

NOTE: Keep in mind that QuickTime movies play best when the window dimensions are multiples of 4 pixels, and that the left edge of the window is on a pixel that is also a multiple of 4.

No matter whether you shoot your own video or use someone else's, whether you have audio or not, or even whether you have any special effects, by taking just a little bit more time, you can "polish" your final product into something that may be just a bit more than the client expected. We can point to several cases where this extra effort on our part turned into additional jobs from a client, or someone they showed that project to.

As we started this chapter by saying, there is no huge, master set of special techniques involved in desktop video production. There is a lot of common sense that must be exercised—but there are advantages to using uncommon approaches. There are a number of things you can do along the way that might positively or negatively affect the final result, and we have discussed some of these in this chapter and throughout the book.

Actually, you don't have to do anything special to any piece of video or audio. You don't have to do any special effects or tricky editing. As long as you take care of what you do, and as long as you understand the process, you can turn out good work within a limited budget. There is tons of work out there for people and companies with basic desktop video studios.

You don't *have* to take time to understand the whole project, including the delivery and playback considerations. But if you *don't* take the time to understand, what you might end up with is something acceptable, but possibly not what the client expected. In the worst cases, what the client gets is unusable (read: *OUCH!*).

We have bid against, and lost to, contractors with basic desktop video studios, who simply capture video from tape into their AV Macintosh computers using the built-in video and audio connectors, and use a single piece of software for the capture, editing, and compression. In some cases, that was the most acceptable approach for the client; their needs—quality and cost—were fulfilled by these other contractors.

In one such case, however, the client expected something more. When they didn't get it, they came back to us. They were disappointed with what the other people produced and wanted to know if we could fix it—make it run smoothly and look better. And could we do it all that afternoon?

It took several hours of show-and-tell to educate them in the entire process and to help them understand what is and is *not* possible. *Then* they understood why we couldn't make the already-processed material look any better. Unfortunately, they had neither the money nor the time to let us go back to square one and produce it the way they wanted.

They ended up going back to the first contractor and demanding that the entire project be done over. We don't know what happened, but we are willing to bet that *we'll* get the call from that client when they want to do another project.

Is there a lesson in the previous paragraphs? Probably. If so, it goes something like: "Understand the capabilities and limits of your own studio. Always try to push the envelope, but don't bite off more than you can chew, or than your client will want to swallow."

We know there is a gross-sounding analogy in there. Sorry, but it's true.

6

Case Studies

This chapter highlights six case studies taken from projects produced at Toucan Studios during 1994. We have selected these projects because, although they all use digital video in some fashion, each has either a different end result or a special combination of hardware and software used to achieve the desired results.

The projects range from capturing and editing several hours of vacation video into a twenty-minute movie through simple conversion of digital video from one format to another, up to the development of an interactive "edutainment" title due out in 1995.

In each case, we provide:

- A description of the basic project, the end result of the project, and its intended use

- A screen shot from the project

- Lists of the different hardware and software products used in the project

- A description of major steps taken to produce this project along with the specifications of the digital video

- A list of any lessons we learned during the project

Although no two projects are exactly alike, you will notice similarities in our approach to many of the projects in these case studies. We have found that certain techniques, coupled with standardized hardware and software combinations, seem to keep popping up. But we don't limit ourselves to just a single combination. In many cases, including a few of these, we have begun a project using one set of hardware and software, and have ended using a different set.

This approach is time consuming, but there are certain projects or materials that just don't work the way you expect at the outset. Since this is our livelihood, we are forced to bite the bullet and start over.

This might not have been the case two years ago; when we were just starting Toucan Studios, we rarely used more than a single application and did all our capture directly into the newly introduced Quadra 840AV computer. That limited what we could do, and we recognized those limitations early on; that recognition prompted us to go searching for a more complete set of tools.

As we mentioned, the half-dozen case studies range from quick and easy video editing and saving to tape (or so we thought going into the project) to the creation of CD-ROM–based retail products.

One of the case studies deals with a prototype for a future project. Although the actual project—assuming that our bid is accepted—will be developed using other software tools, we sometimes find it necessary to create a quick prototype for a potential customer. Creating prototypes for every job will be a waste of your time, but you may find that certain projects are detailed enough, or that the customer cannot visualize what you propose, unless you do so.

Don't hesitate to spend some time creating a prototype; even if you don't get that project, chances are that you can use the same shell for other prototypes in the future. There is one final thing we would like to pass along about prototypes: Create them using materials that match or are complementary to those of your potential client. Never use materials that are in any way competitive to your client. A bit of research goes a long way here.

A word of warning as you begin looking through these case studies: Although you may run into projects that are similar to these, please do not just duplicate what we have done. Each project, each video source, deserves special attention and experimentation to get the best possible results from your particular setup.

That being said, on to the studies . . .

Case Study Number 1:
Editing and Saving Video Back to Tape

Project Description

The intent of this project was to take almost three hours of vacation video shot on Hi-8 tape, edit it down to a manageable and meaningful twenty-minute presentation, and then save the results back out to Hi-8 tape so that it could be duplicated and sent to friends and relatives.

Although this is a relatively uncomplicated task, and well within the scope of almost every desktop video producer, it was not without its share of pain and agony.

The first task was to go through all of the material and develop a basic outline and script (so the final results would make sense and be in some semblance of order). During that scan of the tapes, a rough edit list was made to pare down the 170-plus minutes to about 28 minutes. This was important because, due to other projects already under way, we didn't have enough hard-disk space to capture more than about twenty-five minutes at full-screen size. Fortunately, most vacation video features slow pans and zooms and people just standing in front of buildings, waving and smiling. (See Figure 6.1.)

Tools

Hardware	Software
Hi-8 Camcorder with S-Video output	Adobe Premiere
Macintosh Quadra 840AV	ConvertToMovie
Radius StudioVision card set	Alaska Software DigiTrax

**Figure 6.1
A typical frame from the vacation movie.**

AM 2:20:31

Step by Step

1. As mentioned, only the segments identified by first viewing the entire set of tapes was captured at full-screen (640 × 480) 15 fps, using JPEG capture. We would have preferred capturing at 30 fps, but disk space did not allow this. (We received the client's agreement prior to making this decision.)

2. In manageable groups (since the typical shot was about fifteen seconds), the unedited clips were loaded into Premiere, where in and out points were identified, some minor transitions were added (simple A→B fades and a couple of wipes), and two-to-three-minute groups were processed and saved.

3. All the edited segments were loaded into ConvertToMovie and processed into a single movie using no further compression and no limit to the data rate.

4. The end result was previewed, and it was determined that the original thought of adding just a music track would not be enough. Along with several pieces of music captured at 44.1 MHz, we recorded a running narrative track to DAT tape and edited it in DigiTrax, maintaining the original 48 MHz sampling of the DAT. All of the final audio tracks were placed into DigiTrax and saved out as a single 22 KHz, 16-bit stereo track.

5. The final video movie (now somewhere near the twenty-minute target) and the music track were combined using Premiere.

6. The final result was saved to Hi-8 tape using S-Video and stereo audio cables. That tape was then duplicated in real time, using the camcorder and its S-Video/stereo audio outputs to a SVHS deck (onto standard VHS tapes).

The results were pretty good, considering the generational loss of going down to VHS. Only about one minute of the total twenty-two minutes had any noticeable problems related to the slower frame rate, but since this was a quick piece for family and friends, the 15 fps was acceptable for this project.

Lessons Learned

During this project, we learned three important things:

1. Hi-8 is a pretty good source for this type of video.

2. If you have the ability to discuss things with your clients prior to their taking the actual video, suggest slow pans, slow zooms, and lots of shots of people standing in front of buildings waving—slowly—and smiling. Also, tell them to white-balance their camera whenever they change locations or subjects. (There were several scenes where this was not the case, and the results were scenes that tended to be a bit green.)

3. Plan to have enough hard-disk space for capturing all your targeted source video clips so that you are not forced to drop your recording to 15 fps as we did.

Case Study Number 2: Transferring Director to QuickTime

Project Description

The intent of this project was to take 100-plus Director movies and transfer them to QuickTime movies, maintaining the frame rate and visual quality. (See Figure 6.2.) The end results would then be turned over to a programmer for use in new training products to be run from single-speed CD-ROM drives. Both Macintosh-only and cross-platform QuickTime movies were required.

Although this seemed a simple task on the outside, preliminary testing showed that about 25 percent of the Director movies were created in some manner as to be incompatible with Director's own "transfer to QuickTime" functions. And several of the remaining movies did not play at acceptable frame rates (witnessed by jumping or missing frames).

Tools

Hardware	Software
Macintosh Quadra 840AV	Macromedia Director 4.0
	Apple MoviePlayer 2.0
	Adobe Photoshop
	ConvertToMovie

Step by Step

1. All segments were viewed and approximate frame rates were computed.

2. Each movie was opened in Director and exported into QuickTime format. Only about 75 percent of the movies successfully completed this step. (The reasons are still unknown; we would get a system beep and an error message saying that the operation could not be completed.)

3. Those movies that did translate were opened in MoviePlayer and then edited to remove extraneous frames that made many of the movies 25–50 percent longer than the original Director movies. These were saved out as both Macintosh and cross-platform QuickTime movies. (Although we normally would have saved only a single set of finished movies in cross-platform format, we had been advised that the programmer needed the dual data fork for the Macintosh versions.)

**Figure 6.2
A Director
movie about to
be converted to
QuickTime.**

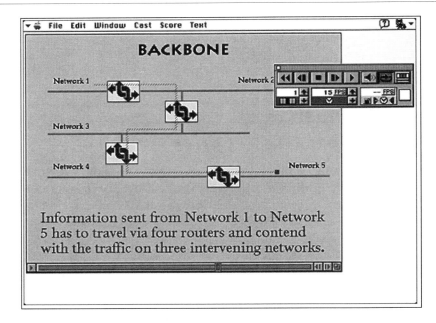

4. The remaining Director movies were opened in Photoshop and saved out as a stack of still frames.

5. Individual frames from each movie were opened in MoviePlayer and reassembled into a movie. These were saved.

6. The reassembled movies were opened in ConvertToMovie, where an appropriate frame rate was set so the final movie would match the originals in their running time. These were saved as both Macintosh and cross-platform QuickTime movies.

**Lessons
Learned**

During this project, we learned three important things:

1. Not all Director movies seem to translate easily into QuickTime—and we don't know why.

2. It would have been to our advantage to be able to connect with the original developer of the Director presentations, to solve the export problem, but that was not possible on this project.

3. Plan contingencies for any project. We did not anticipate the problems encountered exporting from Director and therefore spent an extra two days making this project work.

Case Study Number 3:
Creating an Interactive Kiosk Prototype

Project Description

The intent of this project was to create an interactive kiosk prototype to demonstrate the kinds of media and interactivity possible for potential use in a state park.

The materials that would be available for the finished kiosk included photographs (both historical new photos to be taken), videos (ranging from 8-mm home movies to new Hi-8 video to be shot), scanned documents, new text, and an audio narrative to be recorded, edited, and saved as part of the individual sections of the presentation.

The actual screen size is 640 × 480 with a 320 × 240 window appearing on about 75 percent of the screens, allowing the display of 15 fps, CinePak-compressed movies, each between fifteen seconds and two minutes. (See Figure 6.3.)

Tools

Hardware	Software
3/4-inch U-Matic deck	Avid VideoShop
Hi-8 camera with S-Video output	Apple MoviePlayer 2.0
Macintosh Quadra 840AV	Adobe Photoshop
	ConvertToMovie
Radius StudioVision card set	A custom authoring tool

Step by Step

1. Sample video segments were captured in VideoShop from two different 3/4-inch tapes and from a single Hi-8 tape, at quarter-screen (320 × 240) 15 fps, using JPEG capture. It was necessary to rebalance the video signal for each source tape using a TBC, vectorscope, and known-good color bars.

2. Each video was rough-edited using MoviePlayer.

3. Individual segments were re-edited in MoviePlayer to create the final sample movies and were saved as self-contained movies on a clean, defragmented hard drive. Existing audio tracks were removed and new music tracks were added during this stage.

4. Movies were compressed using ConvertToMovie at 15 fps, CinePak-compressed, with key frames every fifteen frames. Because this was to be played from a hard drive, no data rate limit was set. When this is done, CinePak generally stays in the 300–400 kps range.

**Figure 6.3
A frame from
the kiosk
prototype.**

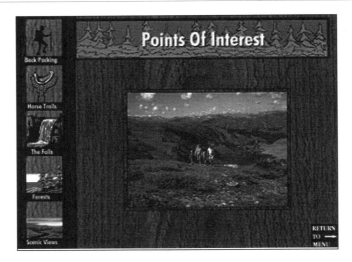

5. The interface screens were created using Photoshop with the movie window positioned so that the left edge is on a multiple of 4 pixels.

6. Various still frames were either saved from QuickTime movies or scanned at 72 dpi on an 8-bit color scanner.

7. All still images were processed using Photoshop to achieve a standard brightness and contrast, plus balanced color from still to still.

8. An interactive shell was developed with a custom authoring tool we use for fast prototyping. All links were developed using the actual edited movies and stills.

9. The final prototype was saved to a clean, defragmented hard drive and shown to the potential customer. Ultimately, the customer decided to produce a videotape in-house. They loved the prototype but didn't have enough funding for the full-scale project.

**Lessons
Learned**

During this project, we learned three important things:

1. Whenever you have more than one source tape, especially if they are different formats, perform color balancing each time you change sources. This goes for still photographs as well. Import them into a program such as Photoshop and adjust the color balance and brightness/contrast of any pictures that are noticeably different from the majority.

2. Know enough about your potential clients to be able to identify and use sample materials that are similar to their own circumstances. This will help them visualize what their actual project will look like.

3. A good prototype shell can be adapted for use for other clients (changing all the graphics, of course!).

Case Study Number 4: A Desktop Seminar

Project Description

The intent of this project was to create a replacement for a speaker-led seminar. This "desktop seminar" needed to be created using a specific development tool, with video shot for another project, PICT files from a third source, and a script developed by yet another party. (See Figure 6.4.)

The end result needed to be playable from a single-speed CD-ROM drive, on Macintosh computers using 68030 processors running at 20 MHz.

The development tool, Desktop Seminar Toolkit from Apple, lets you create a text and visuals script in HyperCard, then it assembles and saves out a shell application that calls up each text, audio, and visual element as required. Although somewhat slow, it has the advantage of being easy to use and creates a reasonable end product.

Tools

Hardware	Software
BetaCam SP deck	Avid VideoShop
Macintosh Quadra 840AV	Apple MoviePlayer 2.0
Radius StudioVision card set	Alaska Software DigiTrax
	Apple Desktop Seminar Toolkit
	ConvertToMovie

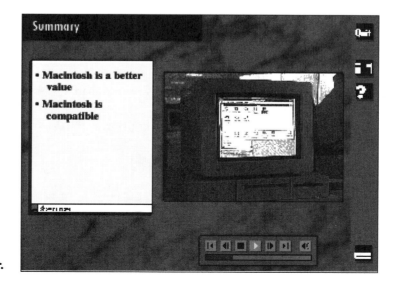

**Figure 6.4
A frame from a desktop seminar.**

Step by Step

1. All applicable video segments were identified and captured using VideoShop from a duplicate master BetaCam SP tape, at quarter-screen (320 × 240) 15 fps, using JPEG capture. It was necessary to balance and brighten the video signal considerably.

2. Each movie was edited to a rough length using MoviePlayer. Desktop Seminar Toolkit has the ability to set individual in and out points for any video, so exact editing was not necessary.

3. The audio track from the complete videotape was recorded and processed using DigiTrax to 11 KHz, 8-bit mono to allow a data rate for the audio of around 10 kps.

4. The original movie format accepted by Desktop Seminar Toolkit was 240 × 180. This size was determined to be too small to represent the visual information contained in both the movies and the PICT files. So we spent one whole night (6:00 P.M. until 5:00 A.M.) rewriting the code in the Toolkit with the assistance of a valued friend, Sean Stewart. The new window size, 320 × 240, allows us to keep the original movie size with very little else necessary other than compression to meet the playback requirements.

5. Movies were compressed using ConvertToMovie at 15 fps, CinePak-compressed, with key frames every fifteen frames. Because this was to be played from a slow CD-ROM drive, the data rate limit was set to 100 kps. This project was created pre–QuickTime 2.0 (QuickTime 1.6 had just been released), and thus the lower data rate.

6. The interface screen in Desktop Seminar Toolkit is user-selectable from a list of about one dozen preset patterns, so there was no need to create a custom interface; we only needed to ensure that the movie window was positioned so that the left edge was on a multiple of 4 pixels. (In a future use of the DS Toolkit, we did go back in and insert a new, custom interface in the list.)

7. Once all of the elements were processed individually and the Hyper-Card script was finalized, a press of a button assembled the entire thing.

Lessons Learned

During this project, we learned four important things:

1. Unless it is unavoidable, anything smaller than 320 × 240 screen size doesn't allow most screen text within a movie to be readable.

2. If clients insist on a specific development and playback application, be sure they understand the plusses and minuses of that environment. Our client was slightly surprised at how slow the end product ran when played from a CD-ROM (even though we had discussed this up front).

3. Understand the performance characteristics of the authoring tool you

use, because this one required that the movies have no audio for the first second or so. This caused us to reprocess several movies.

4. Not all video works well in smaller-screen formats. The source video for this project was from a completed video presentation. It was very dark with stark lighting. This posed a few problems in the final video, which tended to become even darker and more stark during compression.

NOTE: As of this writing, Apple Computer, Inc. has halted the sale of the Desktop Seminar Toolkit. If you already have or can get a copy of it, it is a good tool for creating projects where there is material to be presented with only a small amount of interactivity on the part of the user. DS Toolkit also provides the ability to create tests based on the materials presented.

Case Study Number 5: Producing a Special Effects Content CD for Multimedia Use

Project Description

The intent of this project was to take sets of 100 effects clips ranging between five and sixty seconds and converting them into 15 fps QuickTime for Macintosh, QuickTime for Windows, and Video for Windows movies. The original clips were created using frame-by-frame animation, saved to 35-mm film, then transferred to BetaCam SP tape. The end result is to create a salable product featuring high-quality JPEG, 320 × 240, 15 fps movies that may be used as animated backgrounds and transitions in multimedia productions and products, plus highest-quality CinePak, 160 × 120, 15 fps movies to be used in a visual database, or for applications where the 160 × 120 size is immediately applicable. (See Figure 6.5.)

The end results also required that a clip identity screen with individual numbering and titling, plus a black frame, be created and added to the beginning of each clip. These clips, along with fifty audio tracks in both AIFF and WAV formats, were then recorded onto sets of two CD-ROMs.

Tools

Hardware	Software
BetaCam SP deck	Avid VideoShop
Macintosh Quadra 840AV	Adobe Photoshop
Radius StudioVision card set	Adobe Premiere
	Apple MovieShop
	Kodak Shoebox

**Figure 6.5
A frame from a
Select Effects
movie.**

Step by Step

1. All video segments were captured with VideoShop from the BetaCam SP tapes at quarter-screen (320 × 240) 15 fps, using JPEG capture.

2. A title or identity screen was developed using Photoshop and saved out in both 320 × 240 and 160 × 120 sizes, saved as PICT files. A black frame was also created in Photoshop and saved as a PICT file.

3. Segments were loaded into Premiere, with appropriate in and out points selected.

4. The title screen PICT and black frame PICT were imported and positioned in Premiere. The title frame was opened and the appropriate text information added.

5. The assembled script was then saved in 320 × 240 size, JPEG compression selected, but not processed.

6. The assembled script was then saved in 160 × 120 size, CinePak compression selected, but not processed.

7. The next movie and title screen were processed and the scripts saved, until all 100 clips had scripts in both screen sizes.

8. Premiere was used to batch process (in groups of 10) all of the scripts. A QuickTime single data fork (cross-platform playability) was selected. Since the larger movies are not designed to play from the CD-ROM, the 320 × 240 files were saved with no additional compression, at 15 fps, using highest-quality JPEG. The smaller, 160 × 120 clips

were compressed using CinePak at 15 fps, with key frames every fifteen frames and the data rate limited to 240 kps. The resulting movies were saved to a clean, defragmented hard drive.

9. The 320 × 240 JPEG QuickTime clips were batch processed into AVI files using the VfW Converter utility. Microsoft's Video 1 codec was selected as the target data type. Because of their single data fork nature, the QuickTime for Macintosh files were deemed playable using the QuickTime for Windows player.

10. All movies were arranged and named in accordance with proper Macintosh (up to 31 characters) and Windows (8.3) conventions.

11. A cross-platform visual database was created using Kodak's Shoebox software. Indexing and multiple keyword search information was entered for each clip. Each movie and audio clip was imported into the database. The data was exported and the whole process re-created on the Windows platform.

12. Several cycles of test CD-ROM one-offs were created and tested. Revisions were made to correct all anomalies.

13. The QuickTime for Windows files played almost as expected; the Video for Windows AVI files played in a jerky manner, and both required reprocessing at a lower data rate.

Lessons Learned

During this project, we learned three important things:

1. Setting up all of the scripts in Premiere is time-consuming and a bit ponderous, but the ability to batch process the end results (at night and in between other uses of the computer system) more than made up for the time spent.

2. QuickTime for Windows files, although the same structure as QuickTime for Macintosh, must be reprocessed at a lower data rate (180 kps maximum) in order to play from a Windows CD-ROM.

3. Because of the lower data rate mandated in Windows CD-ROM playback situations, the quality of the AVI clips is slightly compromised compared with that of the Macintosh clips.

Case Study Number 6: Creating a Retail Product

Project Description

The intent of this project was to create an entertaining and educational retail product based on an annual race held for the past twenty-five years in northern California. Just as a bit of background, this race features as many as seventy-five human-powered (read: *pedal power*) works of art, created by artists from around the world. For the twenty-fifth race, these sculptures ranged from a one-man *USS Enterprise* NCC-1701 up to a 90-foot long, multiperson carp, with themes such as a giant sardine can, a Flintstones car, and an armadillo in between. The three-day race requires each kinetic vehicle to traverse thirty-eight miles of city streets, freeways, mud bogs, swamps, and sand dunes and a couple trips across a saltwater bay. It is an extremely fun and environmentally aware race, run "for the glory" of just being there, rather than going for the win. In fact, the big prize winner is the team that comes in dead middle! Enough advertising.

The final product is a CD-ROM featuring over forty-five minutes of video highlights from most of the twenty-five-year history of the race, audio interviews, color and black-and-white PICTs, and lots of text. The video sources ranged from old 8-mm film through Hi-8 through BetaCam SP; the audio sources ranged from Hi-8 to MiniDisc. Over seventy-five hours of new and archived video material was distilled down for the final product. (See Figure 6.6.)

Tools

Hardware	Software
BetaCam SP deck	Adobe Premiere
Hi-8 camcorder with S-Video output	Apple MoviePlayer 2.0
SVHS deck with S-Video output	ConvertToMovie
Macintosh Quadra 840AV	Alaska Software DigiTrax
Radius StudioVision card set	Apple Media Tool
	Fractal Design Painter 3.0
	Adobe Photoshop

Step by Step

1. The distillation of all the video was captured at quarter screen (320 × 240) 15 fps, using JPEG capture.
2. Where multiple clips needed to be combined, each clip was loaded into Premiere, where in and out points were identified, some minor

**Figure 6.6
A frame from a
Select Effects
movie.**

transitions were added (simple A→B fades), and the groups were processed and saved.

3. All of the edited segments were loaded into ConvertToMovie and processed using CinePak compression with a limit to the data rate of 180 kps. Because this product was to be cross-platform, all movies were saved as single data fork files.

4. All of the audio tracks were processed using DigiTrax. Differences in fidelity and input settings were overcome through the use of the built-in equalizer. In the case of videos with very "noisy" audio, some audio was extracted from the movies, processed in DigiTrax, and added back to the movie using MoviePlayer when possible and using Premiere when exact synchronization was required.

5. The interactive design had been created prior to starting this project with all branching and interactivity identified. The actual shell for this product was created using Apple Media Tool. Custom graphics were created in Photoshop and Fractal Design's Painter.

6. The final videos, audios, and text files were assembled in Apple Media Tool with all linking of elements accomplished as each element was added.

7. A test CD-ROM one-off was created and tested. Several links were identified as being inoperative and were corrected. At the same time, several elements were deemed to be inappropriate for the final prod-

uct, and a number of places identified where new elements need to be created and added. Each of these will be created using the same techniques as used for the original materials.

8. This project is still in development.

During this project, we learned five important things:

1. Creating a retail product is harder than it looks!

2. You really need to have access to someone with experience in lengthy interactive presentations. The best type of individual to locate is an instructional designer—someone who understands how people learn and follow information. Without such expertise, you are taking a big shot in the dark trying to guess how the average person will use your product.

3. Shoot for the end product. Have a good idea of what you need for your product before you go out, and either shoot your own video or have someone else do it. If you don't, you will need to go through far too much video in an effort to distill down to the usable stuff. You will go mad!

4. It will be worth your time to learn Apple Media Tool if you intend to create Macintosh or cross-platform interactive projects. Once you get the hang of it, and learn some of its little peccadilloes, you can assemble a project relatively quickly and painlessly.

5. If you want to create a retail product, look for a publisher either before you create the product or as you are creating it. If you can put together a prototype, you will be doing yourself a great favor. A good publisher can help you with the promotion, distribution, and sales of your product; some publishers will even go so far as to help fund interesting projects in return for exclusive rights.

Summary

These are just six of our past and current projects. Something that we have done with several of these, plus a few others we haven't mentioned here, was to create a demonstration CD-ROM. We created a variation of the kiosk prototype shell using new custom graphics, processed everything to run on CD-ROM (some of our projects were not originally meant to run at that data rate), added some music tracks, and ended up with a disk that we send to many prospective clients.

At first, we would individually cut CD-ROM one-offs to send, but at $13–$15 apiece, that got a bit expensive. We recently had a run of several hundred produced for us at a very reasonable price. If your desktop video studio is going to be your business, we suggest that you take some of your best projects and create a demo disk.

One alternative to creating a CD-ROM of your work, especially if you are just starting out and are on a limited budget, is to create a slideshow of still frames of some of your work and save it to a high-density floppy diskette. Some of our end products have been exactly this—a series of ten to fifteen still frames saved out as a QuickTime or AVI movie. Actually, this approach gives you a high degree of flexibility. You can change the mix of slides in your demo "movie" to suit the potential client.

Part Three

PRODUCT REVIEWS

7

Software Product Reviews

No book on a specialty subject such as desktop digital video would be complete without a listing of the products available. Although we can't promise that the list of products we have and will discuss is exhaustive, we have made an effort to go out and find many of the mainstream offerings available as of the beginning of 1995.

The reviews in these two final chapters of the book are not of the "we both gave it two hot buttered popcorns" school. We don't want anybody to be angry if we give their product less of a glowing report than they feel it deserves. To be honest, we haven't found any *bad* products out there. Some, however, are more applicable to a broader range of projects than others.

Our system of review is to let you know what standard features you would expect in a particular type of application and what unique special features a particular product might have. We also will tell you what sorts of projects or processes we use a product for.

We also give the minimum system requirements as listed by the manufacturer. These are the basic requirements to boot and nominally use the application. As we have discussed in several places in this book, many desktop video applications are memory gluttons; you should understand that you will probably require a higher level of system setup (more memory, possibly a faster processor, and so forth) if you are to get full use from some of these products.

The final part of each review is our gut reaction to the product: Is it typical for its class? Does it shine like a shaft of light from above? Is there anything we wish the vendor would do for the next update?

Even if we have lots of good things to say about an application, remember what we have stated all along: Not every product is going to be right for every project. Read these reviews, go to a good software store (or two or three), and look at as many applications as you can. Mentally measure what you see against what you do. If you like what you see, it probably is a good product for your desktop video studio.

NOTE: Although this is not a guarantee, the chances are good that if a product is at version 2.x or 3.x or higher, the vendor is interested in updating and upgrading the software periodically. This is a good thing; it generally means that the vendor is actively supporting its products (and possibly the users, too) and is investing in the future of that application. It also means that there may be low-cost upgrades available to you as the next revisions come out.

We cover software products in three categories:

- Video and audio editors
- Audio processors
- Graphics editors

We will indicate where on the user scale each product fits. We use three symbols to categorize products (Figure 7.1).

The E represents entry-level (the "pro-sumer"), M is used for mid-level (the multimedia professional), and H indicates high-level (corporate development) products. If you are just starting out, and have a tight budget, don't limit yourself to looking at only the entry-level products. Depending on your needs, you may want to invest in a more costly product. On the other hand, even if you consider yourself to be in the video professional range, do not discount the capabilities of the entry-level products.

There are a few products in this chapter that we have just received in the process of writing this book. Although we haven't yet used them in an actual project, we have used them to edit, reprocess, and manipulate known

**Figure 7.1
Entry-level,
midrange, and
high-level user
icons.**

materials so that we might judge them against something we have already done. We identify these products in the "How We Use This Product" section of each review.

Adobe Photoshop

Adobe Systems

For: √ Macintosh   √ Windows

Included on the CD-ROM

Photoshop is a graphic processing tool and is probably one of the best known. Over the several years it has been available, it has gone through some major changes, all of them adding functionality and features. (See Figure 7.2.) This review is based on version 3.0.

Adobe Photoshop 3.0

Minimum Requirements (Macintosh): Macintosh, 2.5 MB of free-application RAM, 4–8 MB hard-disk space (depending on how many features and plug-ins you install), System 7.1 (or later).

Minimum Requirements (Windows): 386/486/Pentium, DOS 5.0 and Windows 3.1, 256-color capable monitor (24-bit card and monitor recommended), 8 MB of free-application RAM (16 MB recommended), and 20 MB free hard-disk drive space.

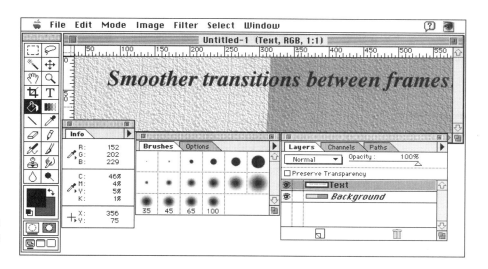

**Figure 7.2
Photoshop with its new layering capabilities.**

**Basic
Features**

- Opens and works with most current and past graphic file formats
- Generate new graphics
- Process (edit, adjust, and so forth) graphics
- Add special effects to graphics
- Translates files between major platforms
- Can use all available Photoshop compatible plug-ins and filters

**Unique
Features**

- Create or add elements in layers, individually addressable at any time
- Adjust color levels, hue, contrast, brightness, and so forth
- Process QuickTime movies (converted into filmstrips) frame by frame with all the same capabilities Photoshop provides to still images

**How We Use
This Product**

We use Photoshop both to create high-quality graphics and to process existing graphics and photos, all for use in our multimedia projects. Version 3.0 has added the one feature that has been conspicuous in its absence in all previous versions—addressable layers. Finally, we can add text to graphics that can easily be changed at a later date. As long as we save the graphic in the Photoshop 3.0 format, these layers remain addressable. Once we finalize on a graphic, we can save it out as a single-layer PICT or EPS (or any of more than a dozen other file types) file.

We use it to create master graphics that can easily be changed to suit individual needs. We use this and previous versions of Photoshop in about 80 percent of our projects.

**Some Things
We Have
Found**

Photoshop has offered plug-ins that have become the standard in the industry. These allow you to do everything from simple blurs to very advanced effects. The newest version is slightly different from previous versions, with some features being added and some being combined, and required about three hours of experimentation to catch on to how to use the new layering. Since we received it just a few days prior to the final submission of this book, we have many things yet to discover.

**The Bottom
Line**

Photoshop has always been a staple in our studio. Even before starting Toucan Studios, we individually used Photoshop since version 1.0. Version 3.0 is yet another advance in a product that gets better and better with each version. Although it carries a fairly stiff price tag, this is one of the tools that should find its way into every desktop video studio, whether you are a prosumer or a corporate professional.

This is a product that even the serious home producer should look at, but at a street retail cost of almost $600, this is not priced for the once-in-a-while hobbyist.

Adobe Premiere

Adobe Systems

For: √ Macintosh   √ Windows

Included on the CD-ROM

Premiere is a full-fledged video and audio editing application. It is the industry reference standard for editing and transition effects. (See Figure 7.3.) This review is based on version 4.0.

Minimum Requirements (Macintosh): 68020, System 7.0, 16 MB application RAM, 80 MB hard-disk drive (larger recommended for full-screen video).

Minimum Requirements (Windows): 486/Pentium, DOS 5.0 and Windows 3.1, 24-bit display adapter and monitor, video capture card compatible with Video for Windows, 16 MB of RAM, sound card and speakers, and a large-capacity hard-disk drive.

Basic Features

The basic and unique features of Premiere are too numerous to cover all in the space of a paragraph or two, so only a few are listed here.

- Digitize video directly from within Premiere (requires digitizing hardware)
- Complete frame-accurate edit window with multiple layers of video and audio control
- Function-rich transitions
- Keying and matting of video and graphics layers

Unique Features

- Batch capture and processing of movie projects
- Control of tape decks via third-party plug-in modules
- Title creation with any font, style, size, and so forth
- Ability to create EDLs (edit decision lists)
- Infinite layering of effects
- Lets you save graphic elements and text as addressable objects, rather than as a permanent part of the movie
- Movie info and analysis
- Digital waveform and vectorscope

**Figure 7.3
The Premiere
main display
with several
editing and
transitions
windows.**

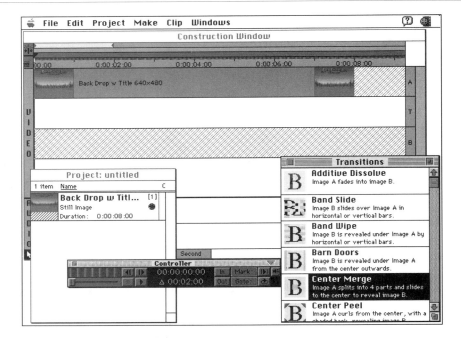

How We Use This Product

We use Premiere on practically every project we produce. It is a required tool in our application library. We have used it to capture, edit, and compress everything from our Select Effects library of animated movies, to turning a forty-five-minute linear information video into many small movies with added graphics, titles, and effects that were produced into an interactive sales and customer training CD-ROM.

Some Things We Have Found

Premiere is a feature-rich workhorse, and sometimes it is just plain overkill for some small projects or simple movie editing tasks. In these cases, we generally use other applications.

Some of the capabilities are multistep procedures that we feel could be streamlined. This is definitely not a beginner's tool; the learning curve is moderate, but we do not recommend this as the hobbyist's first editor application.

There are hundreds of transition plug-ins available from third-party companies that will keep Premiere fresh for a long time.

The Bottom Line

This is a must-have for the multimedia professional. Premiere is even strong enough to cut broadcast-quality commercials, music videos, and documentaries. We expect—and have heard rumors—that there are production houses that are using Premiere to cut their television programs together. The esoteric functions will require the manual for support, but the mainstream capabilities will be very intuitive to the video editor.

AfterEffects

Adobe/Aldus/CoSA

(CoSA was purchased by Aldus, and Aldus merged with Adobe.)

For: √ Macintosh

AfterEffects is a powerful post production tool for compositing, graphics, and special effects. AfterEffects is very fast (PowerPC native) and feature rich. It is designed for use by both multi-media and broadcast professionals. Our review is based on version 2.0.1. (See Figure 7.4.)

Minimum Requirements: Macintosh II or greater, 8 MB of RAM (or more), 80 MB hard drive, System 7.0 (or later), QuickTime 1.6.1 (or later).

Basic Features

- Video layering with an unlimited number of layers
- Animate and control movement of all PICT and video elements
- Plug-in special effects; supports Photoshop-compatible filters

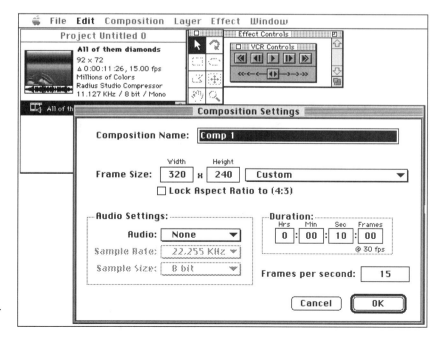

Figure 7.4 The AfterEffects Composition Settings window.

- Frame sizes up to 4,000 × 4,000 pixels
- Keying and alpha channel support

Unique Features

- Sub-pixel positioning of objects for smooth and accurate motion
- Anti-aliasing of titles and objects for smooth edges
- Field rendering for high quality, smooth video playback
- Time blending and motion blur
- Editable motion paths

How We Use This Product

AfterEffects is to QuickTime movies what Photoshop is to still images. It is the most powerful compositing and movie-processing application we have found to date. One of the very useful but minor capabilities of AfterEffects that we use quite often is the capability to apply of filters to movies, particularly Gaussian Blur. We use this method to remove noise, which makes compressing the movie with CinePak more efficient. Karen Dillon's sidebar article in Chapter 3 addresses this use.

We have also used the Image Control feature to adjust the contrast and brightness of dark clips, but these are just two of the dozens of things that can be done with AfterEffects.

We admit that we have not nearly tapped the full functionality or potential of AfterEffects, but this gives us plenty of room to use its features over time and many projects.

Some Things We Have Found

The interface is not the easiest through which to navigate. It does not always conform to the "normal" Macintosh user interface guidelines. The differences are not insurmountable, just something about which the user must be aware.

AfterEffects is very fast in processing filters, effects, and compositing. It is even faster if you use a PowerMac since much of the application is native code.

Expect to make a lot of trial-and-error movies before you have mastered it.

The Bottom Line

This is not a tool for the novice, nor is it priced that way. Although the interface is complex and requires a high degree of knowledge of graphics, compositing, and animation, the Photoshop professional with multimedia experience will soon feel right at home.

This application is a "must have" for the multimedia professional. If it is outside your budget range, we suggest looking at its little brother, AfterImage. AfterImage is based on an earlier version of AfterEffects and is significantly lower in cost, yet with many of the same features.

AfterImage
Adobe/Aldus

For: √ Macintosh

AfterImage is the little brother of AfterEffects. Although not all of the capabilities are offered, it contains many of the most popular features from AfterEffects letting you perform effects, animation, and layering effects on QuickTime movies and still images. (See Figure 7.5.) This review is based on version 1.0.

Minimum Requirements: Macintosh II, System 7, 8 MB of RAM, QuickTime 1.5, and a floating-point coprocessor for some effects.

Basic Features

- Import multiple video and audio tracks into a project
- Create text overlays
- Perform basic video and audio editing
- Offers scalable resolution settings

Unique Features

- Layering of multiple movies
- Create multiple key frames over a period of time
- Uses plug-in effects

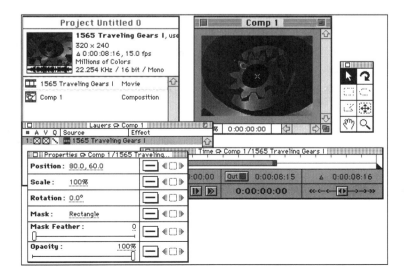

Figure 7.5 AfterImage and some of the settings and control windows.

How We Use This Product

Since we already use AfterEffects, we have not used AfterImage as part of a project. We have tested it side by side with AfterEffects and have found it to be a very good editing and effects tool.

Some Things We Have Found

You can get lost in all of the windows that can appear or be called up if you have only a standard 640 × 480 display. A solution is to keep open only the few windows you actually need at any given time.

The Tutorial and User Guide are well written and fairly easy to follow. They contain step-by-step procedures for using most of AfterImage's capabilities.

This is a fairly powerful program. Anyone using other editor programs will find it easy to understand and use most of the capabilities in AfterImage. For those with no experience in editing, it may take a while to catch on, but the learning curve is pretty fast.

The Bottom Line

For the home and pro-sumer markets, this is a fine alternative to the larger, more costly packages—including AfterEffects. This may be just a bit less than the video professional wants and needs in the way of a full-fledged editor, so that segment may want to look to the big brother product or one of its peers.

Apple Media Tool

Apple Computer, Inc.

For: √ Macintosh

Included on the CD-ROM

Apple Media Tool (AMT) lets you assemble different media elements into interactive presentations and products—all without knowledge of scripting or programming. (See Figure 7.6.). This review is based on version 1.1.

Minimum Requirements: Macintosh IIci, System 7.1, 8 MB of RAM, CD-ROM drive, and a hard-disk drive.

Basic Features

- Imports and uses PICT graphics; QuickTime movies; AIFF, WAV, and SND audio formats; and text
- Allows elements to be assembled into running presentations
- Provides for visual assembly of elements in a flow-diagram

**Figure 7.6
Building a pre-
sentation with
Apple Media
Tool.**

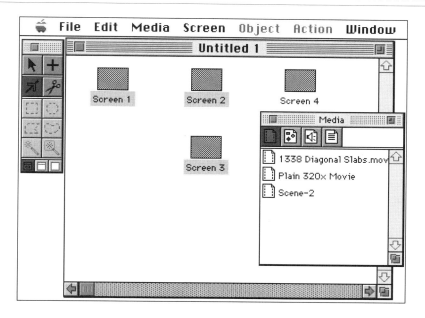

**Unique
Features**

- Allows elements to be assembled into interactive projects and products
- Advanced functionality achievable through the use of add-on programming
- Can create final output for use on either Macintosh or Windows platforms

---

**How We Use
This Product**

We have created several prototypes and projects using AMT in the past several months. AMT's basic import-position-interconnect ease lets us create these prototypes from existing elements in very little time.

We are developing an entertainment/education retail product using AMT. This product is highly interactive and must be deliverable on a single CD-ROM and playable on both Macintosh and Windows machines. AMT fits our needs with only a small amount of custom programming necessary (for printing and some search functions).

We are also preparing to take on a project for another company that currently has a Windows product developed in such a manner that it can't be directly translated into a Macintosh version. We will be using AMT with custom programming to re-create the entire product.

**Some Things
We Have
Found**

Learning how to use AMT takes a little time and experimentation. The manual is good and fairly well written, but only really covers the normal functions of AMT. Like HyperCard, it has a lot of undiscovered capabilities that require a programmer; unlike HyperCard, it takes a fairly skilled programmer to create any of the new code necessary to address these advanced functions.

The Bottom Line

Because of its ability to create cross-platform presentations, AMT is a very good tool for the video professional and corporate developer. It might be nice if it included every bit of code required to let you do everything possible, but then it would probably cost ten times as much. Besides, for the typical user, Apple Media Tool's out-of-the-box capabilities are quite sufficient.

It is impossible to accurately portray this and other development tools fully. Hopefully, you live in an area where you can get a demonstration of AMT.

Audioshop

Opcode Systems, Inc.

For: √ Macintosh

Audioshop is an audio recording and editing program. It features a virtual CD player control panel display that provides access to most of the features of the application. (See Figure 7.7.) This review is based on version 2.0.

Minimum Requirements: 68030, System 7.0, 4 MB of RAM.

Basic Features

- Input and export files in different formats including SND, AIFF, and QuickTime
- Lets users develop a "playlist" detailing all of their recorded sounds, or a catalog of their own audio CDs
- Plays audio CDs
- Drag-and-drop editing functions
- Resample and mix audio tracks

Unique Features

- Slider controls for special audio effects
- Can create Macintosh startup sounds
- Has a "headphone jack" option that lets the current selection begin playing as soon as actual headphones are plugged into the back of the computer (works only on Macintosh computers that are designed to sense when a plug has been inserted)

**Figure 7.7
The Audioshop
control panel.**

**How We Use
This Product**

For a project that required the digitization and cataloging of about fifty audio tracks, we required an audio "index." We developed this index in Audioshop, using the playlist feature and four-to-five-second captured clips. Sampled down to 8-bit mono tracks, the entire index fit on an HD floppy.

We have also used Audioshop as a CD player on different systems in the offices.

**Some Things
We Have
Found**

Although there is not a lot that is unique about this product, it has one of the nicer and better looking interfaces in its category. We have shown this product to many acquaintances, and everybody remarks about the ease of use and instant familiarity of the basic controls.

The playlist function is nice, but it requires manually entering information. Because we are basically lazy, we don't foresee using this function to catalog our personal CD collections of hundreds of discs, but we *are* beginning to use it to catalog our studio CDs full of music tracks that we use in projects.

If you do create a playlist, the list appears in a window on the control panel that can be grabbed and moved around your screen. Once moved, it may be stretched out to reveal all sorts of information about each track. The one thing we find fault with in this window is that we can't seem to stretch it far enough to reveal all of the track information, and there isn't a scroll left-right function.

**The Bottom
Line**

For the home and beginner desktop digital studio, this is a product to investigate. It offers basic capture, edit, effects, and export capabilities that should meet most of your needs. If your needs are for a higher level of functionality, you may want to look at one of the other audio capture and edit packages. If you are looking for something to use to catalog your audio clips and CDs, and if you don't mind a bit of manual labor, take a good look at Audioshop.

Batch It!

Gryphon Software Corp.

For: √ Macintosh

This is a batch-processing tool to automate repetitive graphic processing tasks. It is a visually oriented program that lets you graphically build your processes on screen. (See Figure 7.8.) This review is based on version 1.0.

Minimum Requirements: Macintosh II, 4 MB of free-application RAM, System 7.1, and a hard drive with 10 MB free space.

Basic Features

- Automated batch processing to convert graphic file formats
- Supports PICT, TIFF, Photoshop, and other file formats
- Allows cropping, sharpening images, adjusting colors, and forty other functions

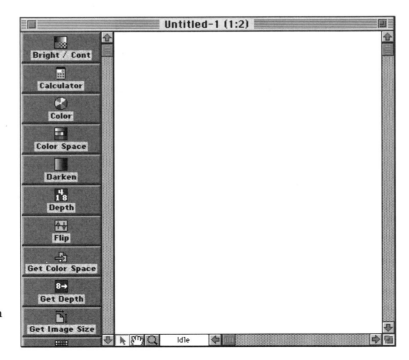

Figure 7.8 Batch It! and ten of its 40+ settings buttons.

Unique Features

- Allows you to build your processes graphically on screen and create links
- Renames and saves new files after they are processed

How We Use This Product

We only recently received Batch It! and have not used it in an actual project. We have tested it by re-creating certain batches we have performed in another batch-processing application to check for ease of use and quality of process.

Some Things We Have Found

The user interface is interesting; most applications that offer these capabilities require that you make menu selections, fill in blanks, and click "Go For It!" buttons. Batch It! gives you visual representations of each of the steps you assign to any given processing job.

The available filters and effects are fairly complete and offer a good variety to the average user.

Since we perform lots of processing on QuickTime movies, it would be nice if Batch It! could work with that file format.

The Bottom Line

Although there is another batch-processing application reviewed in this book that we prefer for our own use, this is a fine tool for the pro-sumer digital video producer. It offers lots of features and is certainly easier to master than many applications that offer this level of complex functions.

ConvertToMovie

Apple Computer, Inc.

For: √ Macintosh

ConvertToMovie is a utility program designed to perform multiple processes on a movie file. ConvertToMovie will do all of the standard compression tasks, plus it allows you to flatten your movie, make it cross-platform, and scale or crop the movie as desired. This review is based on version 2.0. (See Figure 7.9.)

Minimum Requirements: Macintosh computer, System 7.0, 4 MB of RAM (requires at least 2 MB free-application RAM but works best with 5 MB free RAM or more), QuickTime 1.6.1.

Basic Features

- Compression into all QuickTime-supported codecs
- Set quality (in applicable codecs)
- Set frame rate (in applicable codecs)

- Set key frames (in applicable codecs)
- Set data rate (in applicable codecs)
- Save movies as cross-platform capable

Unique Features

- Allows scaling of movies in X and Y dimensions
- Allows cropping of movies
- Allows creation of custom palette for 256-color playback

How We Use This Product

We use ConvertToMovie on almost every project. It really shines in its ability to grab a series of still PICTs and create a QuickTime movie, and in its ability to crop movies. Frequently, when we capture from SVHS and even some other tape formats, a few lines of head scan and other garbage appear at the bottom or sides of the movie. ConvertToMovie lets us crop out these offending lines and pixels.

Some Things We Have Found

When we crop or resize a movie, we must do so for the entire movie, even if there is only a single scene that must be processed. Because of this, we either use ConvertToMovie on individual scenes prior to editing them together (without using compression), or we accept the fact that we will be cropping or resizing everything.

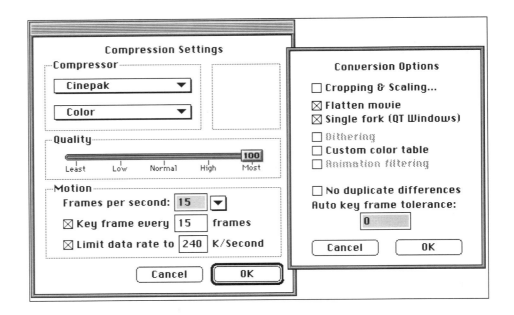

Figure 7.9 ConvertTo-Movie.

The Bottom Line

This is one of our "always ready" tools—something we keep on the desktop so we don't have to go looking for it. ConvertToMovie is an Apple utility, and is generally only found on their Developer CD-ROMs. If you are an Apple developer, you have this utility somewhere. If you're not, we've told the folks in the QuickTime group at Apple that this and other utilities ought to be made available in the next QuickTime retail product. Please stand by . . .

DeBabelizer

Equilibrium Technologies

For: √ Macintosh

Demo and lite version included on the CD-ROM

DeBabelizer is a batch-processing tool to automate repetitive graphic processing tasks. (See Figure 7.10.) Although we have used several versions of DeBabelizer during this past year, this review is based on version 1.5.52. Be advised that version 1.6 should be available by the time this book is published. It is slated to be a "native" application that takes advantage of the PowerPC processors in Power Macintosh computers.

Minimum Requirements: Macintosh II, 1 MB of free-application RAM, hard disk recommended, System 6.0.7 (or later); System 7–compatible and 32-bit clean; supports AppleScript and AppleEvents.

Basic Features

- Automated batch processing to convert graphic file formats
- Creation of custom palettes
- Dithering and color palette reduction
- Opens and works with more than forty graphics file types and formats
- Translates files between major platforms
- Processes animations and QuickTime movies as well as still graphics

Unique Features

- Creation of "super palettes" to provide the best single palette of your graphics files
- Can use Photoshop-compatible plug-ins and filters
- Supports AppleScript for automation of repeatable tasks

**Figure 7.10
DeBabelizer and
two of the set-
tings windows.**

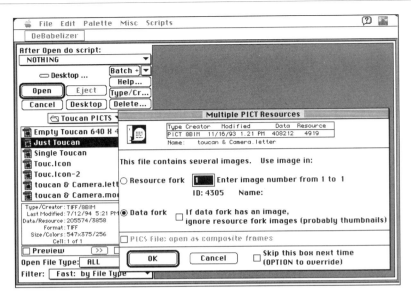

- Lets you change file and creator types of files
- Creation of a visual catalog by placing multiple thumbnail images on a single page

**How We Use
This Product**

We use DeBabelizer for everything from simple file translation to the creation of large batch processes. It has come in particularly handy for processing batches of PhotoCD images (100+ images per batch) where color balance and cropping of each image is necessary. We have even used it to convert over 5,000 images from a PC bitmap format to Macintosh PICTs in a single session!

We take advantage of its ability to change file and creator types of some graphic images. We also use it to create custom 256-color super palettes for our cross-platform projects.

**Some Things
We Have
Found**

The user interface is slightly nonstandard Macintosh. There is a very high use of dialog boxes, and dialogs within dialogs. Many of these dialog boxes can be checked off so they do not appear after the first time—a nice feature.

Some of the palette features of DeBabelizer may not make immediate sense when you first try them. One example of this is in the Palette menu. Under Options, there is a listing for *Color Reduction and Remapping,* whereas further down the menu there is a listing for *Reduce Colors.* Until you read the manual, you may not know the difference.

Also, developing batch lists is not a skill for the first-time user. The manual is all-important in understanding the intricacies of DeBabelizer.

The Bottom Line

This is the Swiss army knife of batch-based image processing utilities. We haven't seen a better batch processor yet. As time goes by, DeBabelizer seems to grow to meet most of our needs. If it lacks anything, it is in its lack of simplicity. But always keep the manual close at hand. If you have any repetitive image-processing tasks, this tool is a must-have product for the desktop video studio.

DigiTrax

Alaska Software

For: √ Macintosh

DigiTrax is an audio editing, mixing, and processing "studio" on your Macintosh. This application lets you record and import multiple tracks and then mix down to a final product. (See Figure 7.11.) This review is based on version 1.1.

Minimum Requirements: Macintosh 660AV or 840AV model or other Macintosh with an Apple Real Time Architecture (ARTA) compatible audio card, color monitor, System 7.1, 8 MB of RAM, QuickTime 1.6.1, and a hard-disk drive for storing audio. (44.1 KHz audio requires about 10 MB for a one-minute stereo audio file.)

Basic Features

- Import multiple tracks, placing them in any order
- Record up to six tracks directly into DigiTrax
- On-screen "LED" displays signal characteristics
- Slider-bar controls for input control
- Full CD "player" controls

Unique Features

- Lets you name each track for identification purposes
- Play existing tracks while recording additional tracks
- Full time-code display
- Graphic equalization of audio tracks on an individual basis
- Sync audio to QuickTime movies with movie window

**Figure 7.11
The DigiTrax
Mixer and
Transport Con-
trols windows.**

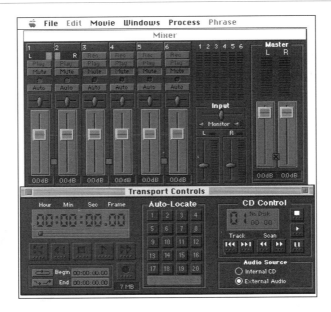

**How We Use
This Product**

Practically everything we have produced that includes music has been touched by DigiTrax. We use it to record and mix music, mix down stereo tracks to mono, and change the sampling rates and bit-depths of music. We have also used the equalizer capabilities to "punch up" some poor audio and to remove hiss from tape sources.

**Some Things
We Have
Found**

There are a few nits that might be picked, such as the closeness or location of certain buttons so that we accidentally click them while trying to do things such as closing windows, but there is not much that we haven't been able to do with DigiTrax. If you have worked with any type of audio mixer before, the interface will be very familiar. Even if you haven't, the interface is practically intuitive.

We had one project that used seven tracks. DigiTrax can import a maximum of six at one time, so we had to do things in two stages. This is not a deal-breaker since we rarely work with more than four tracks, but it would have been nice to have more.

Also, but this is mostly due to the file format, importing lengthy AIFF files takes several minutes. Fortunately, there is a slider bar that tells you how far you still have to go.

**The Bottom
Line**

We have been using DigiTrax since we became a beta test site. Each time we received a newer version it got better. Because very few video editors offer much in the way of audio processing, we strongly suggest the purchase of an audio editor; DigiTrax is at the top of our list.

Disc to Disk

Optical Media International

For: √ Macintosh

Demo included on the CD-ROM

Disc to Disk is an audio capture tool that allows you to smoothly capture audio tracks from CDs directly into your hard disk. Select what you want to capture, and Disc to Disk does the rest automatically. (See Figure 7.12.) This review is based on version 1.1.1.

Minimum Requirements: Macintosh Plus or greater (including PowerBook), 68020 or higher processor recommended, 5 MB of RAM, SCSI hard-disk drive (requires up to 10 MB of space per minute of audio), and SCSI CD-ROM drive.

**Basic
Features**

- Works without any added hardware
- Samples at 11, 22, and 44.1 KHz in both 8-bit and 16-bit
- Copy any sound to your clipboard for playback through the computer's internal speaker
- Provides a waveform display of the audio
- Save sessions to your drive for future use

**Figure 7.12
The Disc to Disc
main screen
and its Options
menu.**

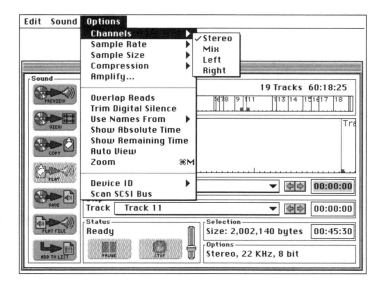

Unique Features

- Can address tracks on either audio-only CDs or mixed-mode CD-ROMs
- Offers control down to 4/75-second accuracy
- Displays your selections in both time and bytes
- Can save files out in Windows WAV format

How We Use This Product

We have not used Disc to Disk during an actual project. We have used it to capture several known audio tracks for comparison and have found it to be accurate and clean.

Some Things We Have Found

All documentation refers to this as an intuitive, easy-to-use interface. Although it is easy to use once you understand what everything does, we still feel that this is a "read the instructions before you use" product. People with experience with other audio capture and mixing programs seem to have an easier time than novices with this program.

One thing we frequently require in our work with audio is the ability to address more than two tracks. This program was designed to capture stereo, left-only, right-only, or mono (left + right), but only to a maximum of two tracks, and it does a fine job of that.

The Bottom Line

We have as yet to use this product in an actual project, but we believe it would have been applicable to several of our previous jobs. It may not be as feature rich or have as attractive an interface as other audio capture and editing packages, but for the pro-sumer level desktop studio, this can be an appropriate tool.

Dynamic Effects

Gryphon Software Corp.

For: √ Macintosh

Demo included on the CD-ROM

Gryphon's Dynamic Effects is a series of effects add-ons to Adobe Premiere. They are the equivalent of plug-ins to Photoshop and offer more than twenty different special effects you can use on your video projects. (See Figure 7.13.) This review is based on volume 1.

Minimum Requirements: Macintosh capable of running Adobe Premiere 2.0, Premiere version 2.0 software, and a hard drive to save your files.

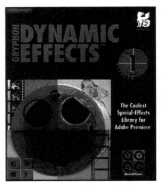

Figure 7.13 One of the new smooth transitions from Dynamic Effects.

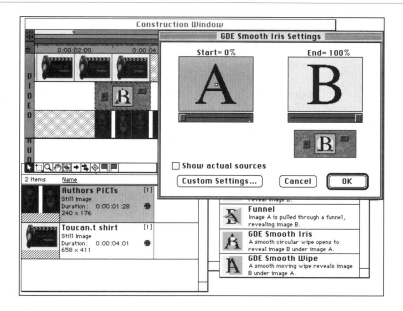

Basic Features

The available effects include, among others:

- Channel delay
- Duotone
- Dust
- Dynamic solarize
- Dynamic twirl
- Luminance jitter
- Soft focus
- Smooth wipe
- Tunnel

How We Use This Product

We only had the opportunity to use this product once prior to submission of this book. We dropped all of the effects into Premiere and imported a known video clip. Once in, we selected a series of different effects (see the preceding list) and made preview movies of each.

Since we use Premiere quite a bit, we foresee using many of these effects on future projects.

Some Things We Have Found

Installation really can't be simpler. You just drag and drop into your Premiere plug-ins folder.

Two of the effects are transitions that offer smoother effects than their Premiere counterparts (Smooth Iris and Smooth Wipe).

Some of the effects are really useful, and some are cute but somewhat less viable for professional projects. If you get this product, try out the Channel Delay effect right in the middle of a head shot (and then uncross your eyes).

The Bottom Line

We love products that allow for plug-ins (Photoshop and Premiere are the two biggies) and really appreciate when someone takes the time to create new plug-ins that extend capabilities.

Although some plug-ins are of dubious use in our business, these seem to be well thought out and executed. We look forward to more of the "smoothed" transitions in future volumes.

Elastic Reality

Elastic Reality, Inc. (formerly ASDG)

For: √ Macintosh   √ Windows

Demo included on the CD-ROM

Elastic Reality is a digital video effects program. Along with its own series of built-in effects, it lets you create your own effects in a WYSIWYG environment. (See Figure 7.14.) This review is based on version 1.2.1.

Minimum Requirements (Macintosh): Color Macintosh with FPU (floating-point coprocessor), 256 colors or better, 8 MB of RAM, System 7.0.1 or later, QuickTime 1.5 or later, and a hard-disk drive.

Recommended Options (Macintosh): 68040-based Macintosh, 24-bit display, additional memory.

Minimum Requirements (Windows): 386/486/Pentium, Windows 3.1, 4 MB RAM, 6 MB free hard-disk space.

Basic Features

- Warping and morphing effects
- Allows creation of shapes with freehand and structured tool set
- Still and full-motion compositing
- Reads and writes in multiple formats including TARGA, PICT, TIFF, GIF, BMP, Alias, Sun Raster, X Windows
- Imports and exports Video for Windows files
- Features a very complete on-line help manual

**Figure 7.14
Creating a simple Elastic Reality morph.**

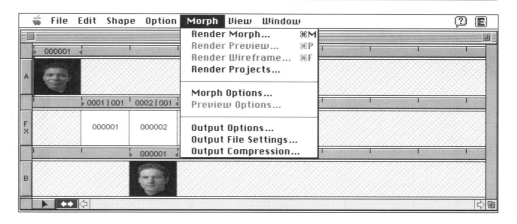

**Unique
Features**

- Allows cel-based and stop-motion animation
- Creates "tweens" using an automatic shape interpolation routine
- Allows elements to be layered within a project so that each one can be addressed independently
- Permits each element (shape) to create its own matte for use in effects
- Permits all shapes to be scaled, rotated, moved, and so forth

**How We Use
This Product**

Many recognizable scenes from television and recent movies have been created using the Silicon Graphics version of Elastic Reality. We have used the warping and morphing capabilities to enhance projects and prototypes.

We also used it to create an animation for one project that called for a logo to morph into a product ID and then into the product itself, all while moving across the screen and settling down in a new location.

**Some Things
We Have
Found**

This has a lot of features, and you shouldn't expect to master all of them in a short time. Certainly you can do a quick morph with just a few minutes of experimentation, but creating a professional morph (one you would put in a project for a client) requires hours and hours of experimentation and work. If you have the need to create such effects, this is a great tool.

The built-in help manual is invaluable when you get hung up.

**The Bottom
Line**

Beginners, beware. This is not a simple "open the file, click on the effect, and *voilà!* Instant success" product. It takes some time and effort to use it to its full potential. Heck, even we haven't used it to its fullest yet. If you are serious about producing Hollywood-style effects for your desktop presentations, there isn't a better software product today.

Media Factory

NUTS Technologies

For: √ Macintosh

Demo included on the CD-ROM

Media Factory is a video editing and transitions effects program. It lets you import and integrate video clips, audio tracks, and graphics. It is designed to bring many of the capabilities of more costly editor applications down to the price level and learning curve of the home or pro-sumer desktop. (See Figure 7.15.) This review is based on version 1.0.

Minimum Requirements: Macintosh II, color monitor with 16- or 24-bit support recommended, System 7.0, 4 MB of free RAM, QuickTime 1.5, video digitizing board or AV capable recommended, CD-ROM drive optional, and a large-capacity hard-disk drive for file storage.

Basic Features

- Imports and utilizes PICS, PICT, QuickTime, and audio files
- Includes more than two dozen transitions and effects
- Allows use of predigitized video clips or capture of new video clips (with appropriately upgraded system)

Unique Features

- Provides a full range of image controls for capture: hue, contrast, brightness, sharpness, white-and-black level, and so forth.
- Movie preview capability with frame-grab button
- Text generation and placement within a clip

How We Use This Product

We received this product only recently and have not had the opportunity to use it in a project. We have used it with known source materials for comparison purposes and have found it to be a fine editor and transition tool.

Some Things We Have Found

For a product aimed at the home and office market, this has a surprising number of effects, filters, and transitions. A couple of the tools have really caught our eye and we look forward to using them in future projects. The two we want to work with are the Reshape and Scaler buttons. These affect the shape and size of a video track.

**Figure 7.15
The basic Media
Factory editing
and effects win-
dows.**

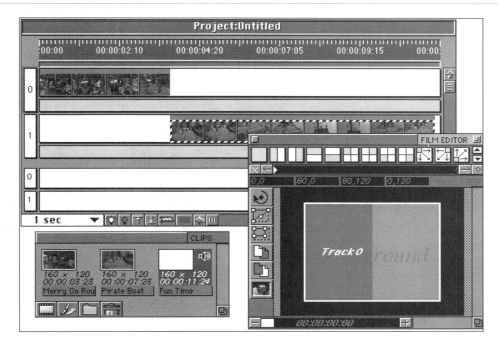

**The Bottom
Line**

From what we have seen, this is something that home and pro-sumer producers should take a look at. You may also want to add this to your application library for those occasions where the full-fledged packages may be
overkill.

Morph

Gryphon Technologies

For: √ Macintosh

Demo included on the CD-ROM

Morph is an application that does just what its
name implies. It creates morphings between
pictures, just like you see on television and in
movies. (See Figure 7.16.) This review is based
on version 2.5.

Minimum Requirements: Macintosh II, color
monitor, 5 MB of RAM, System 7, and 2 MB of
free hard-disk space.

**Figure 7.16
Setting up the
key comparison
points between
two pho-
tographs.**

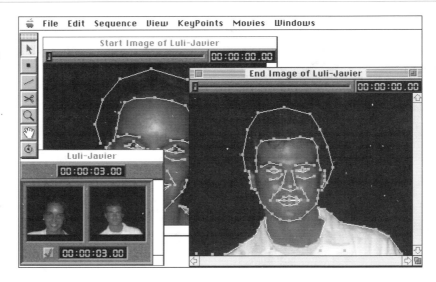

**Basic
Features**

- Supports scanned photograph and graphics formats such as PICT, TIFF, PICS, and Photoshop as well as QuickTime movie file formats
- Creation of straight morphs, image warps, cross-fades, and so forth

---

**Unique
Features**

- Creation of morphs from dynamic (moving) sources
- Adjustment of timing of morph sequences as well as image positioning and color shifts
- Allows you to save morphs out as QuickTime movies, including compressing using any of the standard QuickTime codecs (CinePak, Video, Graphics, JPEG, and so forth)
- Duplicates sequences for use in more than one place
- Allows morphed movies to be created for use with the After Dark screen saver

---

**How We Use
This Product**

We have used Morph to create transitions between still images (fairly easy to do) and for dynamic transitions during QuickTime movies (much more detailed).

For one project in mid-1994, we worked with the folks at Gryphon to develop a subset of the Morph product for use in a permanent display at EPCOT Center to take a person's picture and create a morph in just a few seconds, without any setup or other input.

**Some Things
We Have
Found**

This is a product that can be used with some level of success right out of the box with only a few minutes of orientation. However—and this is a BIG however—if you expect to be able to create Hollywood-quality morphs, you will need to devote a chunk of time to learning and experimentation. The reason is simple and understandable—quality morphing requires careful alignment and selection of key points so the software knows what to do.

The setup time to create a quality morph can be fairly short for a simple one-picture-to-another where both subjects are about the same relative size and are positioned within the frame similarly. Conversely, this time can be very great if you are doing complex, moving morphs between scenes. If you take the time to do it right, you won't be disappointed by the output of this product.

One final point: We tried a fairly long (two-second) morph between two moving sources and compared it against a faster morph of the same subjects (about one-half second) to see what was visually more appealing. To our eyes, the quicker morph looked smoother and was more effective.

**The Bottom
Line**

Morph is a powerful product and is not for the beginner or hobbyist. This is a serious package for the digital video producer who is willing to spend some time learning the application. If you are going to create morphs, this is one of the products you need to look at.

MovieAnalyzer

Apple Computer, Inc.

For: √ Macintosh

MovieAnalyzer is a utility program designed to check and display the playability characteristics of a movie file. It is an important tool to use when you create presentations that will be played from low-data-rate media, such as CD-ROMs. (See Figure 7.17.) This review is based on version 1.1.3.

Minimum Requirements: Macintosh computer, System 7.0, 2 MB of free RAM (but we suggest 5–8 MB of free RAM), QuickTime 1.6.1.

**Basic
Features**

- Loads and analyzes QuickTime movies
- Displays both video and audio characteristics and playability
- Graphs playability of your movies

Figure 7.17 MovieAnalyzer and several of its windows showing the characteristics of a movie.

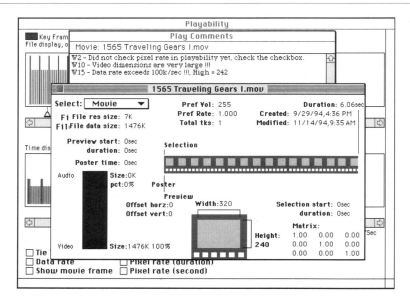

Unique Features

- Analyzes the playability of a movie
- Provides precise frames-per-second readings (to the second decimal point)

How We Use This Product

Whenever we create a movie that is to be played from any limited-data-rate medium, including both CD-ROMs and floppy diskettes, we run the movies through MovieAnalyzer. Although MovieAnalyzer was designed to analyze movies for single-speed CD-ROM drives, it is easy to interpret the numbers for both Macintosh and Windows playback on newer, faster drives.

Some Things We Have Found

Because this is an older utility, it sometimes has problems loading and analyzing more than one movie in a row when using newer system versions. That is easy to get around with a simple Quit and relaunch.

As mentioned, this was designed to analyze movies for playback on single-speed CD-ROM drives and QuickTime 1.5 capabilities. The reporting it provides is based on 110 Kps data transfer maximum. As long as you know what the maximum sustainable playback rates should be for your needs, you can interpret the readings for 2X, 4X, or greater drives.

The Bottom Line

Because this is an older utility, it is not supported and there doesn't seem to be anything new coming to replace it. If you have it, or can find it, use it for now because it is a valuable tool. If you like it and believe it should be updated, write to Apple Computer.

The closest utility we have found to compare to MovieAnalyzer is MovieInfo. MovieInfo is a shareware utility application by Futoshi Ebata. It has many, but not all, of MovieAnalyzer's functions. You can find MovieInfo on our companion CD-ROM. It is one of several QuickTime applications Ebata has written. They can be found on most of the popular commercial on-line services.

MovieWorks

Interactive Solutions, Inc.

For: √ Macintosh

MovieWorks is a set of programs designed to help you create, edit, and compose multimedia presentations. It is divided into a text editor, a paint program, a sound editor, a composer program, and a player. (See Figure 7.18.) This review is based on version 2.2.1.

Minimum Requirements: Macintosh LC, color monitor, System 6.0.7, 4 MB of RAM (8 MB recommended), QuickTime 1.6.1.

Basic Features

The five main components of this package include:

- Text editing for titles and overlays—Text
- 8-bit and 24-bit color graphics creation and processing—Paint
- Audio editing and effects—Sound
- Composition of all elements into multimedia presentations—Composer
- A player application—Play

Unique Features

- Link buttons to different media tracks for interactivity
- Anti-alias text and graphics
- Text editor supports bit map and TrueType fonts
- Paint editor supports PICT, TIFF, and MacPaint files
- Audio editor supports AIFF, QuickTime, and SND files

**Figure 7.18
The MovieWorks
Composer
program.**

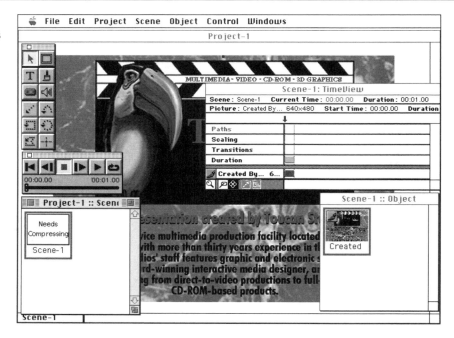

**How We Use
This Product**

Although we haven't used the entire set of programs together for any project, we have used the text editor to create an overlay imported into the Composer, and have used each of the others individually.

We have also used the Sound editor to cut together sample audio files for use as quickie previews for clients.

**Some Things
We Have
Found**

None of the individual programs is especially unique, but each one is fairly solid in its capabilities. By themselves they can be effective tools, but their strength lies in their combined use. The authors of these programs have, thankfully, used standard Macintosh interface guidelines, so each is easily learned in a minimum of time.

For performing basic audio editing and effects, the Sound program is quick and very easy.

**The Bottom
Line**

While there are all-in-one editors available for the video professional or the corporate video producer, many are too expensive for the average home and pro-sumer. This package seems to provide a set of tools to perform good, basic multimedia editing and production.

If we have any comment about this and other sets of programs or utilities, it is that we wish that paint and text-editing capabilities would be combined into a single program with each type of element being in an editable layer.

Multimedia Utilities

Motion Works

For: √ Macintosh

Multimedia Utilities is a set of six utility programs designed to help you create and edit graphic and audio elements. Individual utilities can be used to augment your other multimedia tools. (See Figure 7.19.) This review is based on release 1 of the tools.

Minimum Requirements: Macintosh II computer, System 7.0, 4 MB of RAM (8 MB recommended), QuickTime 1.5.

Basic Features

The functions of the utilities included in the package are:

- Screen recording—CameraMan
- Cel animation—MotionPaint
- Audio editing and processing—SoundMate
- Interactive QuickTime—MovieClick
- QuickTime editing—QuickEdit
- Morphing—QuickMorph

Unique Features

Although none of the individual utilities has any truly unique features or capabilities, the complete set offers a total capability that is equal to many desktop editor applications and even surpasses some.

How We Use This Product

We have used CameraMan for screen grabs for almost a year. It allows both still and motion grabs, which we have utilized in several projects. The rest of the utilities have been used during the prototyping and development of several of our recent jobs.

Some Things We Have Found

CameraMan is a great utility, but we must always remember to turn it off when performing video capture; it seems to slow down the system to the point where we begin to lose frames. This is easy to do with Extension Manager, so we don't count this as a negative, just something you should be aware of.

MotionPaint is a fun tool for creating simple animations. It really can't replace a high-quality animation package for doing fine-detail animations, but it doesn't pretend to.

**Figure 7.19
Four of the Mul-
timedia Utilities
(clockwise from
upper left):
QuickMorph,
MotionPaint,
SoundMate, and
QuickEdit.**

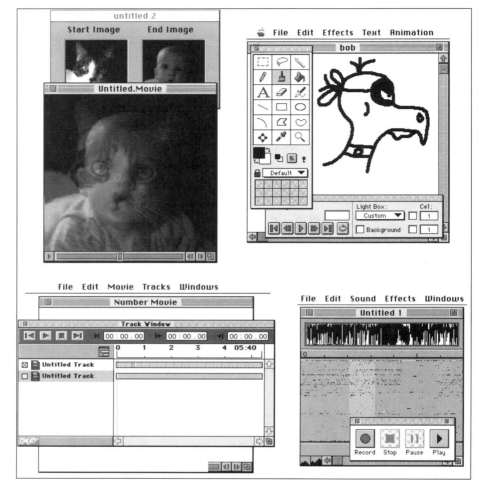

We prefer other audio editing packages for our own use, but the Sound-Mate utility offers quite a few features for such a "simple" program.

We are still experimenting with some of these utilities, such as the interactive QuickTime and morphing utilities. Concerning the QuickMorph utility, we have found that it only seems to work effectively when the two subjects in your source pictures are already lined up.

The Bottom Line

For the price, these are very good tools to have on hand, especially for the pro-sumer level video producer. You will find that you can do things with these utilities in just a few minutes that are as clean and as effective as what you would get with a high-priced application.

For the video professional and the corporate developer, these are interesting tools that should be investigated. After all, you don't always have to fire up a high-priced editing application in order to perform typical video and audio edits.

Painter 3

Fractal Design

For: √ Macintosh   √ Windows

Demo included on the CD-ROM

Painter 3 is a highly capable graphics and art and animation package. Its main calling is as a digital equivalent of natural painting tools. Like previous versions of Painter and Painter X2, it allows you to take existing art and work with it as well as generating new art from scratch. A feature allowing animation and QuickTime movie creation has been added. (See Figure 7.20.) This review is based on the initial release of Painter 3.

Minimum Requirements (Macintosh): 68030, System 6.0.7, 6 MB of RAM (8 MB if using a Power Macintosh), and an FPU for some effects.

Minimum Requirements (Windows): 386/486/Pentium, SVGA or 24-bit color monitor and card, Windows 3.1, 8 MB of RAM, and a math coprocessor. A Pentium computer is preferred for Windows use of Painter 3.

Basic Features

- Dozens of brush types and hundreds of variants
- Image cloning
- Dozens of paper textures
- Robust image processing and filter effects
- Object layering

Unique Features

- Image hose allows painting with sequences of art objects
- Rotoscoping
- A tissue-paper format for creating animations where you can see through the different layers, pick certain layers up, and drop them back to check your positioning
- Session recordings allow for re-creating artwork step by step; great for teaching techniques

**Figure 7.20
Painter 3 with
several of its
windows.**

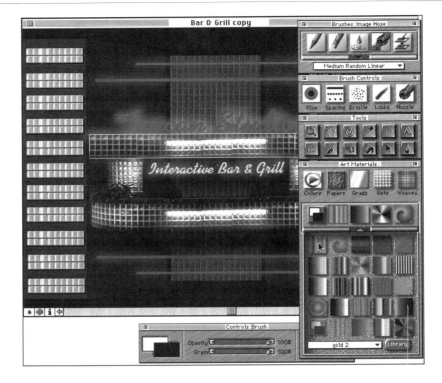

**How We Use
This Product**

Although we have used all the earlier versions of Painter, we are just start-ing to use this new release in our daily business. We have already used it to create some visually stunning graphics for at least two prototype presentations.

**Some Things
We Have
Found**

Painter 3 is a great step forward from previous versions. The new capabilities are useful, and all of the new menus and windows are colorful.

Certainly anyone can dabble in art, but it requires an artist to really make Painter 3 shine. One very nice feature is that Painter 3 easily recognizes when you use a graphics tablet (which we recommend as an addition when using Painter 3).

You really need to use this product on a large monitor (greater than 640 × 480 pixels) because of all of the windows that open up all over the screen. Smaller screens don't leave a lot of room for your actual art.

One nit: We realize that this is a product that competes at certain levels with Photoshop, but it would be very nice if Painter 3 could open Photo-shop 3.0 *layered* documents without the need to go into Photoshop, save the graphic as a single-layered PICT file, then open it in Painter 3, still as a single layer.

The Bottom Line

After working with Painter 2, we were surprised at the number of changes in Painter 3. There are so many changes that we haven't gotten around to exploring all of them.

If you are an artist or you own and have used previous Painter versions, you will probably want to upgrade to Painter 3. If you haven't used Painter before, if you are not a graphic artist, and if you don't require a top-of-the-line art program, this may be more than you need.

Quick Flix!

Radius, Inc.

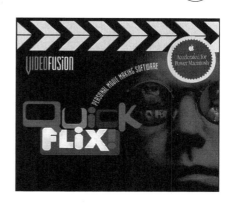

For: √ Macintosh

Quick Flix! is the little brother to Video-Fusion, also reviewed in this book. Where VideoFusion is aimed at the mid to high range of users, Quick Flix! is aimed at the home market. It lets you record, compose, edit, and apply transitions and effects to your digital videos. (See Figure 7.21.) This review is based on version 1.1.1.

Minimum Requirements: Macintosh II, 256 colors or better monitor, 3 MB of free RAM, System 7, QuickTime 1.5 (included), and a hard-disk drive.

Basic Features

- Imports multiple movies for edits and effects
- Input video from still video cameras, your VCR, television, video camera, CD-ROMs, laserdiscs, and so forth
- Effects include wipes, dissolves, fades, slow motion, zooms, and so forth
- Edit and resize movies

Unique Features

- Allows layering of one movie over another
- Apply color effects to your movies
- Includes audio capture and conversion capabilities
- Overlay text

**Figure 7.21
The Quick Flix!
transitions
window.**

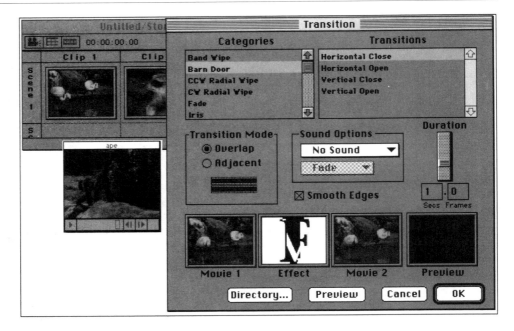

**How We Use
This Product**

We use VideoFusion quite a bit, so this is really a subset of what we already use in ongoing projects. To test this, we processed some movies in Quick Flix! that we previously had processed in VideoFusion. For the basic processing, no difference!

**Some Things
We Have
Found**

This has a lot of features, and most of them are straightforward and easy to use. The transitions window offers quite a few selections and probably will require anyone just starting out with this product to go through the manual in order to understand everything fully.

Speaking of which, it features a nice user's guide, filled with useful step-by-step examples of how to perform each of the product's functions.

**The Bottom
Line**

If we were a home or pro-sumer video producer, we would look seriously at Quick Flix! It provides many of the features of its big brother at a reasonable price. This is also a great video editor for education purposes, allowing students to investigate mainstream capabilities in an easy-to-understand environment.

SoundEdit 16

Macromedia

For: √ Macintosh

Included on the CD-ROM

SoundEdit 16 is an audio editing and processing application. It supports audio files in most major formats and can be effectively used as a file translation utility. It also features the ability to add video tracks to your audio. (See Figure 7.22.) This review is based on version 1.0.

Minimum Requirements: Any 68030 Macintosh, System 7.0 (this is Power Macintosh compatible in emulation mode), 5 MB RAM, and 16-bit sound input hardware necessary to record 16-bit sound.

Basic Features

- Open or import multiple tracks, including from CDs
- Opens, edits, and saves files in almost a dozen formats including AIFF, WAV, AIFC, Resource, and so forth
- Uses Macintosh standard Cut, Copy, and Paste editing simplicity
- Includes audio effects such as fade-in, face-out, flange, echo, amplify, backwards, smooth, shift pitch, and so forth
- Downsamples audio files

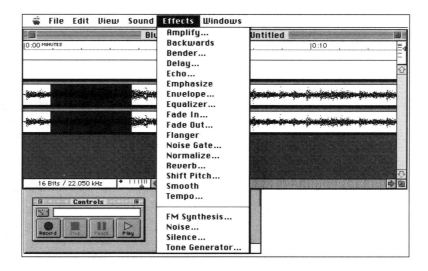

Figure 7.22 The SoundEdit 16 editing display with the Effects menu.

Unique Features

- Fourteen special audio effects
- Can save audio files directly out as QuickTime movies, including QuickTime for Windows
- Can open QuickTime video files, allowing for the exact insertion and matching of a soundtrack file
- Capable of MACE 3:1 and 6:1 compression
- Dynamic spectral views of the sound waveform

How We Use This Product

We use this product to edit together many of our QuickTime-based audio files and to preview some potential audio/video combinations. We also use it for projects where an audio track must be playable as either a QuickTime for Windows file or a WAV format file. We like the easy fade-in and fade-out features and have used them on several projects.

Some Things We Have Found

SoundEdit has a nifty little feature called the Sound Edit window, which tells you how much disk space your file will take up and how much you will save by trying different bit depths, sampling rates, compression, and mono versus stereo.

One thing we would like to see is a Preferences list to retain our preferred save as file format. It always defaults to SoundEdit 16 format; we almost always use QuickTime Movie format.

The Bottom Line

For rapid-fire, quick editing and file translation of audio tracks, SoundEdit 16 is a great tool. Its ability to save directly to QuickTime Movie files is a boon and often reduces the total number of steps needed to create a finished piece. The ability to add video to the audio tracks is nice, but we only use that feature to preview work, preferring to do video and audio assembly (and adding video effects) in a full-fledged video editor.

Special Delivery

Interactive Media Corp.

For: √ Macintosh

Demo included on the CD-ROM

Special Delivery is a powerful multimedia authoring tool used to create presentations and interactive multimedia projects. It is visually based and requires no scripting or flowchart development to use. (See Figure 7.23.) This review is based on version 2.0.

Minimum Requirements: 68020 Macintosh or Power Macintosh, color monitor recommended, System 7.0, 4 MB of RAM, QuickTime 2.0 (included), and a hard-disk drive.

**Figure 7.23
Building a
presentation
with Special
Delivery.**

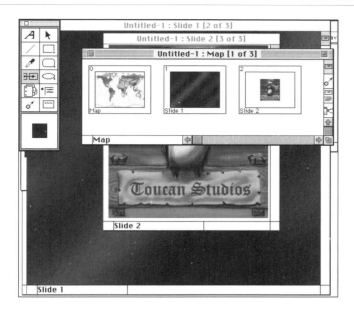

**Basic
Features**

- Allows placement and interactive use of text, graphics, movies, and audio tracks
- Creates presentations as a series of interactive slides, and allows the designation of navigation between slides and interactivity between slides
- Provides complete control over movies, sounds, and the appearance of images and text
- Provides full control over scaling and positioning of movies, pictures, and text
- Allows control of timing and synchronization of individual elements or entire presentations
- Can utilize PowerPoint and Persuasion slides

**Unique
Features**

- Simple, graphical linking to create buttons and interactivity
- Supports presentations on multiple monitors
- Provides three view types to assist in the development of the presentation
- Allows development without the need for programming or scripting skills
- Features full kiosk control capabilities, including keyboard and mouse disabling

---

**How We Use
This Product**

We have used Special Delivery to prototype several presentations, including a training project and an interactive slide show presentation. Because of its visually oriented development environment, it was fairly easy to learn, and was used to create our first project in just a few hours.

Some Things We Have Found

The Tutorial manual that comes with Special Delivery is well written and leads you through most of the major steps you need to know to master the product. We have found that it is best to start with fairly simple presentations, using only a few elements per slide, and not try to get very fancy with the interactivity.

The toolset available to you is simplistic and really doesn't allow much other than positioning elements and setting up the interactivity. You need to create your elements with other applications and import each one as you need it.

The sample backgrounds and buttons that come with the product are good for experimentation purposes, but are somewhat generic for use in actual products. This is not a bad thing; it is great that they have included some of these so you can begin learning how to use the product right away.

Having four different button link types is nice. You can choose between data buttons, navigation buttons, presentation buttons (the VCR-like controls), and portal buttons. Portals contain data, initiate actions, or both, and a portal button defines and controls portals. (This all makes more sense once you begin using the product.)

The Bottom Line

Although not as well known, Special Delivery offers a step up from the basic functions available in Persuasion and PowerPoint. These last two products are beginning to come out with version updates that offer some of these newer functions that have been part of Special Delivery for the past two years or so.

VideoFusion

Radius, Inc.

For: √ Macintosh

Demo included on the CD-ROM

VideoFusion is a video special effects processing application; it is also a movie editor. Its strengths are in its easy way of creating very dazzling MTV-style effects. (See Figure 7.24.) This review is based on version 1.6.1.

Minimum Requirements: Macintosh II or greater, a hard disk, 4 MB of free-application RAM, System 7.0 or later, color monitor, QuickTime 1.0 or later.

**Figure 7.24
VideoFusion's
Pan Zoom
Rotate window.**

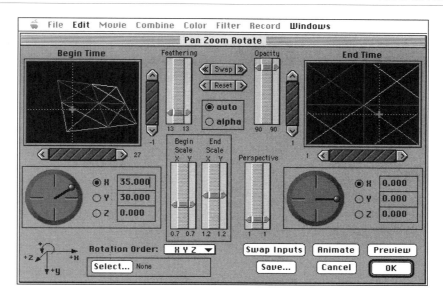

Basic Features

- Large library of special effects, including warp, pan-zoom-rotate, meta-morphosis, and compositing
- Nonlinear editing as well as a storyboard editor and script view
- Record and digitize video and audio analog sources
- Dynamic filters with support for third party filters
- PowerPC native acceleration

Unique Features

- Scalable movie creation; convert frame rate, size, and compression
- 3D rotation and fly-by effects
- Time-based control over effects processes
- Very well designed and easy-to-use effects control interfaces

How We Use This Product

We find this to be a great source capture tool. It is easy and accurate. We use VideoFusion to reprocess movies that need "fixing." In the absence of using (or for the beginner, going out and purchasing) a vectorscope to check and adjust the color, contrast, brightness, and white/black levels of videos, the video settings capabilities let you do more than just "eyeball" your sources for better results. You can also adjust time scale, window crops, frame rates, and more.

We also use it for the built-in effects. As we discussed earlier in the book, we use effects appropriately and sparingly. VideoFusion's wealth of effects capabilities will last us for a very long time.

**Some Things
We Have
Found**

We really like the interface; it is one of the most well-thought-out designs for its purpose we have come across. It actually is fun to use. If you have never used a storyboard-based edit control window, then you will have a slight learning curve, but this is easily mastered.

VideoFusion has one of the best movie information windows available, providing practically all the information about a movie and its tracks that you might want (frame rate, size, compressor, samples, references, and so forth).

Audio editing controls are limited, but it was not intended for audio processing.

**The Bottom
Line**

This is the easiest QuickTime special effects application we have found. It is also a good editor. If you are a multimedia professional and want to add a special flavor to your videos, then this is one of the best ways to get there. If you are a music video producer looking for a special set of effects to complement your artist's music, then this product is perfect for you. (VideoFusion was actually used to add effects to the first desktop-based, digitally edited and produced music video to be aired on MTV.)

VideoShop

Avid Technology

For: √ Macintosh

VideoShop is a video editing, effects, and processing application. It supports video, text, graphics, PhotoCD, and audio files in most major formats. (See Figure 7.25.) This review is based on version 3.0.

Minimum Requirements: Any color-capable Macintosh, 40 MB hard disk, 4 MB of free-application RAM (8 MB or more recommended), System 7.0 or later, color monitor, QuickTime 2.0 or later, Sound Manager 3.0 or later. For video capture: a Quick-Time-compatible digitizer card or AV Macintosh.

**Basic
Features**

- Video and audio recording from analog sources
- Nonlinear digital video editor
- Transitions and special effects
- Unlimited video and audio tracks
- Cataloging of source clips
- Storyboarding of movies

**Figure 7.25
VideoShop.**

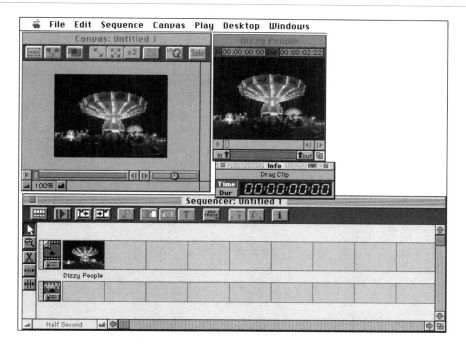

**Unique
Features**

- Built-in titling and scrolling credits
- Unique user interface provides for easy editing; no prior editing knowledge required
- Layer and composite multiple movies at one time
- Batch digitizing and support for timecode
- Device control via ViSCA or Sony serial protocols

**How We Use
This Product**

We use VideoShop for many of its capabilities, from recording and digitizing analog source video and audio to editing and adding effects to our final QuickTime movies. We have used it for CD–ROM–based QuickTime movies as well as for editing full-screen, full-motion video recorded from VideoShop directly out to videotape.

**Some Things
We Have
Found**

VideoShop creates its own desktop in that you have complete access to all of your source files via a Macintosh-like window and folder arrangement. Only the movie-related source files appear in the windows and are represented by "micons"—all other files (non-multimedia related) are hidden. Micons are *moving icons*. If you click once on them, they will play. Double-click and they will open to their normal size. This basic architectural feature of VideoShop is very refreshing compared to the Macintosh Finder.

VideoShop lets you save graphic elements and text as objects, rather than as a permanent part of the picture file. This allows you to move objects and edit the text at a later date (very important). This is a new feature in version 3.0.

The Bottom Line

This is a great QuickTime editing and effects tool suitable for both beginners and experienced multimedia professionals. This is not our only editing application. We use VideoShop alone or in combination with other editor/effects products based upon the type and complexity of the project at hand. If you are not comfortable with a linear frame editing format, then VideoShop's alternate storyboard editor may be just right for you.

8

Hardware Product Reviews

Software doesn't work without hardware. Take that as a given and live with it. Fortunately, there are a large number of software products available for the desktop video studio which work fine with just the computer as the necessary hardware.

There are, however, other pieces of hardware that can add functionality and speed to your work. These are things such as:

- Accelerator boards
- Compression boards
- Cameras

Each of these can, in some way, make your job easier or faster, and some of them can be downright fun to use. Take, for example, the new miniature video cameras such as the QuickCam and the FlexCam Pro. Although designed for such straightforward functions as video conferencing, they can provide alternatives to a big, heavy video camera if all you need is a quick product shot or a video clip.

For the entry-level individual, such as a student or a home producer, the QuickCam by Connectix is a fun, small (about the size of a golf ball), inexpensive (street cost less than $100) 16-grayscale camera. It does have limitations in its frame rate and the number of grays, but it can be put to some good uses. It has the advantage of being highly portable. Just connect it to the serial port of a PowerBook, and you have a complete "field" studio.

As in the previous chapter, each review here features a description of a product's uses, features, unique attributes, and our gut reactions.

We also try to indicate where on the cost scale each of these products fits. Again we use the symbols:

to denote entry-level, mid-range, and high-end products. If you are just starting out, and have a tight budget, don't limit yourself to looking at only the entry-level products. Depending on your needs, you may want to invest in something a bit more expensive. And, if you consider yourself to be in the midrange or high range, do not discount the capabilities of the entry-level products. Because the types of hardware vary so much, we do not categorize them in this chapter. Some of the things you will *not* find in this chapter are reviews of the dozens of CD-ROM drives, audio kits for PCs, and other hardware not directly related to the capture or processing of digital video. We felt it important to stick with products we have used ourselves or have seen demonstrated by the manufacturer.

DigitalFilm

Radius, Inc. (SuperMac)

For: √ Macintosh

The DigitalFilm card was a first-generation video capture and compression board set for Macintosh computers. Although it was one of the first full-screen solutions, it is no longer being marketed. It became one of the first victims of the Radius–SuperMac merger in late 1994. We discuss it here because there is a large installed base of these cards.

Basic Features

- Full-screen video capture with real-time JPEG compression and decompression
- Built-in video and audio I/O and digitizer with support for Macintosh monitors

- External video and audio I/O connector box
- Support for both NTSC and PAL timings

Unique Features

- Built-in 16-bit audio digitizer
- Custom XCMDs for use in HyperCard and Macromedia Director
- Includes DiskExpress II to optimize the "scratch" hard disks to which movies are recorded

How We Use This Product

We used this card in the past for full-screen captures, but have since moved on to other systems.

Some Things We Have Found

This card does not capture true 640 × 480 at 60 fields per second; it will capture 320 × 240 at 60 fields per second and then interpolate that data up to full screen. It will also capture "640 × 480" at 30 fields per second, but it is really only capturing 640 × 240 and then line-doubling to pad out to a display size of 640 × 480. This is a limiting factor when producing videos for broadcast use. The quality of the video output from this card does not compare favorably to the other cards in the broadcast class of product.

If you are producing digital video for multimedia and CD-ROM delivery, especially when that video is to be 320 × 240 or smaller, you will find that this card is well suited for the task.

The Bottom Line

DigitalFilm is a capable performer, but being from the first generation of full-screen, full-motion digitizer and compression cards, it does not compare head-to-head with today's generation of solutions. Although Radius (SuperMac) discontinued this product when they merged, there are still many available at retail, and the close-out price (below $1,500 street), which makes it a good buy for general multimedia production use.

We checked with Radius product management, and they reported that they plan to support the card for some time. Given Radius and SuperMac's excellent history of supporting and servicing discontinued products, we expect that this card will be useful for years to come.

FlexCam Pro

VideoLabs, Inc.

For: √ Macintosh   √ Windows

FlexCam Pro is a unique color CCD camera and microphone designed for desktop video, communication, and multimedia use. This camera provides full-screen, full-motion video to your digitizer, monitor, or VCR.

Basic Features

- Composite and S-Video outputs compatible with any NTSC or PAL digitizer or video monitor/VCR
- Focus ring on lens adjustable between less than an inch out to infinity
- Low light, f/2.0 lens with filtering
- CCD resolution of 510 × 492 (NTSC) and 500 × 582 (PAL)

Unique Features

- Has a flexible gooseneck (its signature feature), allowing it to be twisted, positioned, and pointed in any direction
- Built-in line-level stereo audio microphone
- Automatic exposure level and white balance
- Adjustable audio gain control

How We Use This Product

We have used this camera for everything from interviews (head shots) to product shots to video conferencing. For interviews, the small size of the actual camera head means that it may be positioned to "peek" over the interviewer's shoulder without drawing the attention of the interview subject.

For product shots where the product must be photographed from above, the camera neck can be twisted so the lens points straight down. It is a robust and "flexible" camera.

Some Things We Have Found

The video signal is clean, sharp, and more than sufficient for many close-range tasks. Although we know that this would add to the price, it might be nice for a future version to offer a zoom feature.

One thing that we would like to see changed is the audio connectors. Currently these are a pair of RCA-type plugs. For all Macintosh computers and most PC audio cards, the connector of choice is the stereo miniplug. At least they should include an adapter, as they do for converting S-Video into composite (RCA).

The Bottom Line

This camera is rugged and easy to use. We found it convenient and a time saver (saving us from setting up our more expensive gear when that would be overkill for the purpose). It is a little pricey, as *some* camcorders can be purchased for the same price. We expect that this camera will have lower-priced competition from other sources in the near future.

Media 100

Data Translation

For: √ Macintosh

Media 100 is a professional digital video production system. It includes both hardware and software written specifically for the product, yet it is compatible with a host of Macintosh video and multimedia applications.

Basic Features

- Video and audio I/O box with composite, S-Video, and BNC component connectors
- Full-screen, full-motion real-time JPEG compression and DSP audio processing
- Complete custom all-in-one software interface for access to all system functionality
- Full set of cable assemblies for connecting video and audio equipment

Unique Features

- A suite of hardware and software options, including component video, character generation, DVE special effects, EDL list generation, and HDR (high data rate) compression
- Built-in Encoder/Decoder using highest quality YUV 4:2:2 data format
- Real-time subsampler to simultaneously see the digital video on the Macintosh monitor and the video monitor

How We Use This Product

We received a loan of a Media 100 to review for this book. We used it with both our Quadra 840AV and our Power Macintosh 8100. We used FWB's SledgeHammer 4 GB fast/wide array during the tests with the Media 100.

We captured video from our Select Effects library on a BetaCam SP deck into the software's bin window and edited several minutes of video together with various different transitions between clips to get the feel of the system's capabilities.

Some Things We Have Found

We found it very easy to adapt to this product's software interface. We also were impressed with the speed and smooth control of the digital video streams. The hard-disk management of old clips, discarded transitions, and special effects was practically transparent. This system is productive, and at the same time is fun to use.

When we used the system on our Power Macintosh 8100, we found that we could not view the digital video on the Macintosh monitor. After reviewing the documentation we found that, although the system is compatible (and can be used) with an 8100, it doesn't display the video preview on the built-in video of the 8100. It expects a third-party NuBus 24-bit display card to send the video preview through. We hope that this is something that Data Translation can overcome in future revisions.

The Bottom Line

For the professional video producer on a budget, this system (in conjunction with one or more FWB SledgeHammer drives) is an excellent choice. For the midrange developers out there, this can provide you with lots of things over which you might drool, but the cost may prohibit you from jumping in right now.

MoviePak2 Pro Suite

RasterOps

For: √ Macintosh

MoviePak Pro Suite is a full-motion, full-screen Quick-Time digital video production system.

Basic Features

- Real-time capture and compression at 30 and 60 fps at 640 × 480 (NTSC) and 25 and 50 fps 768 × 576 (PAL)

- JPEG hardware compression ratios from 2:1 through 100:1
- Video and audio connector I/O box with RGB, S-Video, composite, and stereo audio inputs and outputs
- Supports Macintosh monitors up to 21" at 1152 × 870 resolution; captures in 24-bit even on 8-bit displays

**Unique
Features**

- Professional device control via RS-422 interface
- MediaGrabber™ digital video recording software
- Supports recording at four resolutions: standard 320 × 240; full horizontal 640 × 240 (one field per frame); full vertical 320 × 480 (both fields, but pixel doubles the vertical); and full-frame 640 × 480 (both fields per frame)
- Dynamic-Q feature allows limiting of data rate; varies the amount of compression on the fly to minimize frame dropping

**How We Use
This Product**

Although we do not count this product among our studio staples, we have used our review system with several sample projects.

**Some Things
We Have
Found**

This is a revised version of the original MoviePak product, which was a first-generation solution (like DigitalFilm). This second-generation version supports recording true 640 × 480, 60 fps digital video.

We found on several occasions that the card dropped frames during the digitizing and compression process. We don't know whether this is a problem with the card or with using it in conjunction with QuickTime 2.0 (some card manufacturers have reported frame-dropping problems that had not occurred before QT 2.0 was released). If you are using this card to create less than full-frame-rate movies, then this should not pose a problem.

**The Bottom
Line**

The question is which of the two RasterOps products will prevail? RasterOps owns Truevision, which produces the new Targa 2000 for the Macintosh. We feel that RasterOps will have to reprice the MoviePak2 Pro Suite, or it could fall victim to the Targa 2000 and other competitors. The MoviePak2 Pro Suite would be a great buy at a low to midrange price.

PowerPro 601

Daystar Digital

(E) (M)

For: √ Macintosh

PowerPro 601 is an upgrade board for Macintosh Quadra computers. It features a 601 PowerPC microprocessor and effectively turns your computer into a PowerPC Macintosh, increasing your Macintosh computer's performance by 200 to 500 percent.

Basic Features

- NuBus and PDS slot card with a PPC 601 processor
- 100 percent compatible, licensed Apple PowerPC ROMs
- Uses the existing RAM in your Macintosh, plus you can add up to 128 MB directly on the card

Unique Features

- Includes PowerPC native filters and plug-ins for applications that use Adobe Photoshop plug-in technology
- Lets you boot the Macintosh in either 68040 or PPC 601 mode
- Add up to 1 MB of FastCache to increase performance even further

How We Use This Product

It may seem odd reviewing a CPU upgrade in this book, but we felt it was warranted. This is because the codecs in QuickTime 2.0 are now PowerPC-native. Anyone who has sat for hours waiting for CinePak to compress a movie will understand the benefit. Buying the PowerPro 601 just to speed up CinePak compression times by over 300 percent can be worth the price alone. It is less expensive than buying a new PowerPC Macintosh.

We have used the PowerPro 601 in a Quadra 700 (which had previously been relegated to CD-ROM one-off pressing) to batch-compress hundreds of movies from JPEG to CinePak. This has greatly improved our turnaround time on movie processing as well as freeing up our other computers for other production tasks.

Some Things We Have Found

We have found this card to be transparent in its usage, and to live up to its performance claims. We had an occasional system lockup when we first received and installed the card, but that was remedied when we received a software update from Daystar.

The Bottom Line

If you are looking to greatly improve the performance of an older Macintosh Quadra model, if you don't want to shell out for a new computer, and if selling the old Macintosh for pennies on the dollar makes you feel sick, then this card is an excellent solution.

Even if you have already purchased a newer, faster computer, the value gained by bringing your older Quadra back into use as a processing platform can easily be worth the cost.

QuickCam

Connectix

For: √ Macintosh

QuickCam is a small, grayscale video camera for personal multimedia and teleconferencing use. It offers speeds of up to 15 frames per second of video capture.

Basic Features

- Selectable 1 frame per hour to 15 frames per second rate
- Offers 65 degree angle of view
- Weighs just 3.3 ounces
- Has 16-shade grayscale output
- Built-in microphone

Unique Features

- Includes video capture and editing software
- Requires only the power available from your computer's serial port
- Street price of around $100

How We Use This Product

We have experimented with this camera to see what it can do. So far we haven't had the opportunity to use it in a project where its limited video quality would be applicable.

One possible use may come about by the time this book is published when the daughter of one of the Toucan Studios partners will be creating a student project for her computer multimedia class. She intends to connect the camera to a PowerBook 165c to shoot all of her footage, then edit it right on the PowerBook into the final project. She will be able to show the final movie on the PowerBook as well.

**Some Things
We Have
Found**

This is not the camera for those who want a high-quality output. But this is a very nice camera for the beginner or the student videographer.

You can use this as a low-cost cinema vérité camera to add interesting footage to existing movies.

The software that comes with the camera is effective for basic edits. It also includes capabilities for low-cost video teleconferencing.

**The Bottom
Line**

Its size, flexibility, and price all make QuickCam an attractive option for the entry-level market. We expect that a color version of the camera is not far off.

SledgeHammer

FWB, Inc.

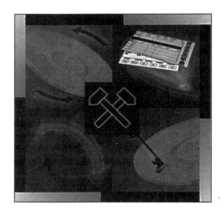

For: √ Macintosh   √ Windows

SledgeHammer is a family of high-performance, high-capacity hard-disk drives for multimedia and video production use.

**Basic
Features**

- AV rated (designed for audio and video recording)
- Rugged metal case design to protect drive mechanism
- Very high spindle speeds and very short access and seek times

**Unique
Features**

- High-performance JackHammer SCSI interface card available with arrays
- HDT software for formatting and partitioning

**How We Use
This Product**

We used these drives with all the software and hardware that we have reviewed for this book. The drives were used to master our Select Effects library of special-effects QuickTime movies.

**Some Things
We Have
Found**

These drives are basically bulletproof. We use them along with the FWB JackHammer card (an accelerated 16-bit SCSI II NuBus interface) to record 3 and 4 MB per second digital video data streams. We can continue, without interruption, until the total of 4 GB of storage space on the drive is full. So far, we have not detected a single dropped frame.

We standardized on the FWB Hard Disk Toolkit software that comes with the drives as our formatting and partitioning software over a year ago. We have tested a 4 GB array, 1.8 GB fast/wide drive, and a 900 MB hard disk. All have performed without any problems.

The Bottom Line

Our only wish is that the drives were less expensive (and that we didn't have to return the 4 GB drive). Hard-drive prices are falling rapidly, and bare drives can be purchased for as little as 35 cents per MB, but that won't get you an FWB drive. These are high-performance, AV-rated drives, controllers, enclosures, and software, all working together. We feel that you are getting your money's worth with one of these drives.

Spigot II Tape

Radius, Inc. (SuperMac)

Ⓔ

For: √ Macintosh

Spigot II Tape is an effective video capture board for Macintosh computers. It features software-compression capabilities and will play your digitized and edited movies back out to videotape.

Basic Features

- Captures live video to a hard disk
- NTSC video output to record digital video to tape
- Composite and S-video inputs and outputs
- Captures video in multiple window sizes and frame rates
- Allows cropping of the record window to digitize just what is wanted

Unique Features

- Custom software compressor to record full-motion video while decreasing overall data size
- Hardware interpolation on video out to fill screen with 320 × 240 movies (pixel doubling)
- Includes simple and easy-to-use ScreenPlay™ recording and playback software

How We Use This Product

Spigot II Tape is designed to meet the needs of the home multimedia market. We tend to use much higher-performance products in our business.

In preparation for this book, we began using the card to digitize from various video sources that might be available to the home or student multimedia producer (VHS, SVHS, Hi-8, and from laserdisc). Although the final results looked absolutely fine for the needs of entry-level multimedia production, it was not (and not expected to be) of the professional quality our clients would expect.

Some Things We Have Found

This card has no sound digitizing capability, but this is not a problem for most Macintosh owners. The vast majority of Macintosh models have built-in sound I/O capability. This card works fine with both built-in and card-based sound I/O.

Spigot II Tape is not a hardware-compression product. It does include a software precompressor with the card called "Spigot II Tape Rough." This codec does a mild form of compression, a balance between keeping the frame rate up and the data size to disk down. The performance of this product will vary with the computer and hard disks used. Be prepared to use between 60 and 120 MB per minute of captured video.

The ScreenPlay software that comes with the card makes it very easy to capture and view the movies. The settings and controls are like those you would find on almost any VCR.

The Bottom Line

Spigot II Tape is an excellent entry-level product for the individual who is getting started on a limited budget. It is fine for home movie editing (you'll need very large hard disks) or for creating QuickTime movies to add to a presentation. You won't make a broadcast video with this, but it has everything you need to make good QuickTime movies for school, presentations, or demos, or for editing your home movies.

SpigotPower AV

Radius, Inc. (SuperMac)

For: √ Macintosh

SpigotPower AV is a full-screen, full-motion video-compression board designed for use in Macintosh AV computers. It is significantly less expensive than other full-screen compression cards because it does not include the video I/O circuitry that the others have. It relies on the AV I/O features of the Macintosh 660AV and 840AV, as well as the Power Macintosh 7100AV and 8100AV.

Basic Features

- JPEG video compression, 60 or 50 fields per second capture rate from NTSC or PAL, respectively
- Synchronizes with the audio I/O of the AV Macintosh computer's built-in audio
- 24-bit color capture up to full screen

Unique Features

- Uses the DAV slot of the AV Macintosh model to pass the digital video I/O
- Print-to-tape via the AV Macintosh model's I/O ports
- User-selectable data rates for optimal performance

How We Use This Product

Many of the example movies we have supplied on the CD-ROM that comes with this book were captured and digitized using this card. Our introduction movies were also processed through this card on a Macintosh 8100AV. We have found this card to be simple, convenient, and transparent in its use.

Some Things We Have Found

One of the few limitations encountered when using this product is not its fault. The video output from the AV computer compressed via this card is 16-bit color, not 24-bit. This is because the video I/O of the Macintosh AV models is only 16-bit color. The internal JPEG data remains in 24-bit format. In fact, if you transcode a movie compressed with the SpigotPower AV to CinePak, the resulting movie will be 24-bit color.

Even with this limitation, this a great compression card for the multimedia producer where the results are for quarter-screen (or smaller) movies. However, if you plan to produce full-screen, full-motion videotapes from your productions, the results will be 16-bit color, which is fine for most home, industrial, and corporate preview uses.

As of this writing, the card is not yet compatible with QuickTime 2.0. SpigotPower AV is completely compatible with QuickTime 1.6.2, the release just prior to 2.0. What would seem to be a compatibility failure on the part of the manufacturer is really only a product-introduction problem. This is an example of what sometimes happens in our industry when two companies bring out products at the same time. Radius is completing development of the software necessary to make the card QuickTime 2.0 compliant , which should be available by the time you are reading this book.

The Bottom Line

If you own an AV Macintosh and are looking for a full-screen compression product, but you are on a budget, then this card is for you. At under $1,000, it is very competitive. If you don't own an AV Macintosh, you are out of luck in this category, as Radius does not have a low-priced solution for you. If you need full 24-bit I/O for professional video productions, then you should be looking at a higher-priced solution category.

Targa 2000

Truevision (RasterOps)

For: √ Macintosh   √ Windows

Targa 2000 is a full-screen, full-motion video and audio capture, and real-time compression card for Macintosh and PC computers.

Basic Features

- Real-time video capture at up to 640 × 486 at 30 and 60 fps (NTSC) and 768 × 576 at 25 and 50 fps (PAL)

- Real-time variable JPEG compression, with dynamic quantization

- 16-bit, CD-quality stereo audio digitizer

Unique Features

- Full CCIR 601 input and output standards compliance
- Simultaneous built-in Macintosh and Video monitor usage
- Able to genlock to the reference sync source being used in a studio

How We Use This Product

At press time we had not yet used this product. Nevertheless, we felt that it was important to include some basic information about the Targa 2000 in these reviews. The information is drawn from product literature, specification sheets, and a demo we received at Macworld in January 1995.

Some Things We Have Found

This new product for the Macintosh (a PC version has been available for several months) is Truevision's entry into the midrange digital video solution category. From the demo we saw, this product looks as if it will compete head-to-head with the Radius Studio products.

The Bottom Line

Truevision has an excellent track record with the products they build for the PC video market. Although they have built Macintosh cards before, they are a late entrant into the Macintosh digital video arena. If they have applied the same level of engineering talent to this new card as they have for their PC products, then this will be a strong contender. If you are considering a full-screen full-motion JPEG solution for video production, you should consider this card.

VideoCube

ImMIX

For: √ Macintosh

VideoCube is a high-end, nonlinear digital video system solution—a combination of hardware and software that may be used to edit and produce professional and broadcast-quality videos. This system is different from all the others in several ways. One of the most significant is that it is completely turnkey. You don't even need to own a Macintosh; it comes with the system. The other nonlinear editing systems are add-ons to a Macintosh. With ImMIX, it's the Macintosh that gets added to the VideoCube!

Basic Features

- Media Processor has storage for one hour of digital video and two hours of CD audio
- Multi-stream, real-time video processing includes two video channels, four stereo audio channels, and an independent title track
- Digital audio mixer with four stereo channels; includes features such as pan, reverb, equalization, and independent gain

Unique Features

- Custom, ergonomic editing control panel (and we don't mean software)
- Dozens of real-time DVE transitions and effects
- Anti-aliased real-time character generator
- Up to five storage modules can be added to the VideoCube; each can store one hour of video and two hours of CD audio

How We Use This Product

We were able to get a lengthy demo of the system from ImMIX's art director at a local post house, from which this information is derived.

Some Things We Have Found

The controller box provides all of the transport control functions of the Cube at your fingers, much like the shuttle controls of a professional video deck, only better. We were amazed at the speed (read: *basically real time*) of the effects and transitions. Several other systems require off-line rendering time to complete their transitions and effects.

The software interface on the Macintosh was elegant. Maybe too visually elegant. In fact, that's probably our only complaint. The interface has a colored parchment paper look to the background of all the controls. This made finding some elements in the interface a little hard on the eyes because there were no solid edges.

The Bottom Line

We are looking into how we can finance, barter, beg, borrow, or give our eyeteeth to get a VideoCube for our own use, permanently. This system is the fastest, most powerful, and elegant nonlinear system we have ever seen. The designers of the VideoCube are from the broadcast industry (including companies such as Grass Valley Group), and they have created a system that exceeds the high quality requirements of that industry.

This system is not for producing multimedia, but is designed to produce up to full-length television shows. If you think a broadcast edit suite can't be had for less than several hundred grand, get ready for a surprise. This system starts at under fifty thousand!

VideoVision Studio

Radius, Inc. (SuperMac)

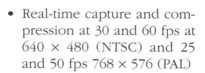

For: √ Macintosh

VideoVision Studio is a professional-quality full-screen, full-motion, video capture and compression card solution.

Basic Features

- Real-time capture and compression at 30 and 60 fps at 640 × 480 (NTSC) and 25 and 50 fps 768 × 576 (PAL)
- JPEG hardware-compression ratios from 6:1 through 50:1
- Video and audio connector I/O panel with two sets of S-Video, composite, and stereo audio inputs, and one set of similar outputs
- Supports Macintosh monitors up to 24-bit color; captures in 24-bit even on 8-bit displays

Unique Features

- External genlock option, and device control capability
- Mix Macintosh audio with digital movie audio
- Real-time standards conversion (NTSC to PAL and reverse)
- Built-in stereo audio digitizer

How We Use This Product

VideoVision Studio is the staple of our production system. We have two Quadra 840AV systems with VideoVision Studio cards installed. Most of our major productions and all of our digital video to tape are based on Video-Vision Studio. All of our Select Effects Library CDs (see the sampler on the accompanying CD-ROM) were produced with VideoVision Studio and Beta-Cam SP decks.

Some Things We Have Found

Although not a limitation in our current projects, the card only supports 24-bit video on monitors displaying 640 ¥ 480 pixels. It will support larger monitors, but only at 16- or 8-bit color. (But the video is still digitized at 24-bits.)

Audio digitizing is 8-bit only, which is not a problem for newer Macintosh models with 16-bit audio built in. We find that the majority of the audio that must be captured from a source tape is generally spoken word or background sounds. These are just fine when sampled at 8-bit, 22 KHz. If we must have higher-quality audio, we will capture it separately and mix it back into the video.

The Bottom Line

At today's midrange price there is no equal. With the introduction of Telecast, Radius has provided an upward migration path for the VideoVision Studio user. There are other systems out there—and we have reviewed several—but for our money at the midrange, the Radius VideoVision products are the best overall performers.

VideoVision Telecast

Radius, Inc. (SuperMac)

For: √ Macintosh

VideoVision Telecast is the most recent step up in quality and performance that Radius has made in the desktop video studio arena. It is a nonlinear digital video production system.

Basic Features

- Component BetaCam SP quality video recording to, and playback from, hard disk
- External video and audio I/O box with professional component, S-Video, and composite inputs and outputs with NTSC, PAL, and SECAM video standards
- JPEG compression ratios of 3:1 to 50:1

Unique Features

- Upgrade path for VideoVision and VideoVision Studio owners to Telecast
- Radius Edit, a custom all-in-one, nonlinear editing application
- Up to four tracks of stereo audio synchronized to video
- Rack-mount design for easy studio integration
- Device control of RS-422 compliant video decks

How We Use This Product

This product has just been introduced as we are finishing the book, and we were unable to get one of the very few units available for review. We felt, however, that it was important to include information about the Telecast in the reviews. This information is drawn from product literature, specification sheets, and a demo we received at the January 1995 Macworld tradeshow.

Some Things We Have Found

Radius has a new software application to go with Telecast. It is called Radius Edit. This will be shipped with all Telecast systems, and we expect that it will be available separately for use with any QuickTime-compatible digital video cards. It was created by the same folks who wrote VideoFusion. From our limited demo, we found it to be very robust and feature rich, yet the interface was not overburdened with extras. The controls will be very familiar to the traditional tape editor.

The Bottom Line

Radius has a proven track record in creating high-quality digital video products. Their new direction in creating all-in-one digital video solutions (including producing Macintosh clones) will, in all likelihood, continue their record. If you are looking for a high-end system, we suggest evaluating the Telecast.

Appendix A
Other Reading

Walk into almost any bookstore and you will find a computer section with dozens of books on multimedia, digital video, and related topics. Each book is written based on a particular author's experiences and preferences.

Since we believe in the sharing of ideas, we would be remiss if we did not provide a short list of other books and periodicals you may wish to peruse. Please note that magazine subscription prices are subject to change.

Books

Demystifying Multimedia
Apple Computer, Inc., and vivid studios
Random House Electronic Publishing, 1995

The Home Video Maker's Handbook
Lewis, Roland
Crown Publishers, Inc., 1987

The Independent Film & Videomakers Guide
Weise, Michael
Michael Wiese Productions, 1981; revised 1990

Multimedia Power Tools
Peter Jerram and Michael Gosney
Random House Electronic Publishing, 1993

Periodicals

Converge—The Multimedia Developer's Companion
Multi-Facet Communications, Inc.
Published monthly; $179/year
800/959-5276

DV—Digital Video Magazine
Techmedia Publishing
Published monthly; $29.97/year
603/924-0100

Interactivity
GPI Publications—Miller Freeman, Inc.
Published bimonthly; $29.95/year
415/905-2200

NewMedia Magazine
HyperMedia Communications, Inc.
Published 13 times annually; $38.00/year
609/786-4430

Appendix B
Vendors

We have discussed a number of different software and hardware products in this book. You may wish to contact their manufacturers and publishers, so we include this list of names and addresses, in alphabetical order by product name:

Action!
Macromedia
600 Townsend Street
San Francisco, CA 94103
800/945-9169

Adobe Photoshop
Adobe Systems, Inc.
P.O. Box 7900
Mountain View, CA 94039-7900
800/833-6687

Adobe Premiere
Adobe Systems, Inc.
P.O. Box 7900
Mountain View, CA 94039-7900
800/833-6687

AfterEffects
After Image
Aldus Corp.
411 First Avenue South
Seattle, WA 98104-2871
206/628-2320

Apple Media Tool
Apple Computer, Inc.
1 Infinite Loop
Cupertino, CA 95014
408/996-1010

APS Drives
APS Technologies
P.O. Box 4987
Kansas City, KS 64120-0087
816/483-4187

Astound
Gold Disk, Inc.
3350 Scott Boulevard
Santa Clara, CA 95054
800/982-9888

Audio Shop
Opcode Systems, Inc.
3950 Fabian Way, Suite 100
Palo Alto, CA 94303
415/856-3333

Batch It!
Gryphon Software Corp.
7220 Trade Street, Suite 120
San Diego, CA 92121
619/536-8815

ConvertToMovie
Apple Computer, Inc.
1 Infinite Loop
Cupertino, CA 95014
408/996-1010

DeBabelizer
Equilibrium Technologies
475 Gate Five Road, Suite 225
Sausalito, CA 94965
800/524-8651

DigitalFilm
Radius
215 Moffett Park Drive
Sunnyvale, CA 94089
800/541-7680

DigiTrax
Alaska Software
1197 Pomela Court
Sunnyvale, CA 94087
800/500-3320

Director
Macromedia
600 Townsend Street
San Francisco, CA 94103
800/945-9169

Disc to Disk
Optical Media International
180 Knowles Drive
Los Gatos, CA 95030
408/376-3511

Elastic Reality
Elastic Reality
925 Stewart Street
Madison, WI 53713
608/273-6585

FlexCam Pro
VideoLabs, Inc.
10925 Bren Road East
Minneapolis, MN 55343
612/897-1995

JackHammer
PocketHammer
SledgeHammer
FWB Incorporated
2040 Polk Street, Suite 215
San Francisco, CA 94109
415/464-8055

KAI's Power Tools
HSC Software
1661 Lincoln Boulevard, Suite 101
Santa Monica, CA 90404
310/392-8441

Kodak Shoebox
Eastman Kodak Company
343 State Street
Rochester, NY 14650-0536
800/242-2424 ext. 53 (U.S. only)
716/724-1021 ext. 53 (outside U.S.)

Media 100
Data Translations
100 Locke Drive
Marlboro, MA 01752-1192
508/460-1600

Micropolis Drives
Micropolis
21211 Nordhoff Street
Chatsworth, CA 91311
818/718-5264

Morph
Gryphon Software Corp.
7220 Trade Street, Suite 120
San Diego, CA 92121
619/536-8815

MovieAnalyzer
Movie Converter
MoviePlayer
MovieShop
Apple Computer, Inc.
1 Infinite Loop
Cupertino, CA 95014
408/996-1010

MoviePak2 Pro Suite
RasterOps Corp.
2500 Walsh Avenue
Santa Clara, CA 95051
800/729-2656

MovieWorks
Interactive Solutions, Inc.
5776 Stoneridge Mall Road, Suite 333
Pleasanton, CA 94588
510/734-0730

MultiMedia Utilities
  CameraMan
  MotionPaint
  MovieClick
  QuickEdit
  QuickMorph
  SoundMate
Motion Works International
1020 Mainland Street, Suite 130
Vancouver, BC V6V 2T4
CANADA
604/685-9975

Painter 3
Fractal Design
335 Spreckles Drive, Suite F
Aptos, CA 95003
408/688-5300

PowerPro 601
Daystar Digital
5556 Atlanta Highway
Flowery Branch, CA 90542
404/967-2077

QuickCam
Connectix
2600 Campus Drive
San Mateo, CA 94403-2520
800/950-5880

Quick Flix!
VideoFusion
1722 Indian Wood Circle, Suite H
Maumee, OH 43537
419/891-1090

Ray Dream Designer
Ray Dream, Inc.
1804 North Shoreline Boulevard
Mountain View, CA 94943
415/960-0768

SoundEdit 16
Macromedia
600 Townsend Street
San Francisco, CA 94103
800/945-9169

Special Delivery
Interactive Media Corp.
P.O. Box 0089
Los Altos, CA 94023-0089
415/948-0745

Spigot II Tape
Spigot Power AV
SuperMac Technology, Inc.
215 Moffett Park Drive
Sunnyvale, CA 94089
408/541-6100

Strata Studio Pro
Strata, Inc.
2 West St. George Boulevard, Suite 2000
St. George, UT 84770
801/628-5218

TARGA 2000
TruewVision, Inc.
7340 Shapeland Station
Indianapolis, IN 46256
317/841-0332

Telecast
Radius
215 Moffett Park Drive
Sunnyvale, CA 94089
800/541-7680

VideoCube
ImMIX
644 East Fort Avenue, Suite 207
Baltimore, MD 21230
410/783-0600

Video Director
Gold Disk, Inc.
3350 Scott Boulevard
Santa Clara, CA 95054
800/982-9888

VideoFusion
VideoFusion
1722 Indian Wood Circle, Suite H
Maumee, OH 43537
419/891-1090

VideoShop
Avid Technology, Inc.
Metropolitan Technology Park
One Park West
Tewksbury, MA 01876
800/949-2843

VideoStudio
Radius
215 Moffett Park Drive
Sunnyvale, CA 94089
800/541-7680

Video Toolkit
Abbate Video
14 Ross Avenue, Floor 3
Millis, MA 02054
508/376-3712

And last but not least . . .

The Apple Multimedia Program
1 Infinite Loop, MS: 303-2D
Cupertino, CA 95014
Tel 408-974-4897
AppleLink DEVSUPPORT
Internet DEVSUPPORT@APPLELINK.APPLE.COM

The Apple Multimedia Program (AMP). AMP is designed for multimedia consultants, educators, designers, desktop video professionals, information/content providers, in-house developers, interactive musicians, marketers, production services companies, systems integrators, and title publishers. Amenities include: market research reports, technical guidebooks and resource directories; CD-ROMs and videos; "Members Only" online bulletin board; discounts on Apple and third-party products, training and multimedia events; co-marketing and networking opportunities and tradeshow participation; and invitations to multimedia events.

Glossary

Every industry and specialization has its own jargon, and digital video is no exception. Although this glossary may not be absolutely definitive, we have attempted to cover all of the terms used in this book that may not be familiar to someone just entering this business.

AC3. Dolby Laboratory's digital audio-compression standard.

ADPCM. *A*daptive *D*ifferential *P*ulse *C*ode *M*odulation. An audio-compression standard that automatically varies itself to best meet the needs of the sound being compressed.

AIFF. *A*udio *I*nterchange *F*ile *F*ormat. Apple Computer's standardized Macintosh file format for storage and playback of digital audio. Other, non-Macintosh platforms have begun accepting and using AIFF files.

Alias. A small file in Macintosh System 7 that points back to the location of the original. An alias may be placed anywhere on the desktop and looks and acts just like the original file, but it contains only the directions on how to find and open that file; it is not a duplicate of the file.

Alpha Channel. The last eight bits in each thirty-two bits of data of a 32-bit-per-pixel image. Many digital video and image-processing applications use it for masking or keying.

Analog. Video or audio signals recorded or played as a continuous sine wave where the peaks and valleys of the wave denote the video or audio information. Videotape formats including VHS and Beta, as well as audio formats such as LPs and cassette tapes, utilize

analog information. The human voice is another example of an analog signal.

Animation Compressor. The Animation compressor is based on RLE (*R*un *L*ength *E*ncoding) principles to compress computer-generated animation sequences from one to thirty-two bits in depth. Compression ratios vary greatly based on the content. It provides acceptable playback speeds of animation files on lower-performance computers.

Anti-Aliasing. A software-based routine for smoothing the edges between pixels. This provides a more natural-looking image. Anti-aliasing can be applied to both picture images and text.

Asymmetric Compression. A compression scheme that requires longer to compress than decompress. Asymmetric compression generally offers superior playback quality. CinePak is an example of an asymmetric compression scheme.

AVI. *A*udio *V*ideo *I*nterleave. Microsoft Corporation's digital video file format designed to support Video for Windows.

BetaCam. An industry-standard, high-quality video-tape record and playback scheme. BetaCam may be either analog (ED Beta, BetaCam SP) or digital (Digital BetaCam).

Bit Depth. The number of data bits used to create a pixel. The higher the number, the greater the range of color capability. Most recent computers are capable of 24-bit (millions of colors), although some platforms support only 8-bit (256 colors) or 16-bit (over 65,000 colors).

CD-ROM. Compact Disk—Read Only Memory. A compact disc used to store digital information. This may be text, graphics, sounds, or any other type of file, and usually is recorded as a continuous data track. As with audio CDs, this format may only be read ("played") and cannot be recorded to. A CD-ROM may also contain standard CD audio tracks along with its data track.

Chrominance. Sometimes abbreviated as *chroma.* This is the color component of a video signal.

CinePak. The Apple CinePak compressor was a joint development between Apple and SuperMac and is based on a combination of a VQ (*Vector Quantization*) algorithm and frame differencing. It provides a significant increase in image quality, playback rate, frame size, and compression of digitized video when compared with the Apple Video Compressor.

Codec. A *CO*mpressor/*DEC*ompressor used to compress or expand digital data. Codecs may be in the form of software, hardware, or a combination of both.

Component Video. Generally used to refer to RGB (red, green, blue) analog or digital signals in video.

Composite Video. A system of combining the chrominance, luminance, and synchronization information of a video signal across a single cable. This is the "standard" used in practically every piece of consumer video gear. Composite video cables usually have RCA-type jacks on each end of the wire.

Compression. The act of taking existing digital data and removing unnecessary or unchanging data in order to make a digital video or audio file smaller or to run on a machine not capable of playback of real-time data.

Compressor. An algorithm (software or hardware) used to compress data (video, graphics, and so forth) into a smaller size.

Data Rate. The amount of digital data transferred during recording or playback. The higher the data rate, the greater the amount of information available and the higher quality the image or sound.

Dialog Box. A window displayed by software on the computer screen providing a message or requesting user input, or both.

Digital. Video or audio signals recorded or played back as a series of 1s and 0s. Generally, the greater the amount of digital data used to represent a specific signal, the higher the quality.

Digital Audio. Audio information represented in digital form. The most familiar format for digital audio is the compact disc, along with Digital Audio Tape (DAT) and the MiniDisc.

Digital Video. Video information represented in digital form. Digital video source formats range from digital videotape (D1, D2, and so forth) to laserdiscs. Digital video also applies to any video file saved in computer form. (See *Digitizing.*)

Digitizer. The hardware that converts an analog signal into digital data.

Digitizing. The process of converting an analog signal (from tape, direct camera feed, and so forth) into digital data. This is then stored as a file, much as if it is a word-processed document or spreadsheet.

Dithering. The use of a limited set of colors in such a way as to give the impression to the eye that there are more colors in an image than there actually are. This is similar to the half-toning found in newspaper photographs where the eye "sees" many shades of gray, when in fact only black and white are present.

Dropout. A loss of video quality generally caused by the absence of a consistent surface on a videotape. Dropouts are almost unavoidable in cheaper tapes, so don't scrimp; you won't save!

DSS. *Digital Satellite System.* The newest television system. A series of geosynchronous satellites providing more than 150 channels using digital transmission. These signals are encoded using MPEG, in real time, and are transmitted to eighteen-inch receiver dishes that can be mounted on your house or apartment where a set top box decodes them, also in real time, and plays them on your television.

Editor. (1) A person performing the act of editing individual audio and video source components into a single or series of master components. (2) A device or piece of software used in the act of editing.

Effect. The use of one or more techniques to modify or change an image or video.

Fields. The scan lines that make up a television picture are represented in two equal sets (fields) of lines, each field containing only every other line. Display of these fields alternates with a total of sixty fields broadcast for each second of video. Since each field contains only half of the picture, it takes two alternate fields to make one complete frame (60 fields ÷ 2 = 30 frames per second).

fps. *Frames Per Second.* The number of physical picture frames (analog or equivalent digital information) either recorded or played over a period of one second. Television uses 30 fps, film-based movies in theaters run at 24 fps, and animation is created using about 12 fps but is transferred to 24 or 30 fps, depending on where it is shown.

Fractal Compression. An algorithm for extreme image compression using fractal mathematics as a part of the technique. Fractal compression is very computer-intensive and highly asymmetric. A unique feature of fractal compression is its apparent capability to endlessly zoom into an image with little loss of image detail.

Frame Differencing. The algorithm used to determine what visual information remains constant from one frame to the next and what information changes. Used during compression to eliminate or reduce the total amount of information that must be stored and used to play back a clip.

Frame Rate. The number of frames of video recorded or played back per second. American (NTSC) television uses 30 fps. Although digital video can be recorded and played at 30 fps, this requires large amounts of storage space, very fast computers, and other specialized hardware and software. Popular digital frame rates include 24, 20, 15, 12, and 10 fps.

Frame Size. The X-Y measurement of a display, usually given in pixels.

Graphics Compressor. A compressor developed by Apple that provides lossless compression of 8-bit (256 colors) images. It differs from Apple's Animation compressor in that it gains compression capability at the expense of decompression speed.

Hardware Assist. The use of some form of hardware assistance or acceleration to improve or speed up a process.

Hi-8. A compact video format used both at the consumer and the pro-sumer levels. This was created as an enhancement to standard 8mm video. The quality of Hi-8 provides a noticeable increase in signal-to-noise over VHS and comes close to the capabilities of 3/4-inch video.

Indeo Compressor. Indeo (AKA: DVI) is a revision of Intel's video-compression algorithm, based upon VQ but also using Motion Estimation and RLE algorithms. Indeo can encode digital video in real time with hardware assistance to data rates of about 300 kps, and play back with software only. It is about two times faster to compress (using software) the same digital video source in Indeo as it is in CinePak.

JPEG. *Joint Photographic Experts Group.* A still-image compression format usually used for compressing still (nonmotion) frames of video. JPEG is designed to compress full-color images and typically gives compression ratios in the range from 4:1 to 10:1 with little or no picture degradation; it can compress up to 25:1 or higher depending on the image content. The Photo compressor is Apple's implementation of JPEG.

Key Frame. A periodic frame where all video information is kept as the reference for compression of the following frame(s). Although it is a balancing act to find the appropriate Key Frame rate for a particular video, popular intervals range from one every frame to one every second.

Lossless. The act of capture/compression/playback where no quality is lost to the viewer. Lossless video generally requires special hardware.

Lossy. The act of capture/compression/playback where some quality is lost. This can be minimized through proper balance of all the compression factors.

Luminance. This is the brightness of an image, generally not related to color. (See *Chrominance.*)

MACE. *M*acintosh *A*udio *C*ompression and *E*xpansion. A form of asymmetric audio compression offering 3:1 and 6:1 compression ratios. This form of compression removes some of the data, so there may be a slight to moderate change in the fidelity of the audio during playback.

MIDI. *M*usic *I*nterchange *D*ynamic *I*nterface. An industry standard for the creation and transfer of music (audio) signals.

Moov. Apple Computer's file format for video, audio, MIDI, text, or anything time-based.

Movie Alias. A Macintosh computer standard pointer-file that may be used to call up the original movie.

Movie Controller. A burly union man usually named Gus, who is the only person around who knows how to turn on the projector. Always smokes large cigars in defiance of local nonsmoking ordinances. Has the amazing ability to change a 450° F projector bulb with his bare hands without getting burned. Also the control bar at the bottom of a QuickTime movie window allowing you to play the movie, advance and back up frame by frame, adjust the volume, stretch or shrink the window, and perform basic cut- or copy-and-paste edits.

Movies. Generic term for audio and video clips. These may be in different formats.

MPEG. *M*otion *P*icture *E*xperts *G*roup. An image-compression format usually used for compressing frames of video that involve moving images. There currently are two levels—MPEG1 and MPEG2. MPEG is the compression scheme used by the new DSS satellite broadcasters allowing more than 150 channels to be compressed, broadcast, and decompressed in real time.

NTSC. *N*ational *T*elevision *S*tandards *C*ommittee. The video broadcast and signal standard used primarily in North America and Japan. This standard utilizes a total of 525 scan lines to make up a single full-screen frame.

PAL. *P*hase *A*lteration *L*ine. The NTSC-equivalent standard used in most of Europe and most of the rest of the world. This standard uses a total of 625 scan lines to make up a single full-screen frame.

Performance. The balanced playback characteristics of a digitized video or audio.

Post-Processing. Processing of digital video or audio sources once they have been edited into final form.

Poster Frame. The single frame used as a visual representation for an entire video movie. The default frame is usually the first frame of the movie but may be changed to the user's choice.

Q-Factor. The quality factor in any compression algorithm. When you adjust the slider bar in a compression dialog, you are setting the Q-Factor.

QuickTime. Apple Computer's standardized architecture for time-based media displayed on Macintosh computers.

QuickTime for Windows. Apple Computer's standardized architecture for time-based media displayed on Intel-based computer platforms.

Sample Rate. The rate at which digital information is recorded. The greater the sample rate, the higher the quality potential of the digitized information.

Scaling. Resizing an existing digital video clip to be either larger or smaller. In general, resizing up creates a lower-quality end product due to the absence of necessary data and should be avoided like the plague. Resizing down may result in a lossy or lossless (see their definitions) end product.

SECAM. *S*ystème *É*lectronique pour *C*ouleur *A*vec *M*émoire. The French equivalent of NTSC or PAL used only in France, Russia, and one or two other Eastern European countries. This broadcast standard is similar to PAL, using 625 scan lines. It differs in its handling of chrominance information.

SMPTE. *Society* of *Motion Picture* and *Television Engineers.* The time code standard used for locating individual frames on a videotape and displayed as HH:MM:SS:FF (Hours:Minutes:Seconds:Frames). A single frame equals 1/30 of a second.

Sound Manager. A Macintosh computer file necessary for the accurate recording and playback of digital audio in non–AV-equipped machines.

Spatial Compression. The amount of compression within a single image or frame of video.

S-Video. An industry signal and connector standard. S-Video cables feature four wires carrying chroma, luminance, brightness, and ground signals. (*Hint:* Apple keyboard cables can be interchanged with S-Video cables in a pinch!) No audio is carried in an S-Video signal.

SVHS. *Super Video Helical Scan.* An upgrade in performance to the VHS standard. This format requires special tapes and record/playback decks. In general, this provides an improvement in the signal-to-noise ratio over standard VHS.

Symmetric Compression. A compression scheme that requires the same amount of time to compress or decompress. Indeo and Apple Video are example of symmetric compression schemes.

Temporal Compression. The amount of compression applied to a sequence of images or frames of video over time.

Third Party. A company or supplier creating and selling products that support other products. An example is a software developer that makes an application for a specific computer.

Tracks. The different streams of digital information that make up a digital video or audio. Video usually requires a single track, although some assembled pieces may contain multiple tracks playing one after the other. Audio may be either a single monaural track or two-track stereo or mono.

Transition. The way in which one image or video changes into another image or video.

VHS. *Video Helical Scan.* The most popular consumer format for videotape, first introduced in the late 1970s. This utilizes a ½-inch tape carrying composite video and analog audio signals.

Video Compressor. The first compression method developed by Apple, which allows digitized video to decompress from CD-ROMs or hard disks in real time, with no additional hardware. Compression ratios range from 5:1 to 25:1.

Video for Windows. Microsoft Corporation's standardized architecture for time-based media. The file format used with Video for Windows is AVI.

WAV. A standardized audio format used in Intel-based platforms.

Window Size. The X-Y pixel count of a digital video display. Among the most popular window sizes are 640 × 480, 320 × 240, 160 × 120, and 80 × 60.

YUV Compressor. YUV stores data in the YUV 4:2:2 format at a compression ratio of 2:1. This algorithm is not lossless, but the resulting quality is extremely high. Several Macintosh AV models can digitize directly into this format. The YUV standard involves encoding the complete range of intensity information along with half of the color information.

Index

This index presents the major occurrences of each key word in the book. You are certain to find some of these words used elsewhere in the book, but we believe these to be the most meaningful locations. In many cases these listings reflect the first occurrence of a term, concept, or product in a section that may stretch for several pages.

You don't need a crystal ball to see where multimedia is going. What you need is a box.

Apple Multimedia Program

Actually, what you see here is more than just a box. Our Starter Kit is your link to the world of multimedia. An annual membership fee connects you to the best minds of the multimedia community, whether you're an educator, designer, publisher, in-house developer or marketer. You'll receive market research reports, technical and how-to guidebooks, co-marketing and networking opportunities, discounts and much more. For worldwide program information, call (408) 974-4897. That way, the future can't happen without you.

The Apple Multimedia Program.

ACD-PCN-KL4546

25.5 picas x 37.6 picas	Art Director: M. Choo
1995 NewMedia Tools Guide	Writer: L. Sequist
Interactive CD	Producer: S. Kassman
Prepared by BBDO, Los Angeles, CA	